ASTROLOGY
ALiVE

A Guide to
Experiential Astrology
and the Healing Arts

BARBARA SCHERMER

THE CROSSING PRESS
FREEDOM, CALIFORNIA

For information on bulk purchases or group discounts for this and other Crossing Press titles, please contact our Special Sales Manager at 800/777-1048.

Visit our Web site on the Internet: **www.crossingpress.com**

Library of Congress Cataloging-in-Publication Data
Schermer, Barbara.
Astrology alive : a guide to experiential astrology and the healing arts / Barbara Schermer.
    p. cm.
  ISBN 0-89594-873-7 (pbk.)
    1.Astrology. 2. Self-realization—Miscellanea. I. Title.
  BF1729.S38S339 1998
  133.5--dc21

                                                    98-5018
                                                     CIP

To Shellyji and those who preceded him;
to Kriyananda and those who came after him.

CONTENTS

ACKNOWLEDGMENTS

I am not one of those who dashes out of the movie theater just as "The End" flashes up on the screen. I often keep my seat as the lights come up and watch the parade of credits, marveling at the number of people it takes to make a film. And now, having written *Astrology Alive,* I look back with wonder at how many people it has taken to truly make a book. To the many who have helped me, I offer these "credits"—and my sincere gratitude.

Shellyji for sharing his deep yogic wisdom and Scorpionic humor—and for his abiding faith in me.

Kriyananda for teaching me to stand on my own two feet.

My father who taught me strength through his gentleness.

Jeff Jawer for the support, encouragement, and inspiration of a colleague and friend.

Clay Bodine, Noel Tyl, Paula Walowitz, and Rick Tarnas for their editing suggestions, sensitive feedback, and sound advice.

Eileen Campbell for being willing to publish my first book.

Bobby Skafish and Dixie Sue Botari for helping me find appropriate planetary music.

B. J. Johnson for her superb illustration of the Kriya Yoga chakra system.

Greg Vlamis for his cosmic connection.

Michael Cox for suggesting that I write this book.

Judith Pynne for a call out of the blue that ultimately led to the publication of this book.

My colleagues and friends, Margie Nicholson, Debra Trimmer, Moira Canes, Betsey Means, Susie Cox, Anne Trompeter, Carl Fitzpatrick, Tom Brady, Ramona Lucero, Dan Urban, Randi Wolferding, and my mom and family who gave me their encouragement, good ideas—and in two cases—allowed me to share their personal stories.

Most of all, I wish to thank my husband, Bob Craft, for his consistent and loving support of me and my work, especially in my moments of frustration and doubt; for his reading and commenting with care upon every chapter, sentence, and word in the book.

INTRODUCTION

In the beginning, astrology was *alive*. Life, and especially that aspect of life we call *mind*, is shaped by the recurrent patterns of relationships between the living and the surrounding world.[1] As humankind evolved, it was always in the context of an existence upon a whirling sphere, cyclically exposed to the sun, moon, planets, and stars, and interactive with them. Thus, we may truly say that the patterns of heavenly movement are inherent in life, in mind, and in humanity. And, as men and women further regarded the stars as their wandering companions, the diverse regularity of the heavens continued to inform them of the subtleties of pattern, as they in turn laid upon the stars a template revealing the qualities of emerging mind.

Human life at the beginning was not separate from the rest of creation. The stars must have been an intimate part of day-to-day life. Yet so little remains to inform us of our ancestors' earliest attempts to grasp the heavens. Did they climb mountains to place themselves closer to the stars? Did they pile up bricks or stones to mark their course through the skies? We know that they did so as much as four thousand years ago in ancient Mesopotamia, and at least by 1500 B.C. at Stonehenge. And who can say how long the Great Medicine Wheel, with its precise astronomical alignment of stones, has stood high in the Bighorn Mountains of Wyoming? In any event, we are safe to assume that in the splendor of the dark, quiet nights, while gazing into the starry vault, early humans were transported—lifted to the realm of the gods. In the first century A.D., the Roman poet Manilius captured what early men and women may have felt:

> *Those moonless nights when even the stars of the sixth magnitude kindle their crowded and gleaming fires, seeds of light amidst the darkness. The glittering temples of the sky shine with torches more numerous than the sands of the seashore, than the flowers of the meadow, than the*

*waves of the forest. If nature had given to this multitude powers in pro-
portion to its numbers, the ether itself would not have been able to support its own flames, and the conflagration of Olympus would have consumed the entire world.* [2]

And later yet (c.1150 A.D.), Ptolemy wrote, "Mortal as I am, I know that I am born for the day, but when I follow the serried multitude of the stars in their circular course, my feet no longer touch the earth; I ascend to Zeus himself to feast me on ambrosia, the food of the gods." [3] Even with the refinements of Greek and Roman civilization, humans remained close to the earth beneath them, and to the stars above. Men and women had a relationship to the natural world, and their contemplation of the heavens was a vital, primal communion which brought meaning to life.

Today we can see that we have lost touch with much of this primal experience. And astrology, child of this union of the contemplative urge with light from the heavens, is in danger of losing its primal vitality by becoming too abstract, theoretical, and analytical. Brain researchers have shown us in the last few years, that we have not one brain but two, with—to risk over-simplification—an analytical, verbal, rational left hemisphere and an intuitive, visual, holistic right one.[4] Our culture's traditional way of educating people has cultivated and encouraged the left brain, touting abstraction, while ignoring the development of our intuitive, imaginative right brain. Math, science, and verbal skills are taught at the expense of art, music, and creative expression. Although some enlightened educators have responded in recognition of this fact, their programs are the first to go when funds are cut.

It is important to point out that many of us do not learn well with words or abstract symbols, but depend on that part of the brain that "paints pictures." "Numerous studies have confirmed the fact that vividly experienced imagery, imagery that is both seen and felt, can substantially affect the brain waves, blood flow, heart rate, skin temperature, gastric secretions, and immune response—in fact, the total physiology." [5] And research continues to point toward the critical role of imagery in learning.[6] The tyranny of left-brain domination has gone too far. Is it any wonder that most children's artistic impulses start disappearing at age nine, when they have been "brainwashed" from age six onwards to use only their left brain? The present educational system abandons children who may be naturally visual, imaginative thinkers.

The conduct of our education in astrology has been no different. In the beginning, most of us sat before a teacher, passively memorizing the planets, signs, houses, and their meanings. Then we passively sat in another class learning how to synthesize those planets, signs, and houses into meaningful interpretation. What other means of learning do we currently have? We have books to read and conferences to attend. Again, most conferences are set up in the familiar left-brain learning style: one active participant, the lecturer, speaking to a passive group of twenty-five listeners. And our books are too often a dry parody of the same format. We have been—and still are being—educated only to *think* about astrology. By now the conclusion must be obvious: to learn an astrology of the right brain we must use its language, a language not of words but of images.

Consider this: You are an astrologer, holding a consultation with a client about transiting Neptune. Instead of talking, you show her a picture of San Francisco shrouded in fog to illustrate her upcoming encounter with that planet. Or, with a group of students, you hand out crayons and have them draw what Mars square Uranus "feels like." You could lead them blindfolded around the block to give a direct experience of the Neptune square Mercury aspect. Or, to better communicate the essence of Pluto, you work with them on a sprawling collage of Pluto images, replete with magicians, world leaders, atomic explosions, and erupting volcanoes. Going even further with a group, you might stimulate the use of the holistic right brain by having members enact their internal images of Mars—with the aid of some energizing dance music, contacting Mars, and giving it expression through movement and dance. (The term *astrodrama* has been given to this form of acting out the planetary energies.) The group may further refine the process by exploring how different the Mars energy feels in Scorpio or Taurus, or by noticing the different feeling tones between expressions of a Mars/Jupiter, Mars/Saturn, or Mars/Uranus conjunction.

Music is perhaps the most time-honored means of communicating with the right brain. Music that elicits the particular energy of each planet can be found. Holst's *The Planets* and Tomita's re-interpretation are classics. The album, *Deep Breakfast*, by Ray Lynch suggests Venus/Jupiter, and the song "Icarus" by various artists conjures up a beautiful Venus. The collection, *Hearing Solar Winds* by David Hykes and the Harmonic Choir profoundly evokes Neptune and Pluto.

Even without these more expressive techniques, you can enhance a right-brain response with the use of verbal images through the skillful employment of metaphors, analogies, and fairy tales. For instance, you might tell a client or a class that Neptune is like "wearing glasses with the wrong prescription." Or illustrate a Saturn return as "a baby chicken breaking out of its shell." Hypnotist par excellence, Milton Erickson, and the NLP (neurolinguistic programming) psychotherapists have shown that the proper use of metaphor more than illustrates—it heals.[7] To sharpen your skills in this area, you might tell the story "The Frog Prince" from Grimm's Fairy Tales to bring to life the transformative nature of Pluto, or you may draw upon Greek and Roman mythology for those stories in which the planetary archetypes themselves are the primary characters.

That ancient tales express astrological archetypes is, of course, no accident, for the understanding that both the planetary energies and the gods have profound influences upon humankind (if indeed they are not identical) springs from the same ancient sources. In fact, *Astrology Alive* argues that the "new" astrology described here is in reality a reemergence of the very old, coming from a time in which the archetypal energies were readily available and deeply felt. Chapter 1 illustrates this point with the Demeter-Persephone myth that—for the Greeks—was the basis for the "Greater Mystery" of Eleusis, a ritual repeated in spectacle, pageantry, and reverence at each consecutive fall equinox for two thousand years! Every year the residents of Athens abandoned the city to walk the fourteen-mile Sacred Way to Eleusis and take part in this "sacred theater" and its rites. As we will see later, this myth had extraordinary power within Greek culture and in the unconscious of the Greek people. And our focus will not remain on the Western traditions alone, since astrology has flourished in the East for centuries, often integrated with spiritual tradition.

Astrology Alive will show the relevance of these myths and rites for a new kind of astrological practice that provides a corrective to the "left-brained bias" of both astrology and the culture at large. Myth contains, in story form, the deepest truths of the culture. Today, in the West, we seem to have an impoverished mythology, weakened by too strict an adherence to the Newtonian-Cartesian scientific world view. And we should suspect that astrology, as an "institution" in that culture, is in a weakened state as well. We who have an interest in astrology have been carried along with the technological tides of our time, often to our benefit—with new methods of computation and research—but also to our detriment. We have forgotten that our original encounter with the heavens was immediate, direct, and alive. Are we not hungering for a deeper knowledge of ourselves and others? Isn't that precisely what astrology purports to offer? Doesn't it put us more in touch with our true nature? All too often, it seems, we have simply gone along with our culture, just *thinking* about astrology. What if we began to *feel* it as well?

With metaphor, music, myth, spiritual practice, and dramatic and artistic expression, we can move into more direct contact with the planetary energies, and in so doing, we rediscover the depths of ourselves. Astrology becomes then, not just a tool for abstraction and intellectualization, but a way of self-knowledge and a means to vital, primal communion with that which is transcendent. And that brings me to the purpose of this book: *Astrology Alive* is intended to introduce and to teach what has come to be called "experiential astrology." It is a book for all of us who are bored with traditional approaches, who want to revive our feelings of planetary connection and communion, and who are willing to pursue deeper levels of experience. It is designed to be of value to anyone learning or teaching astrology, or to anyone from the arts or psychology who is conversant in the language of astrology. If our aim is true, the material will be particularly useful for the growing number of individuals who are beginning to combine astrology with other fields such as Gestalt psychology, psychosynthesis, mythology, the arts, and spirituality to yield new healing forms.

Consider this book as an invitation to a feast, on whose broad table you will find the kind of fare that both tempts the senses and sticks to the ribs—tasty and nurturing ways for you to work and play at bringing astrology alive. Any such table needs support, of course. The four "legs" of our own table include three major thinkers and a "movement." The first thinker is Dane Rudhyar, whose lifelong effort was to develop a "humanistic" astrology. The second is Carl Jung, who—along with ideas from the Jung-inspired archetypal psychology of the soul developed by James Hillman and furthered by, among others, Thomas Moore—gifted us with an enormously fruitful journey into the workings of the human mind. Without his concepts of the archetypes, the self, and the personal and collective unconscious, we would scarcely have a way to talk of important matters of consciousness. The third supporting member is Jacob Moreno and his psychodrama which was a direct stimulus for astrodrama, a particularly well-developed form of experiential astrology. And as Chapter 3 will detail, the fourth source of support is the "human potential movement" that brought psychology to the popular culture in the 1960s.

Astrologer Stephen Arroyo has noted a major stumbling block for both students and practicing astrologers: the lack of guidance for synthesizing the many disparate elements of an astrological inquiry.[8] It is a rare astrology text that succeeds in teaching the blending of chart symbols. However, synthesis yields swiftly to experiential methods that teach by doing, and these will be illustrated by techniques gleaned from my own experiences in experiential performance and theater, teaching, counseling, and marathon group therapy sessions.

Part I of Astrology Alive will, after a suitable dose of background and theory, concentrate on conveying to you the basic skills that will help you learn from experience. Later chapters will provide numerous examples from my own experience teaching experiential astrology around the world, including forays into astrodrama, healing work with individuals and groups, imagery and dream work, and the integration of astrology and yoga practice. Part II first introduces and then extensively discusses a planet and their meaningfully related sign or signs. I've given numerous detailed exercises for bringing the planet or sign to full experiential expression. I've also provided films that illustrate each astrological symbol, as well as musical selections that can be used to evoke as well as to understand the appropriate energy. My aim is to place all the tools of experiential astrology in your hands.

It is especially important that you let this book stimulate your sense of exploration, participation, spontaneity, and just plain fun. Harvey Cox states it well: "Man's very survival as a species has been placed in grave jeopardy by our repression of the human celebrative and imaginative faculties.... Man is by his very nature a creature who not only works and thinks but who sings, dances, prays, tells stories, and celebrates. He is *homo festivus*."[9] I invite you then, to join the merrymaking. But be reminded that our play may have serious purpose: Pluto is now transiting through Sagittarius, and with the consequent stirrings deep in the psyche, people are increasingly in need of ways to bring about emergence, from the depths, of those forces that inspire and illuminate. Experiential astrology, as described here, may serve as a tool for that emergence. I invite you to use it wisely, well, and with pleasure.

PART 1

EXPERIENTIAL ASTROLOGY
PRINCIPLES
AND PRACTICES

INTRODUCING EXPERIENTIAL ASTROLOGY

One of the truths of our time is this hunger deep in people all over the planet for coming into relationship with each other. Human consciousness is crossing a threshold as mighty as the one from the Middle Ages to the Renaissance. People are hungering and thirsting after experience that feels true to them on the inside.
—Marilyn Ferguson, *The Aquarian Conspiracy*

Scene One: A young man in a red cape swaggers aggressively up to a large, robust woman. She holds her body rigid, arms folded across her chest, and stands her ground. In the background, the Mars movement from Holst's "The Planets" blares from a hidden speaker. As if swept into action by the frenzy of the music, the young man tries repeatedly to force his way past his opponent. The more he pushes, the more the woman is unmoved. The "hotter" he gets, the "colder" she becomes. Curbing his frustration, he changes his tack, trying to seduce her with sweet words. "Come back when you're grown up!" she commands. As the scene progresses, a look of recognition flashes in the woman's eyes. She suddenly begins to understand the creative impasse she has experienced in her work as an artist during these weeks that Saturn has been squaring her natal Mars.

Scene Two: A group of astrology students are fanned out on a broad, newspaper-strewn floor, sensuously expressing, with finger paint on posterboard, the energy and character of the planet Jupiter. With sticky blue hands, they swirl and spiral through a series of grand, sweeping movements. They are obviously having great fun!

Scene Three: Sitting in the center of a circle (her natal chart), a young woman is surrounded by the eager faces of ten "planets," positioned as they appeared at the moment she was born. One by one, they introduce themselves. Beginning with the first house cusp is her Moon in Cancer. Cuddling at the woman's feet, she coos, "I'm your Moon in Cancer. I'm shy and quiet. I like to pull back from the world to nourish myself. I *love* herbal baths, walks with my lover, and hugging my cat." Each planet, after completing its introduction, begins interacting with the others according to the aspects in the woman's chart. The Moon enters the circle joined by her Pluto in Scorpio. (The woman's Moon trines Pluto.) Responding to Pluto's influence, the Moon moves more sensuously, gracefully, and passionately. Then comes a sudden interruption by a belligerent Mars in Aries. (Our subject's Moon squares Mars.) Taunting the Moon, he roars, "Don't be such a pushover! You're always giving in because of your insecurity and need to be liked. Who cares if they like you? I don't care if they don't!" The young woman's chart unfolds before her eyes, bringing with it the feelings that each combination of aspects produces in her unconscious. By the end of her living horoscope, she is deeply affected, entranced by her uniquely personal drama.

Scene Four: In a gymnasium theater-in-the-round, surrounded by an expanse of window glass, the full moon is rising in the night sky. On the lawn outside, a procession of ten "planets," actors in costume, approach. Although many in the audience know no astrology, each planet, from the Sun out to Pluto, teaches and amuses, and presses each onlooker toward recognition and understanding of its psychic function within.

Scene Five: With learning about the four elements as your objective, you and your students have taken an overnight journey into a forest. To commune with Earth, the group sits on the ground, meditates, and imagines the strength of the earth flowing from the ground and into each still body. To experience Air, all climb to the top of a breezy ridge and take deep, full breaths of the windy air. To encounter Fire, you scatter to fetch kindling and firewood and build a roaring campfire. To experience Water, you take the path to a hot spring and relax tired muscles as the new moon welcomes you in the east.

Scene Six: A young woman contemplates the kaleidoscopically colored circle of images and symbols on the paper before her—a "birth mandala" of her horoscope. She has spent the last two hours in an artistic and reflective process to create this vivid, rich representation of her psyche.

Scene Seven: An earnest young man, sitting in the center of his own natal chart, spine erect, deeply meditative, attunes to the planetary psychic energies within. He knows he has an upcoming transit of Saturn opposite his Sun, and he is about to perform a ritual he created to help soften and neutralize that imbalance.

Each of the vignettes above is an example of a contemporary approach to astrology that may be new to you: the field of experiential astrology. These innovations in this ancient discipline show great promise by adding impact, depth, and meaning to astrology's already extensive repertoire. The chief defining characteristic of experiential astrology is that its methods offer direct participation in the vital energies symbolized by the horoscope. By taking the astrological chart off the page and into movement, encounter, art, drama, and dance, we allow not just participation by the intellect, but involvement of the senses and emotions as well. While its methods can be studied, experiential astrology is in essence an adventure to be experienced!

My own personal set of adventures began in 1979 while teaching a basic astrology class. We were talking about Saturn and its correspondence with old age. Caught up in a desire to get my message across, I stopped talking and just began to walk back and forth in front of the class. Beginning as a blithe young girl with a bounce in my step, I slowly allowed my gait and demeanor to shift toward middle age—a little restrained, more bent over, nursing some new pain in my back. Then, even more wearied by Time, I crept and staggered, until as an old crone, I collapsed into a heap on the floor, clearly dead. The effects of this two-minute drama were palpable. For myself, in my attempt to communicate a planetary symbol, I had actually envisioned my own death and had enacted it, thus having a taste of Saturn's "bitter pill." And the discussion with my students that ensued after a hushed silence showed that their encounter with Saturn had been real, too.

Several months later, while leafing through a magazine, I spotted a photo of an exploding volcano. There was Pluto—more clear now in my mind's eye than any verbal description could make it! Thus inspired with the recognition that images can teach the astrological principles, I spent that week pouring through a stack of old magazines, creating collages of images and photos for each of the ten planets. I put the "image board" I had created of Mercury in front of a group of new students. With no previous understanding of the planet Mercury, they told *me* what Mercury meant!

With these insights came teaching methods that brought a level of interest, energy, and sharing to my classes that I had noticed only fleetingly in my experience as both a teacher and student in the traditional mode. Because my classes encouraged spontaneity and play, the students became more relaxed with each other and found it easier to be themselves. They were more inclined to "tell their own stories" and share their insights with other students. This created an environment of increased group participation, deeper sharing, and intimacy.

Some time later, I read an article by Jeff Jawer in *Astrology Now* about astrodrama and the work he was doing in Atlanta.[1] In "Living the Drama of the Horoscope," Jeff described his first experiences with the acting out of individual aspects in the horoscope, for both teaching and counseling. He cites J. L. Moreno's work with psychodrama and the work of Dane Rudhyar as influences on his practice. Jeff's article gave me new inspiration and a host of ideas to try. He confirmed my own sense of excitement with the potential of an "interactive astrology"—an excitement that we have shared, then as now, through fifteen years of invention and discovery.

From 1982 to 1984, I convened a series of extended workshops in Chicago, during which we enacted the natal charts of at least two group members per week, astrodrama style. One particularly exciting group included two tall, strong, and handsome male students, one dark-featured and the other light, who were also superb dancers. Instead of using their voices to enact their roles (usually the Sun, Mars, or Jupiter), they danced the energy with their bodies! I remember one day while we were warming up in our Mars characters with John McLaughlin's "Birds of Paradise" playing in the background, these two men exploded into the room, running from opposite sides toward each other in great leaps. They were so Marsian the rest of us ducked for cover! Here was another way to enact the planets—*dance them*!

Planetary Theater

October of 1984 brought an opportunity to test out all these new tools for astrology. In that month the "New Center of the Moon" conference occurred, an extraordinary blend of experiential astrology and public theater that the two hundred or so who made it to Santa Fe still fondly remember. The event, organized by Santa Fe astrologer Tom Brady, was played out against a planetary backdrop of transiting Sun/Mercury/Pluto conjunct in late Libra/early Scorpio sextile Neptune in Sagittarius. Tom assembled a unique cast of characters to create and participate in an outdoor astrological theater open to both conference participants and Santa Fe residents. This "Theater of

Planetary Memory" was constructed in Cathedral Park, a spacious outdoor square next to a magnificent old Spanish church. The center of the theater was an inflatable, black-domed planetarium with inside walls that were studded with a luminescent map of the zodiacal belt and other constellations. Around the central theater dome were ten "planetary rooms," each creating an experience of a particular planet, complete with lighting, music, and images. With the aid of a creative video producer, crack lighting technicians, and a crew of carpenters, these rooms came to life. For example, in the red-hued Mars room, a Green Beret soldier in full battle dress stood at silent attention, conveying strength and an undertone of menace. Here was Mars incarnate!

Approaching the grounds, one passed under a huge sign flashing "The Theater of Planetary Memory" and entered a space defined by twelve neon zodiacal signs strung high in the trees overhead. Entering Mercury's room, first stop on the planetary tour, each visitor gave the necessary birth data, which were entered into a computer that calculated his or her chart and transmitted it to a monitor in the starry dome.

Inside, ten actors dressed in their planetary costumes had less than three minutes to find each visitor's key aspects, talk about how they might be portrayed, and scurry into the positions that the planets occupied in the natal chart. Knowing that I had experience with astrodrama and experiential work, Tom had invited me to be the theater's director. My job was to mold the ten planetary actors into an effective astrodrama troupe and to direct the performances in the theater. Only two of the "actors" had theatrical training or performing experience prior to this weekend.

When the actors were ready, our "psychopomp," the clown "Wavy Gravy" of Woodstock Music Festival fame led the expectant subject into the darkened celestial dome to be seated in a tall director's chair at the center. As the lights came up, the visitor was met with the spectacle of his or her own inner life, dynamically portrayed. Arrayed in full costume, complete with makeup and props, the planetary actors played out the particular planetary struggles and cooperations in the visitor's natal chart. In barely three minutes, the troupe was able to enact a number of brief vignettes, rapidly moving from one natal contact to another. By revealing their inner nature, the troupe by turns delighted the participants and moved them to tears. Not having anticipated the power of astrodrama, many left with a look of sheer wonder.

If the effect of the encounter was so great for the visitors, you might imagine the impact it had on those who created the astrodrama. In the two nights that the theater operated, we performers must have presented well over one hundred enactments of natal charts. Each of us played a single planetary energy throughout the twelve signs and in every possible aspectual relationship. We were, by mid-performance, virtually *humming* with our planet's energies, and although time constraints were sometimes stressful, we felt exhilarated, not overwhelmed. Long after the theater had closed for the night, the energy of the actors seemed still to be bouncing around the dome, and we stayed long after the performance, reliving our experiences with an astrology that few had encountered before. The impact of our experiment with astrodrama spread throughout the conference as well, and we players, incognito without our costumes, overheard many conversations praising our efforts. And maybe this and other presentations of experiential astrology have had an even broader effect. We are slowly beginning to see more of our conferences include some form of theater or performance as well as workshops in experiential methods.

The conference weekend was to prove especially important to me for another reason. At one point, Tom Brady mentioned in an offhand way a tidbit of information that was to propel me into an investigation that, to some extent, was to culminate in this book. While researching in the University of New Mexico's library, Tom came across a sampling of early Greek Orphic writings with a cryptic reference to "horoscopes being danced." This notion so captivated my imagination that I began extensive research into the origins of Greek sacred theater and the Graeco-Roman mystery schools. Oddly, the reference itself has remained a mystery—neither Tom nor I have been able to find the quote. Ultimately, I was to spend a month in Greece at a number of the sacred sites. Although Delphi, Epidauros, and Delos each had its magic, I was most drawn to the sacred theater and to the healing rites and ceremonies of Eleusis.

Ancient Mysteries

I was in Eleusis at the Fall Equinox, 1985—the very day on which, so many centuries before, the annual celebration of the "Greater Mystery" in honor of the Great Mother was held. I spent long days alone—envisioning, meditating upon, and "feeling into" what we know, and what we must imagine of those sacred events. From the spectacle of the fourteen-mile processional walk on the Sacred Way to the ritual dancing at the Kallichoron well, participants in the mysteries danced in the ceremonies of initiation, and witnessed the reenactment of the myth of Demeter and Persephone in the

Dromena. I had pored over the books of the experts on Eleusis; now I walked the grounds over and over again, hoping my soul might catch a glimpse of the sights and sounds of the holy dances. I meditated in front of Pluto's cave, the Ploutonion, and performed my own private ritual. From the hill above the city, I gazed down into the ruined outlines of the sacred precinct, trying with my mind's eye to replace column upon pediment, to lay knowledge upon intuition, until at last I believe I was able to comprehend the essence of the place. Eleusis and its mythologically-rooted healing ritual has long since passed away. Yet, on this day, I was able to imagine that the mythic archetypes were being summoned once more. This is what I saw and heard and felt...

Eleusis, Fall Equinox, Boedromonion 20 (530 B.C.)

I dreamed, I danced as far back as I can remember. For that I needed only to be alone, among the small mountain creatures around my native town of Mandra. The flowers and the birds were my audience. The high mountain meadow where I tended my father's sheep was my stage. I was ten when my mother and father took me southward down the mountain to attend the great festival at Eleusis. I shall never forget it. For the first time, I saw my secret joy of dancing shared by others. I remember being barely able to sit in my seat as I watched the dancing in honor of the Corn Goddess. My heart pounded. Though I didn't understand much of the secret meaning of what I saw, my soul was aflame with the magic of the festival.

And tonight, five years later, because of my dream I dance for the first time in honor of the Goddess Demeter. "Demeter"—even her name teaches us: "De" is the "letter of the vulva," the delta, the triangle of the female trinity of virgin, mother, and crone. I have worked hard all year to absorb her teachings, to prepare for this moment, instructed by the priestesses who demand that the dancers keep the traditions in precise detail. There are hundreds of dance movements to learn.[2] Errors rob our ritual of its power. The dance is highly structured and carries us as we wind snakelike through the passage of life to death and back to life again.

Yesterday, Iacchos led the long procession from Athens, and my sisters and I, with thousands of other citizens, escorted the sacred statue of our Great Mother to the temple grounds, the place sanctified by the Goddess herself. Throughout the procession, we sang the ancient calling song:

Come, arise, from sleep awaking,
Come the fiery torches shaking,
Oh Iacchos, Oh Iacchos,
Morning Star that shinest nightly,
Lo, the mead is blazing brightly,
Age forgets its years and sadness,

Aged knees curvet for gladness,
Lift thy flashing torches o'er us,
Marshall all the blameless train,
Lead, Oh lead the way before us.[3]

Tonight is the sixth night of the festival and the first night of the temple dancing and the Dromena, the sacred reenactment. Now I must go. The dance begins.

With a hundred other dancers I pass through the great stone Triumphal Arch, with the inscription I will soon know to be true: "Only Those Who Dance the Mysteries, Know the Mysteries."[4] We enter the new eastern courtyard of the temple, built atop the ancient ruins on which others like us danced for nearly a thousand years. Outside, I can see throngs of people sitting on the sloping eastern terraces around the courtyard, facing the altar to the Goddess in the southwest corner of the square. I feel a gentle breeze from the sea enticing me toward my place at the Kallichoron well, the "Well of Fair Dances." I stand in my place. I look at my bare feet. I am both excited and afraid. My mouth is dry. I feel my heart beginning to beat a quicker rhythm. I keep my eyes on my feet, take a deep breath, and begin with the others.

Slowly, tenderly, we move with measured steps, establishing a rhythm that lulls perception. We take the time needed to set the pattern, weaving in and out, in and out of the labyrinth. I pound out the rhythm of the drums with my feet. In and out. In and out. Repeat. Repeat. Repeat. There is no part of me that is not part of the Goddess. "Move deeper. Use the ritual knowledge." I take each step with loving attention, not forcing, but gently moving beyond my limitations, my weariness, step by step, penetrating to the place of stillness. "Receive the power of the dance." Step. Step. Step. My heart beats in rhythm with the drums and my feet. No longer fettered by fear, my feet dance like the beat of steady rain, sensing they have danced these steps a thousand times before.

There are no longer just a hundred bodies twisting in the dance. Now I can see and feel many more shapes whirling around and around, communing with Her, honoring Her. The shades of my ancestors are dancing with us in the circle.

My feet dart about like fish in tumbling water, my body is the rhythm, the circle, the dance. I breathe in time to my movements, in and out, in and out, as I spiral deeply into the circle and out again to its edges, each repeat of the sacred pattern entrancing me more. Out of me, like the cycle of nature herself, arises an endless succession of new springs from old winters.

My eyes blur as I close them, then open wide, not knowing what it is I see in the enveloping silvery fog. I come to life in the dream I dreamt last spring, living the vision that brought me to this moment! I am whirling with torrents of moving lights, lights circling around and around, and I'm being drawn into a dark, ancient well. I'm afraid of the dark abyss but cannot stop my being sucked into the center, being propelled and drawn nearer and nearer its gaping mouth. I reach inside and sense my strength. With the pressure of whirling forces against my legs, I am able to stand at the abyss. No longer afraid of being swept in, my feet stand firm. My eyes follow a stream of moonbeams up into the night sky to see the full moon gracefully reaching her summit. I bathe in her soft light. She flows into me, through me. I feel her gentle but strong "soul-arms" reach down, embrace, and transform me. As she illumines my face and body, a shadow dances with me—hand-in-hand we pause, decide, then plunge into the abyss!

I reach my core, Her within me, the solid stuff of earth within. Steady. Enduring. I merge with the ancient feminine spiritual root, embracing a lineage millions of years old, back to our ancestors who lived the first principle of harmony. I drink of Her strength and am empowered. I drink of Her healing and am made whole. The steady, eternal breathing of the Great Mother sounds in my ears.

I feel my hair streaming across my eyes as I whirl. I feel the tears drying on my cheeks. The moon overhead overwhelms me. The Goddess is present. The Goddess is here!

I hear a woman's wailing faintly in the distance. The other dancers hear Her, too, and as one, move toward Her cries at the "Mirthless Stone" beside the Sacred way. The Dromena itself begins. Demeter, our Earth Mother, has just discovered that her daughter, Persephone has been kidnapped by Plouton, Lord of the Underworld. Consumed with passion, he has carried the young Persephone through the Gates of Hades to become his Queen. Demeter wails in her grief at the loss of her daughter. I realize I am sobbing, too. I see an image, permanently etched in memory, pass through my mind—it is the day my father died last winter. I see his last breath, his death shudder. I feel helpless, wanting to seize his life force and restore it to him. I cry. She cries. Thousands cry. I rage with the Goddess in anger, storming up and down, shaking, my body bathed in hot sweat. I journey into the cold darkness, facing my fear, my terror, shuddering and trembling. I sink in a heap, utterly exhausted from enduring the mystic catharsis.

I am jolted! A feeling of ecstasy bubbles up within my spine and moves in a wave toward my head. I look up. I look again with my eyes straining at the very edge of the visible. I see there the mist and within it the Vision. I see there the Return. I am jolted again and then transported, lifted to a region of pure light, a place of celestial brilliance, suffused with loving sounds of the holy voices and surrounded by the sacred dancing of the Goddesses. I wander free in this joyful realm in communion with Myself...with Her...with All That Is, fused to the cosmic rhythm. What I truly saw I cannot tell you. There has been a sacred seal placed upon my lips. I must speak no more!

And countless lips did remain sealed, so that the revelation that sustained a host of initiates over two thousand years was lost for all time at the death of the last hierophant. A veil thus descended on Eleusis. The Kallichoron well has gone dry.

What exactly was done at Eleusis to create such a powerful effect? We do not know. We do know the rites brought about an experience of the death-rebirth cycle, stimulating a deeper understanding of the esoteric spiritual meaning of this collective human event. Themistios, drawing upon Plutarch, an initiate of the Mysteries, wrote, "The soul [at the point of death] has the same experience as those who are being initiated into great mysteries."[5] And Pindar wrote, "Happy is he who, having seen these rites, goes below the hollow earth; for he knows the end of life, and he knows its God-sent beginning."[6] George Mylonas concludes his book on Eleusis saying that whatever the substance of the Mysteries was, the fact remains that the rites of Eleusis satisfied the most sincere yearnings and the deepest longings of the human heart.[7]

The ritual at Eleusis built to an ecstatic climax in which the accumulated psychic discord and tension were released. Fear turned to joy, and participants experienced a powerful healing catharsis. The rising action always included intense and repetitive physical activity to produce the proper receptivity. After hours and hours of chanting, singing, dancing, drumming, and musical rhythms, participants were transported out of everyday awareness and opened to more subtle realms. The dancing was preceded by days of purification, fasting, and very little sleep, during which all walked in awe-inspiring processionals with hundreds of like-minded souls. Magnificent ceremonial vestments and holy symbols were displayed, and sacred words and formulas were spoken. The impact of the whole experience reached its peak in a magic moment when the inspired participant had a direct experience of cosmic forces. With *participation* in this manner, a divine communion was made, and the individual was no longer an onlooker of the cosmos but a dynamic, active part of it. The individual became co-creator of the cosmic drama.

Astrology and the Gods

The rites of Eleusis reenacted the death-rebirth experience which astrologers recognize as the process of the archetype of Pluto in the individual psyche. The astrological archetypes and the myths of the gods and goddesses draw from the same pool.

Mythology contains the particular manifestations of the archetypes in their various patterns. Astrology incorporates a basic ten (and many more) of these essential archetypes into a language for understanding.

It is particularly clear, at least for Western culture, that the same cultural and historical forces that produced the myths of the gods and goddesses drove the forge by which astrology was formed. The gods of the Greeks—Uranus, Chronos, Pluto, Poseidon, Hermes, and Aphrodite—are the embodiments of the distinctive psychic qualities of the planetary forces that we now call by their Roman names—Uranus, Saturn, Pluto, Neptune, Mercury, and Venus. Thus Saturn, which can signal death and destruction in the horoscope, is the same power represented by Chronos, who devoured his children and who, in the guise of Time, may in truth be said to destroy whatever has been brought into existence.

Joining in a ritual event and reenacting a myth that resonated with a truth beyond cultural bounds gave the Eleusinian faithful a peak experience of cosmic communion. If, indeed, the astrological archetypes arise from the same deep, unconscious realms of the mind as the gods and goddesses, then vivifying the astrological symbols should provide the same kind of communion. If, for example, we learn to actively express our Pluto, bringing it to life consciously, then we no longer deny or repress its power, and we might avoid the usual explosions of emotion or conflict that characterize Pluto. We learn to use our own Pluto in more conscious ways by embodying the symbolic truth of the planet—penetrating into, transforming, and assimilating its power.

I do not want to imply that astrologers must spend four days dancing and fasting in order to come to know a planetary archetype, although this level of intensity might be an appropriate experience for some astrologers. I *am* suggesting that, like the ancients, we step beyond the boundaries of observation and thought and use direct experience to understand our own internal planetary forces.

In so doing, you pass from seeing the planets as isolated mental images to actually experiencing the vital rhythms of their interactions, which reveal deeper subconscious feelings and previously unexpressed aspects of being. The horoscope, then, is no longer a static, black-and-white, one-dimensional assortment of data with inanimate glyphs and signs. It becomes a moving field of planetary action: vibrant, interactive, and alive!

ANCIENT ROOTS:
NOTHING NEW UNDER THE SUN

You could never arrive at the limits of the soul, no matter how many roads you traveled, so deep is its mystery.

—Heraclitus

I have come to understand that much of what seemed new in the formulation of this book had been anticipated—by 500 years—in the work of Renaissance philosopher Marsilio Ficino! Below, I will introduce Ficino and his method, and then describe the relevance of his thought and experience to our subject. Along the way, I will strengthen the relationship between experiential astrology and Jungian thought, and, especially, the post-Jungian ideas of James Hillman and Thomas Moore. Finally, I will attempt an understanding of Ficino's greatest collaborative effort with Botticelli in the production of *La Primavera*, probably the most-studied, and arguably the most beautiful painting of all time. You may reach the same conclusion as me: that Marsilio Ficino was the First Experiential Astrologer.

The First Experiential Astrologer

Marsilio Ficino was a true "Renaissance Man." He was the primary translator of Plato as well as the translator for the body of philosophical and magical texts attributed to Hermes Trismegistus. He was the first head of the Platonic Academy, established by his patron Lorenzo de' Medici. Prodigiously talented, he was a Christian theologian and cleric, a Hermetic magician, a physician and a psychotherapist, a musician and an astrologer! Eminent Renaissance scholar Eugenio Garin underlines the importance of our subject: "After Ficino there is no writing, no thought, in which a direct or indirect trace of his activity may not be found."[1] Ficino was born near Florence, in Figlini

Valdarno, on October 19, 1433, 12:40 Greenwich Mean Time.[2] He lived in and about Florence until his death on October 1, 1499.[3] And it was in Florence, the rich and tumultuous center of the Italian Renaissance, that Ficino developed a remarkable "therapeia of soul" that included the Platonic ideas, astrology, psychology, Hermetic magic, imagination, contemplation, art, and music.

In his many pursuits, Ficino reserved a central place for "soul," that indefinable yet omnipresent essence that was the focal concern for all those philosophers who, after Plato, would come to be known as the "Neoplatonics." To Ficino and his fellows, "There is nothing so deformed in the whole living world that it has no soul, no gift of soul contained in it."[4] Soul, then, is not just an individual attribute—the body's "ghost"—but is inherent in all that is. Thus, on the one hand, Soul *is* our experience of both our internal and external worlds, the proper mediating factor between spirit and body, the "prime mover," the agent that develops our psychological sensibility through attunement to the multiple presences in our psyche. On the other hand, Psyche, as World Soul, according to Ficino, and following Plato, is everywhere.

Ficino's psychology is also profoundly astrological, in both its terms and its modes of thought. Ficino saw the horoscope as a "theater of soul, a Memory Theater-in-the-Round, an alchemical vessel for the planetary workings of the imagination and a container for the sufferings of psyche."[5] The planets were not merely material entities, or even psychological "energies," but "planetary Gods, each one presiding over certain foods, flowers, animals, metals, and modes of behavior," says Charles Boer, who notes that by making this move, "Ficino lifts the world and human life from the categorical deadness of his Aristotelian contemporaries, and profoundly ensouls it.... Suddenly, everything is reborn, [and]...we see *Renaissance*."[6] These Gods—these planetary *archetypes*, to use the term made familiar by Jung—Ficino sees as multiple presences in the psyche, each having their own personalities that interact with each other and form complex, ever-changing relationships. Each of these archetypes is a pool of limitless and bottomless "imaginal soul stuff" that continually recreates itself in new ways— daily through the life of our own souls and eternally through the World Soul, our *anima mundi*. Succinctly put—to Ficino, planets in motion = psyche in motion.

If soul is the essential substance of Ficino's psychology, *imagination* is its essential process. "Where Ficino is original is in his vast and careful conceptualization of all this physiology and psychology under an imaginary polytheism."[7] Psychologist James

Hillman, to whom we will return, points to Ficino's tripartite division of the psyche into mind or rational intellect, body, and *idolum*—imagination or fantasy, in support of Hillman's emerging archetypal psychology, in which it is through the vehicle of imagination that the archetypes of the soul are known: "The soul is constituted of images...the source of images—dream images, fantasy images, poetic images—is the self-generating activity of the soul itself."[8]

Ficino's astrological psychology teaches us to open ourselves to an archetypal, imaginal, aesthetic perspective on all that we see and experience, learning to *see* the Gods with our imaginal inner eye, transforming and being transformed by all that happens to us and in us into images of soul significance and value. It is precisely this perspective of Ficino's that is so crucial for psychological astrologers today. Ficino encourages us to actively imagine the planetary Gods in our daily lives, and thereby develop both a mythic sensibility and a disciplined imagination. By using imaginal methods to directly contact and experience Soul within, we draw the archetypal images of the Gods and Goddesses out of the chaos and restore them to a recognized internal order. And what happens to each of us when we make this critical change in perspective? We become the *central protagonists* of our own life stories. By learning how to "invite the Gods and Goddesses" into our lives, we begin to co-create our own unique life story with Them; thus we find a place in the cosmos, and recover divine inspiration. Rather than feeling like an isolated, powerless creature at the mercy of life's meanderings, we become archetypal artists, co-creators of our own lives and the actualizers of our horoscopes.

Marsilio Ficino's long-neglected modes of thought have been recently reintroduced into psychology, namely *archetypal* psychology, as developed by James Hillman and his followers. A long-time Jungian analyst, Hillman, in his theoretical writings, eschews Jung's early scientific speculations in favor of the more Neoplatonic ideas that reemerge in later Jungian thought. Hillman's stated aim is "the revisioning of psychology, psychopathology, and psychotherapy in terms of the Western cultural imagination."[9] In so doing, Hillman has drawn upon Ficino and his Neoplatonic kin, notably in "Plotino, Ficino, and Vico," an address contemporaneous with Hillman's seminal *Re-Visioning Psychology*. In the former work, Hillman credits Ficino, especially for the idea of the centrality of the soul, for his understanding of the role of imagination, and for his establishment of both a "depth psychology" and a "psychoanalysis" that teaches one "to place psychic reality first and to consider all events in terms of their meaning and their value for soul."[10] In *Re-Visioning Psychology*, Hillman elaborates and expands upon these ideas to establish a psychology based upon soul and soul-making, centered in the processes of imagination, and intended to "restore the mythical perspective to depth psychology by recognizing the soul's intrinsic affinity with, nay, love for the Gods."[11] Of course, such a psychology has much to contribute to astrology in general, and experiential astrology in particular. I refer the reader to the substantial literature on archetypal psychology—the prolific Hillman himself continues to add to a 1988 "checklist," numbering over two hundred, mostly scholarly publications.[12] In early 1997, Hillman's *The Soul's Code*[13] was a *New York Times* best-seller, preceded by colleague Thomas Moore's *Care of the Soul*[14]. The tenets of archetypal psychology have entered popular culture.

Thomas Moore's earlier work, *The Planets Within*, is most important in direct relation to experiential astrology and is a "must read" for anyone who wishes to go beyond the understandings given here. In effect, Moore derives (from Ficino) and develops (following Hillman) a psychological theory that is most congenial to the experiential approach. Moore is skillful and complete in his presentation of such Ficinian-archetypal ideas as (1) the centrality of the soul, (2) the personified and polytheistic nature of the psyche, (3) the fundamental nature of the archetypal image, (4) the role of imagination as the very method of archetypal work, and (5) the understanding that soul permeates the world as *Anima Mundi*, or World Soul. To many, if not most astrologers, this is a psychology with a familiar ring to it—after all, astrology served for hundreds of years as a container for Neoplatonic ideas and has thus contributed to "saving the phenomena" that a post-Enlightenment, science-dominated world has sought to suppress. Archetypal psychology aims to do the same and is introducing a greater audience to a style of thinking we might consider to be "astrological" while establishing its relevance to contemporary life and thought. Some particular examples from Moore's *The Planets Within* may illustrate what experiential astrologers have to gain from entertaining its ideas.

Chapter 3 introduces three concepts that characterize experiential astrology: *experiencing*, *enacting*, and *embodying*. Here, in connection with the work of Moore and Ficino, I will emphasize an even more fundamental concept: *imagining*. In his discussion of Ficino's ideas, Moore delineates several processes of imaginal activity, including constellation, cultivation, dissolving/congealing, sublimation/condensation, and accommodation. *Constellation* is rather like the counterbalancing technique suggested in Chapter 10, "Balancing Your Difficult Transits"—in essence, lessening the effect of one influence by calling upon its opposite. As Moore notes, "Ficino's advice is twofold: find a way to offset the tendency by inviting an opposite kind of spirit; and, at the same time, experience the powerful daimon [i.e., the "god" in the image] to the hilt," with the intention of "maintain[ing] a variety of spirit without getting rid of the dominant one."[15] The pathological "monotheism" of submission to any single image is opposed in favor of a "polytheism" that makes a place for all the Goddesses and Gods, thus accepting their various gifts. To truly receive these gifts, however, is to engage in the imaginative process of *cultivation* of the environment; that is, to seek out and to experience the soul qualities of the events and material offerings of the world. For Ficino does take delight in the world—his prescriptions for illness and depression, rather than bitter herbs and foul medicaments, favor fine wines, the whitest sugar laced with gold, stimulating company, "the frequent sight of shining water, the sight of green or red colors, the uses of gardens or woods, walks, and rivers."[16] He understands that healing consists of drawing upon the energies of the planetary archetypes as they present themselves in every existing thing. Moore is correct to point out the connection of cultivation with Ficino's embrace of magic and ritual, a theme expanded upon in this volume.

Alchemy, the combining of elements of spirituality and psychology to understand the workings of both matter and the soul, was an allied art to astrology in Ficino's time. Moore argues that the alchemical processes of *dissolving* and *congealing* relate to Ficino's work in that both approaches strive to "keep soul in the middle [and] not let it disappear in mind or in body."[17] For soul makes its special contribution that is too often lost in intellectualizing or in excessive pursuit of remote spiritual ends—or in gross materialism or the soulless indulgence of bodily need that tends toward obsessions and addictions of all sorts. As Moore states, "Alchemy moves in two directions: it spiritualizes what is otherwise dense and literal, and it concretizes that which is intellectual or spiritual."[18] The former is the process of *solutio,* or "dissolving," the latter, *coagulatio,* or "congealing," both of which can help us maintain the central and essential position of soul. Moore uses alchemical *sublimation* and *condensation* to further elucidate the hazards of excess spiritualizing or literalism: "Psychologically, flighty ideas and schemes need concretization (condensation), while excessively literal matters require vaporization (sublimation)."[19]

Accommodation, in Moore's discussion of Ficino, is the last "process of imaginal activity" to be discussed here. To *accommodate* is to carry out the title of Ficino's *De Vita Coelitas Comparanda*—to arrange (or "correlate with" or even "prepare") one's life according to the Heavens. This is the essence of Ficino's message, to bring oneself into harmony with one's astrological context, with the archetypal images expressed through matter, energy, and time, and mediated by the embodied soul. This is, of course, the goal of experiential astrology, if not astrology as a whole. Consistent with his psychological view, Moore directs us beyond astrological symbolism alone:

> We may begin to understand the process of accommodation by studying the planets, along with Ficino, as archetypal images, but we do not have to stop there… A dream will do, or a novel, or science, or a walk in the woods. Everything is metaphor and food for the soul. All of the material world contains sparks of the kindred sky, flashes of the psychological lumen.[20]

We have spent several pages with Moore and Ficino to show the continuity of Ficinian-archetypal psychology with experiential astrology, and to illustrate some of the modes of imaginal activity that may contribute to our understanding of astrology as experience. However, it should be made clear that archetypal psychology and experiential astrology are by no means identical; in fact, as an aspect of astrology, the subject of this book often remains closer to Ficino than Moore and archetypal psychology do. For Ficino is an astrologer by conviction, and though he sometimes wavered, and did condemn the excesses of the astrology of his day, he did not evade taking the position that events on earth are actually and meaningfully correlated with the motions of the heavenly bodies, rather than being "just" psychological, as archetypal psychologists sometimes appear to suggest. Too, Ficino appears to be more affirmative regarding the veridicality of magical practice than are the psychologists. (D. P. Walker, scholar of Renaissance magic, believes that the "less discreet" writings of Ficino's student Diacetto reveal Ficino to be more of a practicing astrological magician than is sometimes supposed.[21]) Regarding magic, my own preference is to leave these matters open to interpretation. Concerning astrology, however, I concur with intellectual historian and astrologer, Richard Tarnas:

> It is not that astrologers have arbitrarily used the stories of the ancients about Venus, Mars, Mercury, and the rest to project symbolic meanings onto the planets, which are in actuality merely material bodies without intrinsic significance. Rather, a considerable body of evidence suggests that the movements of the planets named Venus, Mars, and Mercury tend to coincide with human experience that closely resemble the character of their mythical counterparts. The astrologer's insight is fundamentally an empirical one. This empiricism is given context and meaning by a mythic, archetypal perspective, a perspective that the planetary correlations seem to support and illustrate with remarkable consistency.[22]

In fairness (and with forgiveness that archetypal psychologists rarely cite even the finest and most congenial of modern astrological writings), it should be said that archetypal psychology seems to move at least halfway toward this view, and perhaps for a similar reason—that the Inquisition that caused Ficino to recant some of his ideas[23] has its modern counterpart in exclusion from serious intellectual consideration if one fully endorses astrology. At least since Jung himself, those in the Jungian tradition have sought epistemological positions that could be defended, while saving a host of spiritually vital phenomena. That said, the cautions issued by the psychologists are worthy of serious consideration. We all grant a certain reality to our perceptions and beliefs, and have been caught up at times in "our relative truths held absolutely." *Literalizing* names that unfortunate tendency, at its worst in fundamentalist views, whether religious, scientific, ethnic or political—or even "New Age." As you read this book, I hope that you will keep the flexibility, the openness, and the generous spirit that characterizes Ficino himself when he admonishes the reader impressed with neither his particular medications nor of his appeal to "astronomical images" that "You can, with my permission, or even, if you prefer, with my recommendation, put such things aside."[24] *Spiritualizing*, which "appears as scientific objectivity, as metaphysics, and as theology"[25] is equally suspect in the eyes of the archetypalists, for such carries us upward to a rarefied and ungrounded abstraction that leaves the richness and complexity of life on earth behind. Like Ficino's own psychology, the experiential approach works best when centered in the soul.

Ficino's Astrology and the Astrology of Ficino

If Ficino was indeed the first experiential astrologer, it seems only fair to use astrology to understand the man and the experiences he underwent in becoming so. Toward that end, I will focus upon a particular time span (approximately his late middle years, from 1460 to 1480), and upon the issue of his *melancholia*, to which Ficino on a number of occasions assigned an astrological origin. In a letter to his friend, Giovanni Cavalcanti, he writes, "Saturn seems to have impressed the seal of melancholy on me from the beginning, as it is, almost in the midst of my ascendant Aquarius..."[26] The following is Ficino's natal chart[27] (of course, he was unaware of the outer planets discovered many years later).

FICINO'S NATAL CHART

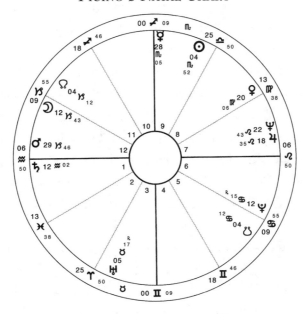

First to catch the astrologer's eye is Ficino's fixed T-square, involving the Sun, Saturn, and Jupiter. His Saturn on his ascendant is a classic indicator of depression, and combined with the square to his Sun in the ninth house, made it likely that darkness would be profoundly present in his mood. He called himself a Saturnian and struggled all his life against the temptation to despondency. That Saturn resided in Aquarius, opposed to Jupiter in Leo, made stability and moderation of mood elusive—he was reported by a number of his friends who saw him regularly to be in one of two states—either serious despair or profound ecstasy.[28] In short, Ficino appeared to be "manic-depressive" or "bipolar" in the current psychiatric parlance. To be sure, there are moderating influences in the chart. The Jupiter in Leo establishes a context for Ficino as a charismatic philosopher and leader of the Platonic Academy, the inspired teacher of music and image who attracted the most "conspicuously brilliant young creative artists and poets of the time—Lorenzo de' Medici, Alberti, Poliziano, Landino, Pico della Mirandola, Botticelli, Michelangelo, Raphael, Dürer, Titian, and many others."[29] And should we be surprised to find Mercury on the midheaven in sextile to Venus trine to Moon for this "philosopher of love"? We do not ignore, of course, that Saturn brings as many gifts to the soul as it does tribulations. Even so, the argument here is that his melancholy is crucial to his character, and that it was Ficino's attempts to deal with his own depression and the agonies and ecstasies of his own soul that brought to birth what we may call his "Therapeia of Soul."

Ficino's *Letters*[30] and the various commentaries upon them give us the dates and events we need to understand the origins of Ficino's "Therapeia." First, consider that between 1466 and 1468, transiting Neptune was conjoined to Ficino's Scorpio Sun, and the confusion and profound challenge to identity we should expect is apparent in the historical record. Translation of much of Plato and of the mystical *Corpus Hermeticum* lay behind him, and "from 1467 to 1469 Ficino was in serious despair... [having] become so captivated, so exhilarated by this new Platonic way of imagining, that he found himself...wanting to revive a pagan religion."[31] These are ideas that could easily lead to the rack or the stake. Yet, with natal Sun in Scorpio, Ficino could not escape or deny the truth that sprang from the depths of his being. *Platonic Theology* took these ideas as far as he dared in print. If the Neptune transit brought confusion, it is also likely to have deepened his commitment to the magic he discovered in the Hermetic writings. We know from many passages in his later *Book of Life* that he practiced magical ritual. D. P. Walker gives a picture of him "nourishing his spirit and making it more celestial" that fits this time:

> He is playing a *lira da braccio* or a lute, decorated with a picture of Orpheus charming animals, trees and rocks; he is singing...the Orphic Hymn of the Sun; he is burning frankincense, and at times he drinks wine; perhaps he contemplates a talisman; in daytime he is in sunlight, and at night he "represents the

sun by fire." He is, in fact, performing a religious or magical rite—"a sacrament profane in the mystery of wine."[32]

About this time, transiting Uranus (in Libra, in trine to his natal Saturn in Aquarius), was planting the seeds for the synthesis of the pagan, magical, and astrological, as well as Christian elements that were to characterize his philosophy, his psychology, and his healing practice. It was somewhere during this time that, in Charles Boer's words, "Ficino crossed an internal boundary—indeed, he crossed over into that area Jung would have called "psychology." And, like the alchemists Jung would later reveal to be supremely psychological, Ficino both created and discovered an imaginal reality of such complexity and depth that it revealed the nature of soul.

The year 1468 was the crucial turning point for Ficino. It was during this depressing time when Ficino was so afflicted with a "bitterness of spirit," that his friend Giovanni Cavalcanti advised him to concentrate and write upon love as a remedy for his illness and to "convert the lovers of transitory beauty to the enjoyment of eternal beauty."[33] Ficino immersed himself in his devotion to the arts, to love and to beauty, thus entering into an extended encounter with Venus. As a result, he wrote the first version of *De Amore*, a commentary on Plato's *Symposium*, that was to become a great classic in the literature on love—indeed, one of the most important treatises of the Renaissance. Thus, not only did Ficino's Venus in Virgo in the 8th house, sextiling his Mercury in Scorpio find its fulfillment through devotion to Love and Beauty, but Mercury in Scorpio, in sextile to Mars in Capricorn allowed him to translate those insights into practical techniques for daily living—and loving. Again, the transits are informative. From 1473–1478 transiting Pluto was conjuncting his Venus in Virgo, sextile Mercury trine Mars; from 1473–1479 transiting Neptune was sextiling his Venus conjunct Mercury sextile Mars, and from 1477–1479, transiting Uranus was sextiling his Venus conjunct Mercury sextile Mars! Wouldn't we imagine that this was the time of the most intense exploration and transformation of his understanding of love? The historical accounts of Ficino confirm that he emerged from his long, deep depression, a transformed and reinvigorated man. Not only did he write his second version of *De Amore*, but he also reinterpreted the *Prisca Theologia* (the ancient theology), published the first edition of the *Corpus Hermeticum* (1471), and began writing the *Book of Life*, a version of all he had learned from his encounter with Saturn—the basis of his Therapeia and the paradigm for experiential astrology. I say *a* version, because the highest expression of Ficino's teaching may be contained in a single image, *La Primavera*—Sandro Botticelli's extraordinary painting, the most familiar, and most honored evocation of Spring.

If ever the essence of a time was captured in paint on canvas, *La Primavera* is that image. One of the most studied paintings, scholars tell us, it was painted in 1479.[34] Historically aware astrologers would immediately agree, for this places its creation at the peak of the astrological configuration that most characterizes the Renaissance— the Uranus-Neptune conjunction, in the last degree of Scorpio of 1478. And there is strong evidence from art historians that the program for Botticelli's painting was provided by none other than his mentor at the Platonic Academy—Marsilio Ficino![35] (Uranus-Neptune was then making an exact conjunction to his Mercury.) To the astrologer, it seems that this Uranus/Neptune conjunction of 1479 acted as a trip wire, setting off an alchemical explosion of profound depth and energy, propelling shards of archetypal substance throughout the Renaissance—throughout history— that, when imagined, assembled, and worked into artful expression by the masters of the time still invokes the magic of their origins. *La Primavera* is such a device—a *talisman* in Ficino's way of thinking—that has drawn down celestial powers that all may now appropriate, if we have the eyes to see and the will to understand. The art of doing so is the practice of experiential astrology.

My conclusion is that *La Primavera*, perhaps along with the *Birth of Venus* and *Pallas and the Centaur*, were probably painted about the same time,[36] and were the visible culmination of Ficino's titanic struggle with melancholia, both an end and a means for the development of his Therapeia, and one of the many ways he conveyed his knowledge of Saturn to the other "Saturnians" of the Academy—and to us all. The subject of the painting is Venus, Goddess of Love and Beauty—who else could soften the blows of Saturn—in all of her manifestations from vulgar to divine, in all her relationships with the celestial archetypes, and with all the qualities that a balanced synthesis of Paganism and Christianity might obtain. I will limit my discussion of the painting, since Thomas Moore (relying on classics scholar Edgar Wind[37]) has done well in his own astrological and psychological interpretation, and because I would prefer that you approach the image *experientially*, as it was intended. That is, according to scholar Frances Yates, "precisely an image to be used in the practice of natural magic, a means of exposure to the spirit of Venus, especially useful, in full accordance with Ficino's own thought, to circumvent the ravaging spirit of Saturn."[38] Moore, following Frances Yates, sees *La Primavera* as a means of educating the memory, and he cites Yates' suggestion "that if a person had such a model or picture in his bedroom, he could go through a day's activities interpreting them through that familiar image."[39] This is the practice I recommend to you as an adventure in experiential astrology.

My husband Bob Craft and I took Frances Yates' suggestion seriously four years ago on the Spring Equinox, when we hung a four- by three-foot copy of *La Primavera* in our bedroom and became students in Botticelli's "school of imagination." With its inspiration, we decided to make a serious study of love—erotic, "Platonic" (Ficino was the first to use the term), and the many nuances from sacred to profane. We made it a weekly practice on Friday nights (governed by Venus, of course) to examine and explore our thoughts and experiences in light of the imagery of *La Primavera*. Layer after layer of meaning began to reveal itself, both in the painting and in our understanding; the beauty and richness of the image seemed to amplify the beauty and complexity of our own experiences. Many of our insights have been carried into our workshops and presentations at astrology conferences; some remain our personal treasures. All of the ways of understanding that we brought to the table—Eastern, Western, shamanic and Native American, Jungian, alchemical, etc., came to bear on this exchange between our awareness and the image-encoded message from 1479. If you choose to do the same, your comprehension will, perhaps, be quite different, shaped by your own knowledge, experience, and modes of knowing. But much of the celestial endowment of the image will emerge—especially if you bring an astrologer's sensibility to the endeavor. Ficino's *Book of Life* or Moore's *Planets Within* may help you with the latter—Moore interprets each character in the painting in light of its symbolic association with the planets. Our own insight from continued exposure to the image is that the structure of the painting is in fact *zodiacal*, moving clockwise (the painting was probably designed to be hung in a space to the right of a door) from the dark-winged Zephyr on the far right, identified with Aries, through the eight figures, each representing all or part of a sign. The following table will give you an idea of the characters as they are described by scholars[40] and the associated signs as I see them:

TABLE 1. LA PRIMAVERA: SIGNS AND CHARACTERS

Character	Sign
Zephyr, the West Wind	Aries (Spring Equinox)
Chloris	Taurus
Flora	Gemini
Venus/Mary	Cancer (Summer Solstice)
The Graces	Leo
Beauty	Leo
Pleasure	Leo
Chastity	Leo/Virgo
Mercury	Virgo (or Libra, Fall Equinox)
Eros/Christ	Center of the Horoscope

Note: Mercury's gesture toward the heavens indicates the last six zodiacal signs (Libra through Pisces) and reflects the Hermetic dictum, "As above, so below."

Bob has a slightly different take on the association of signs to *La Primavera* figures,[41] seeing the first four as I do, but identifying each of the Graces—Pleasure, Chastity, and

Beauty—with Leo, Virgo, and Libra; and Mercury with Scorpio. He then identifies the remaining four "invisible" figures as: Sagittarius = The Centaur (from Botticelli's *Pallas and the Centaur*), Capricorn = Chronos and Jehovah, Aquarius = Ouranos and Prometheus, Pisces = Psyche and Christ in Heaven, and Eros = the Pagan God of Love as well as the incarnated Christ. We continue to debate our respective views.

We do not ask you to choose one or the other of these suggestions, but to encounter *La Primavera* on her own terms. We can surmise what Ficino himself intended from a remarkable letter to the young man for whom the painting was probably commissioned,[42] Lorenzo di Pierfrancesco de' Medici, second cousin of Lorenzo the Great, who was about fifteen years old at the time of the letter. It appears to be a lesson on love and morality, almost entirely in astrological language. First, Ficino asks the young man, "If...I make you a present of the heavens themselves what would be its price?" and notes that, "he would rather not talk about the price, for Love, born from the Graces, gives and accepts everything gratis." He then describes "the happiest man" as one with no bad Moon aspects to Mars and Saturn and good aspects to the Sun, Jupiter, Mercury, and Venus. He goes on to interpret these for Pierfrancesco and to tell him how these should be his guide. "Finally," he says, the Moon in a man should be directed to "fix her eyes on Venus herself, that is to say, on [Humanitas]."[43] Ficino reveals himself as a humanist and seems to be instructing the young man to seek out what is good in humanity and to recognize its origins in divine love. This is the recommended starting point for engaging the message of *La Primavera*. For the rest, you need no more guidance than Ficino's own succinct statement on his central teaching concerning love: "There is one continuous attraction, beginning with God, going to the world, and ending at last in God, an attraction which returns to the same place where it began as though in a kind of circle."[44]

Perhaps as we do, you will see that circle as the zodiac in its timeless renewal of creation. Perhaps you will seek to learn more about Ficino whom you may now agree is the First Experiential Astrologer, or to apply his methods to investing your own life with celestial radiance. Perhaps you will see, through these images from long ago, that your own life is propelled by this endless cycle of love.

3

MODERN ROOTS OF EXPERIENTIAL ASTROLOGY

Dem bones, dem bones, dem dry bones...
—Negro spiritual

Dane Rudhyar and Humanistic Astrology

The modern origins of experiential astrology can be traced to the late 1970s, when the doctrines of the human potential movement in the field of psychology and the culture at large began to find expression in astrology. The work of Dane Rudhyar and the humanistic astrology he developed over a lifetime is fundamental to my approach to the natal chart. His work shifted the focus of astrology from an outdated, predictive, event-oriented, and even fatalistic stance to that of a person-oriented one, emphasizing human growth and accomplishment.

Astrology and the Modern Psyche is perhaps Rudhyar's clearest explication of the relationship between astrology and the "depth psychology" that underlies the modern approach. In his book, Rudhyar traces the development of depth psychology to its origins in the evolutionary theories of Charles Darwin.[1] The classical psychologist, following Plato, sees a particular stone, tree, or person as a pale copy of some preexistent form. For Darwin and those who embraced his ideas, all life, including our own, evolves from more primitive beginnings—"the depths"—and is in a continuing state of re-creation. Thus, as Rudhyar states, "The individual 'I,' instead of being seen as an a priori, archetypal Self—as some 'pattern of perfection' transcendent to life on earth—begins to be understood as the end result of human living, as a victory to be won, as the result of the slow effort of integration and...individuation."[2] Sigmund

Freud was the original master of the probing of the human mind in its instinctual depths, and his work, with that of his followers, underlies much of the modern view of mind and human life.

Rudhyar's interest in depth psychology began in 1932 with his introduction to the works of C. G. Jung, an early associate of Freud.[3] For the astrologer, this signaled the beginning of a lifelong effort to reformulate "classical" astrology along the lines of a developing humanistic psychology, an effort that was to culminate in the now widespread "humanistic astrology" associated with his name. Experiential astrology's debt to Rudhyar is clear; the humanistic orientation provides the essential theoretical framework for the experiential use of astrology for becoming whole, healthy human beings, integrated in body, mind, and soul. But experiential astrology goes beyond Rudhyar's program by a further synthesis of elements from humanistic psychology, and from the arts and ancient spiritual tradition, thus yielding a body of technique for the purposes of self-actualization and self-realization.

Contributions of Jungian Psychology

To introduce astrology into a discussion of Jung is no imposition upon the great psychologist. He spoke often and favorably of the astrologer's art. In his many writings, Jung emphasized that astrology was a "map of the psyche" that included the sum total of all ancient psychological knowledge, describing both the innate predisposition of an individual personality as well as providing an accurate way of anticipating a life crisis. Because of their relevance to experiential astrology, these Jungian ideas demand attention: the process of individuation, concepts of wholeness and polarity, the model of the psyche with its conscious, personal unconscious and collective unconscious levels, and the theory of archetypes. Also, central in Jung's thought is the way he saw mythology as the key for understanding the human mind.

In Jung's view, we each begin life in a state of undifferentiated wholeness. As we mature, we emerge from the cosmic womb of the unconscious, evolving into increasingly complex structures capable of expressing ourselves in more refined and elaborate ways. This is the process of individuation. First to appear is a fundamental polarity. Jung states,

> The psyche consists of two incongruous halves that should properly make a "whole" together...but consciousness and the unconscious do not make a whole

when either is suppressed or damaged by the other. If they must contend, let it be a fair fight with equal right on both sides. Both are aspects of life. Let the consciousness defend its reason and its self-protective ways, and let the chaotic life of the unconscious be given a fair chance to have its own way, as much of it as we can stand. This means at once open conflict and open collaboration.... It is the old play of hammer and anvil: the suffering iron between them will, in the end, be shaped into an unbreakable whole, the individual.[4]

Thus individuation is the result of the continual integration of consciousness and the unconscious, and human growth proceeds by organizing separate elements into a complex whole.

Astrology, no less than Jung, incorporates ancient notions of wholeness and polarity. The astrological chart itself represents the whole of an individual personality. It is composed of two halves, one that represents the conscious, solar, active, masculine, day side of consciousness, and the other—the unconscious, lunar, passive, feminine, night side. As Jung's discourse often centers upon the interaction of paired opposites, i.e. conscious-unconscious, thinking-feeling, sensation-intuition, Animus-Anima, the chart also consists of polarities of similar explanatory power-pairs of opposites of signs (Taurus/Scorpio), of houses (second/eight), and of archetypes (Venus/Mars). And even the most left-brained of astrological consultations has the result of bringing what was unknown into consciousness, thus proceeding towards individuation as Jung describes it. Experiential astrology is intended to provide methods and understandings that go much further toward promoting the "open conflict and open collaboration" between consciousness and the unconscious to which Jung refers.

In 1909, Jung had an extraordinary dream that crystalized his theory that the psyche is composed of three distinct but interactive systems or levels—a conscious mind and an unconscious one that consists of two parts, the personal and the collective unconscious.[5] The dream ultimately led to the publication of Jung's seminal work, *Symbols of Transformation*. Joseph Campbell summarizes the themes of this great effort:

> ...the essential realizations...were, first, that since the archetypes of norms of myth are common to the human species, they are inherently expressive neither of local social circumstances nor of any individual's singular experience, but of common human needs, instincts, and potentials; second, that in the traditions of any specific folk, local circumstance will have provided the imagery through which the archetypal themes are displayed in the supporting myths of the culture; third, that

if the manner of life and thought of an individual so departs from the norms of the species that a pathological state of imbalance ensues of neurosis or psychosis, dreams and fantasies analogous to fragmented myths will appear; and fourth, that such dreams are best interpreted, not by reference backward to repressed infantile memories (reduction to autobiography), but by comparison outward with the analogous mythic forms (amplification to mythology), so that the disturbed individual may learn to see himself depersonalize in the mirror of the human spirit and discover by analogy the way to his own larger fulfillment.[6]

The publication of this book (in its original German edition) signaled Jung's break with Freud, in that the therapeutic method was no longer to consist solely of "reduction to autobiography," the Freudian method, but would emphasize "amplification to mythology," the connection of unconscious contents to the broader expressions of underlying reality—the enduring myths of humankind. And it is just this shift that makes Jungian thought so relevant to experiential astrology. Jung's great insight was that the mind has, as in Freud's view, an unconscious level that contains the repressed contents of one's personal history, but also that "this personal unconscious rests upon a deeper layer, which does not derive from personal experience and is not a personal acquisition but is inborn." Jung called this layer the *collective* unconscious because "this part of the unconscious is not individual but universal; in contrast to the personal psyche, it has contents and modes of behavior that are more or less the same everywhere and in all individuals."[7] Therefore, we all have a level of mind which is "identical in all men and thus constitutes a common psychic substrate of a suprapersonal nature which is present in every one of us."

Chief among the contents of the collective unconscious are the *archetypes*, "the primordial...universal images that have existed since the remotest times."[8] Emphasizing that the archetype predetermines form, not content, Jung offers us the vivid image of the archetype as like "the axial system of a crystal, which preforms the crystalline structure in the mother liquid although it has not material existence of its own."[9] He further explains that these archetypes, which are our universal heritage, may emerge in any individual consciousness, strike a responsive chord in companions, and be elaborated into myth, ritual, and cultural belief as they have throughout our history. They are the source of our shared understandings of the Great Mother, the Hero, the Gods themselves, and, not least, the planetary symbols of astrology.

We can speculate that Jung's recognition of the deeper, mythical level which he called the collective unconscious is a rediscovery of the same level that produced the divine communion experienced by the ancients of Eleusis two thousand years ago. It is apparent that Jung did not devise a concept, but instead uncovered a psychic reality. We humans invent concepts as tools for grasping, categorizing, and taking things apart. We can replace concepts, but the archetypal structures of consciousness are like vital organs: there are no rational substitutes for them. These archetypes are powerful, invisible forces that shape our behavior and influence emotion and belief. Jung—and this is the essence of his therapeutic method—would have us come to know these forms within ourselves and thus become freer and more whole. The Jungian perspective gives us both the rationale and the methodology for employing the astrological symbol as archetype. In experiential astrology, our aim is to put forth methods capable of evoking astrological archetypes so as to advance Jung's goal of awareness, wholeness, and freedom.

Experiential Astrology and the Human Potential Movement

I don't want to leave the impression that experiential astrology was designed by a committee of academics pouring over volumes of Freud, Jung, and Rudhyar. In fact, the typical contributor has spent more time testing the limits of personal growth than languishing in the library. My own background—which includes almost everyone's growth workshop, pilgrimages to Esalen Institute in Big Sur, California, an extended training program in group leadership skills, and fifteen years of the study of Kriya yoga—is not unusual. These are, of course, the opportunities for growth—psychological, spiritual, and artistic—that arose, especially in the United States, as the "human potential movement" of the mid-1960s. So, when we turn to creating elements of an "experiential" astrology, we bring a multitude of theoretical and practical notions whose origins tend to blur. However, some patterns are discernible and will get a brief treatment below under the headings of "experiencing, enactment, and embodiment" after a particular debt is acknowledged to Jacob Moreno and his contribution of "psychodrama."

Astrodrama, a form of experiential astrology that entails "acting out the horoscope" in part owes its inspiration to Jacob Moreno's therapeutic method of psychodrama. Moreno was a Viennese psychiatrist and contemporary of both Freud and Jung. He died in 1974, and thus his life spans almost the entire era of concern to us, although psychodrama has come into special prominence only since the 1960s. Moreno was a director of experimental theater in the 1920s. His interest in the therapeutic uses of the art form began with a marital quarrel among members of his company, which he brought before an audience with remarkable results.[10] From that beginning, Moreno saw the promise of a healing theater and took steps to bring it into being. In effect, Moreno threw out the psychiatrist's couch and substituted an impromptu stage where "individuals could act out their own and the world's problems in the absolute freedom of improvisation."[11] As one observer notes, "Moreno's theories are complex and abstruse, but his method is simple, direct and powerful. A psychodrama performance involves participants who enact scenes from their lives using a variety of techniques to heighten emotions and clarify conflicts. Observers who may not be directly involved often profit from the experience."[12] Where in classical drama the aim was to bring about a *catharsis* (that is, a healing emotional release) in the audience, psychodrama invites that experience in the actors, with great effect. Astrodrama, in its lighter, more performance-oriented form, may be directed toward the audience, or when used as a means of personal growth, it may have all the intensity and immediacy of a psychodrama. In either mode of expression, astrodrama has what astrologers will recognize as the distinct advantage of being informed by "the map of the psyche," the astrological chart.

Rudhyar gives us a humanistic point of view of the natal chart, Jung provides us with a larger theoretical framework within which astrology can creatively operate, and Moreno supports the importance of individual participation as the means to return to the central role of protagonist in one's own unfolding life drama. But there are other influences upon experiential astrology. Out of a great complexity of possibilities, three patterns or themes appear to emerge.

The first influential theme of the human potential movement is "experiencing." We are experiencing when we actively, emotionally attune to ourselves in the moment, particularly in a situation that has opportunities for personal growth. At one extreme, experiencing may include a profound, emotionally cathartic discharge of feelings. Dispassionate and abstract intellectualizing is the near opposite of experiencing. No less an authority than Carl Rogers, the father of non-directive psychotherapy, thought this factor important enough to develop, along with his colleagues, a scale for its measurement.[13] Even casual observation supports the claim that the usual mode of communication about astrology is abstract and dispassionate, perhaps good for transmitting raw data, but not reflective of experiencing, which facilitates growth. Experiential astrology seeks to remedy that.

A second characteristic of growth-oriented practice may be called "enacting." You have seen enacting referred to in its most obvious form in the psychodramatic "acting out" of life episodes in Moreno's work. But enacting includes, especially in the *Gestalt* therapy devised by Fritz Perls, the acting out and integrating of unconscious and disowned contents of the unconscious mind.[14] An intense astrodrama may include these elements as pointed to by particular transits to the chart, but may include the bringing into full emotional expression an archetype such as Venus, the Sun, or Pluto. Enacting makes explicit what is implicit in our unconscious, and thus allows us to give it form and feeling and to integrate it into our being.

"Embodiment" is the third factor that influences experiential astrology. Beginning, perhaps, with Wilhelm Reich, another of Freud's early circle, the West began to rediscover that, in some real sense, we *are* bodies. We don't just have bodies as an unhappy appendage of our minds. Reich's contribution (later elaborated throughout the 1960s and beyond by followers such as Lowen and Keleman) included the recognition that the body is an energetic system with characteristic blocks to the free flow of emotion and feeling. He also devised techniques for removing those blocks.[15] More generally, however, embodiment means that we astrologers can leave the chairs of our consulting rooms and can express the meanings of the astrological archetypes in motion, feeling, dance, and touch—and we'll be richer for it.

Spiritual Traditions and Transpersonal Psychology

The Western humanistic tradition never had complete sway over the content of the human potential movement. From the advent of the movement, spiritual leaders and their ancient traditions (largely from the East) had their place alongside therapists and T-groups. Astrology has a particular affinity for some elements of this spiritual influx, in part due to some common origins. In Kriya Yoga, for example, astrological and yogic precepts have long been intimately intertwined, each illuminating the other.[16] Later in this book, you will encounter yogic aspects of experiential astrology.

The Eastern and Western psychologies named above are combined in a relatively new field termed "transpersonal psychology."[17] The writings of proponents such as

Ken Wilber, Stanislav Grof, and Jean Houston may be sources of continuing inspiration for our pursuits in experiential astrology. Interestingly, the "classical psychology" displaced by humanism is making a return under the aegis of transpersonal psychology. Grof is explicit about this in particular reference to astrology:

> ...astrology, a discipline rejected and ridiculed by Newtonian-Cartesian science can prove to be of unusual value as a source of information about personality development and transformation. It would require a long discussion to explain how and why astrology can function as a remarkable referential system. This possibility seems quite absurd from the point of view of mechanistic science, which treats consciousness as an epiphenomenon of matter. However, for an approach that sees consciousness as a primary element of the universe that is woven into the very fabric of existence, and that *recognizes archetypal structures as something that precedes and determines phenomena in the material world* [my italics], the function of astrology would appear quite logical and comprehensible.[18]

Fortunately, in order to use experiential astrology, we don't have to resolve whether classical or humanistic psychology is the right view, especially since philosophers haven't been able to do so in over three thousand years. Whether we think the archetypes arise in a dimension of reality beyond our own (as might Grof or a follower of Plato), or that they are a manifestation of mind as our shared inheritance as human beings (à la Jung), or even that they are ordinary but extremely important ideas that reflect cultural truths, we can enlist them as a tool for self-understanding and growth.

So we have come full circle in our journey into theory, and yet have touched upon only a few of the influences on experiential astrology. In part, this is due to its diffuse origins, but perhaps even more because what we are attempting has been arrived at by actual living experience rather that by study. Each of you who chooses to explore experiential astrology will have a chance to experience it in your own way, to embody its principles, and to enact them in your own life.

4

USING EXPERIENTIAL ASTROLOGY

We are enacting, telling, witnessing the Story of our Souls.
—James Hillman, Revisioning Psychology

Experiential astrology has been used in four principal ways: as an artistic and expressive form of theater; as a teaching tool for students and practitioners; as a context for therapeutic healing; and, as we'll see in Chapters 5 and 6, for self-study, contemplation, and personal ritual. In ancient times, the portrayal of archetypal planetary energies was integral to public drama. Theater was a sacred, cathartic medium, designed to heal through direct contact with the deepest levels of consciousness. Modern theater, on the other hand, may experiment with the evocation of deep symbols from time to time, but seeks most often to entertain rather than transform. The Astrodrama performance described below was one in a series of steps toward re-creating the healing theater of the past, with astrological symbols as the medium for direct interaction with the unconscious. As you read on, note the healing effects of the form on both audience and actors as well as the ease with which astrodrama communicates astrological information to those who may not know so much as their own Sun sign.

This performance was created to express the astrological influences present at the very moment in which it was enacted. What is described was the first of two connected performances, one staged on the lunar eclipse (full moon), Taurus/Scorpio in May, 1985 for a general audience, and the other on the solar eclipse (new moon) in Scorpio for the NCGR (National Council on Geocosmic Research) Regional Conference in Chicago, in November, 1985.

The setting is the large converted gymnasium of the Noyes Cultural Arts Center in Evanston, Illinois. Large floor-to-ceiling windows line two sides of the room and overlook a broad lawn. It is a beautiful, warm, spring night. As dusk turns to dark, the glow of flickering candles mirrors the star-studded backdrop. The full moon rises lazily in the night sky. An audience of more than one hundred, half of whom know no astrology, settle into their seats to enjoy the performance. Why not join us for the show?

May 4 1985 Theater

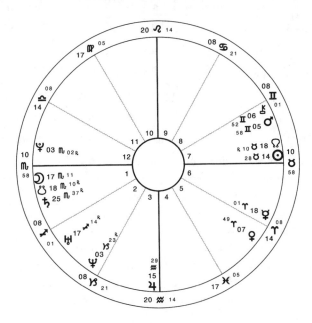

As the lights fade to black, the deep resonant voice of the narrator breaks the silence: "And God created the Sun, the Moon, and the planets...."

A spotlight catches the brightly costumed "planets" as, one by one, they make their entrances. Mars leaps to the stage and thrusts with his sword; Saturn enters with a stately, almost laborious gait. Each planet speaks a three-line "signature": "I am Mercury! I am your power to communicate, the mind behind your brain, the focusing lens through which all others pass. With reason's torch, I search for *truth*." Venus enters in a whirl of pink and green chiffon: "I am Venus! I am all that you love and find dear. I attract through my loving, gentle and harmonious spirit." When they have entered the theater, they spread out, bantering and mingling with the audience. Venus approaches a woman in the back row. "And what sign is your Venus in?" "Taurus," answers the surprised spectator. In a split second she begins to improvise: "Oh we *do* love to eat! Let's go to that new little French restaurant. I hear they have the best *paté de foi gras*. And a great price on a bottle of Pomerol '82!" Chuckling with recognition, the woman grasps Venus' hand warmly. Around her there's a sense of delight and anticipation as the other planets entertain.

Soon, each moves to center stage and finds the point in the circle of the Zodiac that represents their exact position in the sky at that moment. Then Mercury, in the natural role of communicator, points out the four directions, the arc of the Zodiac belt, the rising and setting planets, and the aspects (angular relationships) of each planet to any others on this particular evening. Each then takes three minutes for an introduction, evoking as fully as possible the unique identity of their planet. With body movement, feelings, images, sounds, speech, mannerisms, and facial expressions, they paint a living portrait of their planetary energy. Let's listen as Mercury speaks.

"I am your power to communicate, to think and reflect, to discriminate one experience from another. As Hermes, messenger from the Gods, I am the bridge between your conscious mind and the undiscovered world of the Unconscious.

I am the means by which you speak. I invented all writing, language, books, and libraries. I seek knowledge—and understanding. I search for new ways in which to perceive the world. I ask the ultimate questions: Where have I come from? Why am I here? Where am I going...? I can be your best friend or your worst enemy. As your foe, I can bring you endless distractions to keep you out of touch with your repressed emotions. I keep you busy so you won't *feel*. Emotions are so unreasonable!

In Scorpio, I penetrate to the depths, seeking the core. I know the secrets of magic and Tantra, but what I've discovered I'll never tell *you!* In Virgo, I am clear, precise, and efficient. I recognize error and imperfection, but, I'll admit, I'm much more interested in what I've done wrong than what I've done right.

Tonight, I'm in Aries. I'm bold and brash and impulsive. My thoughts are like shooting stars, exploding in all directions—and tonight, I'll tell you what's on my mind, like it or not!"

When each of the planets has spoken, the lights are dimmed, signaling the next phase of the program, a retelling of the myth of Demeter and Persephone. This myth was chosen because it evokes the strong Taurus/Scorpio energies (betrayal and forgiveness) available to us on this evening.

Scene One introduces Hades, pacing back and forth in uncontrollable anger, ranting and raving, growling and grimacing at the noisy, wrathful Giants imprisoned in

Mt. Etna above him. Determined to restore quiet to his domain, he makes off for the upper world. Arriving there, he spies Persephone in a meadow picking flowers. Viewing the scene from a hillock, Venus, in a moment of irony, sends Cupid to pierce the unsuspecting Hades with the arrow of love. Thus struck, his anger turns to lust for the innocent young girl. Utterly consumed with passion, he circles her, hissing and licking his jowls in anticipation.

A surging drumbeat echoes the rhythm of Persephone's heart as she spots the lustful Hades circling her. Immune to her screams of terror, the dark god seizes the girl, carrying her off into his underworld cave. When Demeter, the maiden's mother, learns what has happened, she first shrieks with rage, then collapses with a convulsive sob, utterly stricken with grief. No one, not even the gods can console her. And for that, all must suffer. As Goddess of the Grains and caretaker of all that lives upon the earth, she neglects her duties. The earth withers. What was once green and beautiful turns brown and bare.

Finally, with the aid of Hermes/Mercury and the intervention of the all powerful Zeus/Jupiter, a bitter compromise is struck. All must reconcile themselves to the new arrangement. The primeval power of Hades and Demeter is played against the innocence of Persephone. The three are bound together against their will by passion and grief. All betrayed and all endured the betrayal of another.

The final words of the play are spoken by Hermes:

"This is a myth that reveals our purity and innocence, our desires and betrayals. It is a story about our tolerance of the intolerable, acceptance of the unacceptable, and ultimately, forgiveness of the unforgivable. It presents the mystery of man which resides in these contradictions, opposites that forever meet in rhythmic and creative interplay of light and dark. The solution resides in man's courage and ability to enter the threshold, meet the demons, and pass through the flame. Man is the fire and the hearth, the log and the sacrifice...."

The lights fade to black. The emotional roller coaster of the last twenty minutes ends with a moment of pregnant, reflective silence, filled, as several audience members will say later, with stirred up feelings and their own remembered experiences of betrayal.

But, swiftly, the tone of the performance changes with the commencement of a series of playful, creative improvisations drawn from the charts of audience members. From the back of the room comes a request to see "Mercury in Gemini, square Uranus in Virgo." After a moment's consultation, Mercury and Uranus move quickly to center stage. Mercury begins an energetic monologue, blurting out her favorite opinions, books she's going to write, and great questions she's found the answer to. Uranus, drawing near Mercury, seems to radiate a kind of erratic energy to which Mercury must respond. She is unrelenting in her criticism of Mercury's ideas, flooding her with wild options to consider. The improvisation ends with an exhausted Mercury begging for peace and quiet.

A request to see "the Sun in Aries opposite the Moon in Libra" invites another spontaneous skit. The Sun and Moon take the floor, engaged in a psychic tug of war over marriage plans. The forceful Sun insists they should schedule the wedding as soon as possible, while the evasive Moon shuffles across the floor with a confused expression. She tells us in an aside what she's thinking: "This guy! He's cute but I *did* just meet him last week. He looks a little like Brad, but he really acts more like Tom." The scene ends without resolution, but with much good-humored applause from the audience.

As the finale of the evening's production nears, each planet steps forward to offer a symbolic gift to the audience. Mercury gives the seed of positive thought; Saturn, clay with which to mold a structure for our lives, Mars, a sword to inspire the courage to cut through what holds us back. The close of the performance bonds the evening's participants, performers, and onlookers in a moment of reflection. The very last words of the evening are spoken by Carl Fitzpatrick as Pluto:

"Nine beautiful gifts. But wasn't there something forgotten? Something you could have had from anyone, but somehow...? Anyway, what can you ask from Pluto, when in my realm I gather all that remains after you have accumulated in Taurus all that you value, stamped your mark on it, and called yourself secure. Some of that refuse rots to poison your depths, and to survive, you'll have to return to me to dig it out and find the power to heal. As for real treasure, you never recognized it. And if I give it to you now, you'll only throw it away again.

The eclipse shows the mystery. The moon is in Scorpio, and you whine and cry because I bring you betrayal and death. But what have you known of trust, or of life? I'll test your shallow innocence in a crucible of suspicion, and maybe then you can learn to commit yourself whole and inspire trust. Betrayal? You bring that on yourself! I call on you to be transformed through your deepest passions so you will know the fullness of life. Death, too, you bring on yourself.

The sun is in Taurus, and you dwell in a block of stone, with me as the sculptor, hacking away at your prison, and it bleeds when you clutch at the pieces of what you have instead of valuing what you are. You can bring me your resentment and bitterness because all you hold precious has been corrupt and stolen. The one gift I'll have for you is the last thing you will ever ask for: your true self!"

Following the performance there's a live band, dancing, drinks, and hors d'oeuvres. It's been an intense, thought-provoking, and emotional evening, reflecting for all the deeper drama that lies behind the familiar symbols of the full moon eclipse in Taurus/Scorpio.

As co-producer, director, and the planet Mercury, my memory of the event is still vivid. Our troupe of players was able to evoke the aspects of the moment and use them to create an astrological "happening." The Mercury sextile Jupiter, trine Uranus allowed us to communicate and teach astrological principles and understandings. The strong Taurus/Scorpio square Jupiter gave us access to a level of consciousness that permitted a healing release; and the Venus sextile and Mars trine to Jupiter ensured the success of the evening-ending celebration and feast. The performance also provided a means to reach not only experienced astrologers, but many who were entirely new to astrology. Rather than touching just one person in the usual one-to-one consulting style, we reached out to more than one hundred. In this time of Pluto in Scorpio, when people were looking for deep, cathartic experience, we were able to show a glimmer of the psychological potential of astrodrama and experiential astrology.

Those who made this undertaking a reality are of particular interest from an astrological perspective. The co-producers of the theater were Clay Bodine (Saturn conjunct Pluto), Betsey Means (Sun in Scorpio), and myself (Saturn conjunct Pluto). Of the ten "planets," four were practicing astrologers, three were actors/actresses, and the remainder were therapists/healers. Five of us had astrology backgrounds. The others had no previous knowledge of astrology. Of the ten "planets," four had Sun in Scorpio; two Moon in Scorpio; two Scorpio rising; and three Saturn conjunct Pluto! What struck me as more than coincidence was the strong Scorpio energy within this group that came together for a performance on a Taurus/Scorpio eclipse. That organizing point seemed to attract a group not only interested in deep, psychological, and emotional experience, but capable of evoking and communicating the powerful energies of the eclipse.

For us in the cast, of course, the experience extended far beyond the evening's performance. We rehearsed twice a week for an intensive eight-week period. Rehearsals included astrology, movement, body awareness, sound, voice, guided imagery, and creative improvisation, in addition to the creation of the play within a play (Demeter and Persephone). We were also fortunate to have available to us the special expertise of two well-known women in the area, sound therapist Vickie Dodd and dance therapist Jane Siegel. Both did much to help performers develop their voices and bodies as instruments of expression. Each planet actor spent many hours literally living with their planetary identities: thinking, sensing, feeling, becoming their planets, and finding ways to communicate what they experienced on the inside. Using inner images, creative imagination, guided meditations, voice, sound, movement, and body imaging, they explored the connection with the archetype within. During the weeks of preparation, the troupe members helped each other develop their planetary roles, refine ideas, write scripts, and design and create costumes and makeup.

We also shared our feelings about our roles. Pluto told about how, on his way home from the first rehearsal, he heard a voice within him crying out, "What are you doing? You haven't acted in anything since eighth grade!" And on another occasion, with tears in her eyes, Neptune shared her struggle to find a way to express her planet: "I realized a part of me has really been out of touch with anything spiritual. It's been hard to open up, and trust that I have it in me."

The effects of the performance were far greater than we might have imagined. Photographer and friend, David Hartwick, made the following observation: "My strongest impression of this experience is that it's healing theater. Those receiving the most healing were the actors themselves. Being able to get out there and *be* those things, that's where the real healing was taking place. I've always been a fan of people's theater with an everyman quality to performance. Down the road in this process, you should look to getting more people directly involved. That is where the greatest healing may ultimately lie. We all need to get up at some time and act out who we are."

David's comments were certainly prophetic in light of the post-performance experiences of the actors: (Associated astrological keywords have been highlighted in italics). The Sun (Clay Bodine), decided to *expand* the number of classes he would teach, and set a goal to *double* his working/theater space, which he did within six months. The Moon (Ann Trompeter) stopped *vacillating* and decided to commit herself to her career as an actress. Mercury (Barbara Schermer) began to *write* this book. Both Venus actresses (Saren O'Hara and Randi Wolferding) decided to get *pregnant*.

Mars (Dennis Brittan), Chicago therapist, became further involved in treating psychological aspects of the *battle* against AIDS.

Saturn (Betsey Means) pointed to three related outcomes: new realizations about the ways in which she had been *restricting* her life, and a new commitment to overcoming those restrictions; her acceptance of a key role in a Chicago play as a *burdened* woman who eventually goes mad, and her catalytic role in helping "Uranus" get her new business *organized*. Uranus (Vicki Dodd) finally accepted herself as a *maverick* therapist and opened a New Age networking center called New Voices Networking. Not surprisingly, Neptune (Gina Bader) had the most *vague* connected experience, although she did say she was recently felt more *inspired*. Jupiter (Jim Redmond) noticed no particular Jupiterian elements in his life, but astrologers would note that any effects were likely to be outweighed by the influence of his Saturn return at 26 degrees Scorpio, and transiting Pluto conjunct his Mars at 4 degrees Scorpio.

Pluto (Carl Fitzpatrick) had the most dramatic experience. Within weeks of his performance, he fell from a forty-foot ladder, fracturing his pelvis, crushing his foot, and breaking his right arm. (Transiting Uranus was conjunct his first house Mars in Sagittarius as Pluto made a sextile to Saturn. Carl feels it was the Pluto sextile that helped save his life.) Here is what Carl wrote about his experience:[1]

> "Shortly after our November performance, which was timed with a solar eclipse in Scorpio, on my birthday, I lived through a serious accident that brought me close to death. It may have seemed to others that Pluto aspects brought me disaster, but in my own heart and mind it was as if my communion with the Pluto archetype prepared me to survive a moment of crisis. Pluto, the healer, gave me the inner strength to survive the crisis almost fully whole.
>
> As we rehearsed, I meditated on the meaning of Pluto and the need for transformation in every life, and I became subliminally conscious that a turning point in my own life was approaching. In retrospect, I can focus on the decision I had been putting off for years that, for many reasons, I should give up the work I'd been doing on ladders. It took a speeding car to literally knock the ladder from under me to help me make my decision. It seems laughable to call this experience a disaster. Who would have suspected that I could fall four stories and escape with only a minor disability. It seems clearer than ever that if accepted with instinctive awareness, Pluto represents a deep liberation of the essential self."

In sum, our astrodrama was an extraordinary group experience. The impact it had on the performers is clear. The effect on the audience was apparent from the good feelings shown at the dance and celebration that followed. People were obviously affected and moved, and were made more aware of their own, deeply personal connection with their cosmic neighbors. Both performers and audience joined together to provide a superb example of a renewed astrological awareness, amplifying and elucidating human experience with a healing touch for all.

Teaching Astrology by Experience

Nearly everyone educated in the Western tradition experienced a common "approved" method for assimilating new information. Learning took place in a classroom where a teacher presented ideas verbally while we, as students, sat quietly at our desks recording them. We have been conditioned to think that this is the only way to learn.

In your first basic astrology class you probably struggled with what seemed an impenetrable mass of data. There were pages and pages of detailed notes about thirty-four new concepts. There were the ten planets, twelve signs, and twelve houses, not to mention the five key aspects. Learning the basics may have impressed you much like your experience of third grade, with concepts implanted largely by rote memorization. Only when the thirty-four symbols were finally memorized did you, probably, begin to get a sense of how all the data fits together to form a cohesive interpretation.

But with experiential teaching methods, we can now learn and teach in ways that communicate to our whole selves simultaneously, rather than just our left brain cognitive side. Not only can we use the "Air mode" (talking) to teach, we can use Fire (action), Earth (sensations, pragmatic tools), and Water (feelings). With multiple approaches, astrology becomes more interactive, making learning easier and synthesis more complete.

Activities

One of the key concepts we learn in beginning astrology classes is the relationship between the four elements: Fire (Aries, Leo, Sagittarius), Air (Gemini, Libra, Aquarius), Water (Cancer, Scorpio, Pisces), and Earth (Taurus, Virgo, Capricorn). Let's see how experiential astrology might approach the elements.

If you're teaching about the elements in the traditional way, you might introduce each element with a verbal description and perhaps draw four triangles with their respective elements and signs on a chalkboard. This approach appeals to the intellect.

To have a more complete experience, why not add an activity for each element that the entire group can participate in.

For the element Fire, we might ask the group to stand up, spread out, and stretch. (You'll need some floor space.) Once they've loosened up, try playing some fiery Aries music—active, insistent, aggressive, rhythms. Then encourage the group to feel, to *be* the Fire quality: move and burn like a fire. Be direct, definite, emphatic. Ask them to move their arms, legs, torsos, and heads. This process can be used to bring their whole selves into synchronism with the Fire element. When the music is over, observe the highly charged energy in the room. Notice the chattering and huffing and puffing to catch a breath. That's *Fire*! To broaden the learning, get feedback by asking the group members what this exercise was like for them. This can lead to a discussion of the Fire element in their charts. A person with a fiery chart will probably have no difficulty in doing this, while a person with a water chart might feel more inhibited.

After a short discussion, move on to the element Air. After talking about Air, give the group an experience of it. Try creating an imaginary situation. Ask your group to suppose that they are having a cocktail party. The guests have just begun arriving and it's their job to see that they're comfortable. Ask them to be the social butterfly, moving from group to group, interacting with everyone. Then turn on some upbeat, jazzy background music to add to the atmosphere. That's *Air*! Once everyone has had the chance to interact, again take a moment to ask what this experience was like for them. Do they have much Air in their charts? Was this easier for those with strong Air charts? Who had the most difficulty with this exercise? Does this reveal anything about the elemental components in their charts?

Move on to the element Earth. Since Earth relies on sensing to form impressions, ask the group to sit cross-legged in a circle, close enough to barely touch knees. Have them close their eyes. Then pass around natural objects they can touch, smell, taste, etc., such as a bag of soil, herbs, stones, clay, gems, iron, incense, gold, a leaf or bark. As each person touches, feels, or smells an object, they are using their Earth element. After a dozen or so objects are all passed around, ask the group to open their eyes. Were any of the objects distasteful? Pleasant? Unidentifiable? That's *Earth*!

Finally, work with the element Water. Ask the group to lie down in a comfortable position on the floor of the room. Then turn off the lights and invite them, through guided imagery, to go to a beach. Let them feel the warm sand and water. As the tide rises they float safely atop the water and out to sea. Play ocean sounds softly in the background. Let everyone melt into this. Be silent for five minutes. Then guide them back into the room, slowly making them aware of their environment. When the time is right, turn on the lights. What was this like? Almost everyone enjoys this kind of passive, introverted Water experience, especially those strong in Water. The more restless ones may have strong Fire, or Fire transits affecting their charts.

Now, let the initial flush of excitement at experiencing the elements open into a further discussion. Students learning experientially are likely to understand elements more deeply. They will not only have an intellectual understanding of Fire, Air, Earth, and Water, they will also have a kinesthetic experience of the elements and how they feel in their bodies.

Image Boards

Image boards for teaching or learning can also create a range of new possibilities. These collages of visual images are effective and stimulating tools for teaching basic astrology to beginners, helping intermediate students to learn aspects and hone their interpretation skills, and even jiggling the creative juices of experienced astrologers preparing client's charts.

For a basic astrology class, you might create an image board for the planet Venus with sensual images like a baby llama sitting in a field of daisies; a photograph of a freshly dipped, chocolate-glazed hand holding a chocolate-covered ice cream cone; a little girl dressed in her mother's hat, purse, and high heels, carrying her doll; a pair of sensuous, wet, woman's lips; a dolphin; two lovers; a beach full of sunbathers; a man peacefully fishing in a boat at dusk; and a ballerina dancing. Show students with little or no knowledge of astrology an image board like this and ask them what Venus symbolizes. They'll tell you!

Then put out an image board of Uranus. On it might be a graphic silhouette of a man with colorful lightning bolts, spirals, meteor streaks, and stars imposed over him; exploding fireworks; an image of computer circuitry; a hi-tech mechanical arm; a spaceship; punky, hip young men with sunglasses; a photo of silicon valley; and a view into deep space. Ask what Uranus represents. Then ask what happens when you blend Venus and Uranus energies together.

When teaching how to integrate aspects, display the boards of Venus and Uranus together. Again, use the combined images to illustrate how these energies interact in a conjunction, sextile, square, trine, or opposition. What do the boards tell students about the quality of relationship a person would seek if he or she had Venus conjunct Uranus in his or her natal chart? What might be a typical sequence of events in a relationship if a client had Venus square Uranus in their natal chart or a transiting Uranus opposite their natal Venus? What kind of a love affair would ensue if their Venus was conjunct their new lover's Uranus?

If you are using image boards therapeutically, have your student or client look at the images of their natal Venus square Uranus. Ask them to spontaneously describe what they're seeing. Can they see a parallel between these images and the way they relate to others in their daily lives? Ask what this energy feels like inside. Can they associate any of these feelings with their current relationship? Can they draw their own image of what this feels like to them? A half-hour investment in this process will reveal much more than a mere description of their Venus square Uranus.

To make image boards, get ten large (at least 12" x 14") pieces of cardboard, a stack of magazines (*Omni*, *Smithsonian*, *National Geographic*, *Newsweek* are good sources), scissors, plastic photo protectors to keep the boards clean, and a glue stick. (By using a glue stick or rubber cement, you can change your image boards frequently to keep both you and your students interested, and make it possible to add better images when you run across them.) When browsing through magazines, keep an eye out for appropriate planetary images. In time, your image boards will really begin to evoke the planets they illustrate.

Astrodrama and Psychotherapy

In my experience, Astrodrama, in conjunction with the methods of psychotherapy, has demonstrated its healing potential time and time again. It can be used with many therapeutic approaches—Jungian, Gestalt, psychosynthesis, etc. Astrology can mesh particularly well with aspects of the Neo-Reichian body therapies and Alexander Lowen's Bioenergetics, particularly when astrologer and therapist work together as a team. My husband, psychotherapist Bob Craft, and I have presented a number of "Astrology and

Psychotherapy" workshops in Chicago for astrologers who want to work more deeply with their charts. The following is an example from a workshop we conducted together.

The group was focused on the chart of a woman who wanted to work with her problem of Saturn/Pluto conjunction in Leo in her seventh house. She had never been married and had a history of running away from commitment when her relationships became intimate. When she was five years old, her brother became critically ill with polio, and for her protection she was sent to live with relatives. She remembers almost never seeing her parents. To her, the family had disintegrated, and she felt abandoned. Now, as an adult, she was becoming aware that the insecurities and doubts surrounding this period of her life contributed to her deep fear of intimate relationships.

Beginning with a brief astrodrama, she responded to her Saturn and Pluto with confusion and frustration. Bob then asked if she would be willing to let him do some body therapy with her. She agreed and followed his instruction to lie down on her back. Because intimacy with a man was a threat for her, I sat alongside for reassurance. When she was comfortable with the situation, Bob placed his hand on her sternum and gently began to press, asking that she focus on whatever feelings emerged.

As he continued to press on her heart area, her eyes teared and soon put forth a gushing stream. She first spoke, haltingly through her tears, of her feelings of hurt in relation to men in her past. Then she began to mobilize herself against Bob. She grasped his hands, trying to push them away. (She had already been told that she could end the exercise at any time by saying "STOP!") He resisted, she pushed harder. She finally pushed him farther away by getting her feet underneath and shoving angrily and defiantly against his chest. With his full weight against her resisting feet, Bob asked her to hold this position for as long as she could and to "stay with her feelings."

Her legs began shaking from the strain of resisting, and she quickly appeared to feel overwhelmed with the effort of keeping him away. She began to show evidence of feeling suffocated and started to hyperventilate. Frightened, she cried, "Don't suffocate me. Don't suffocate me. Leave me alone. Go away. I can't breathe." At this point, as she was to describe it later, she "broke through" and relived a forgotten and repressed near-drowning experience she had in Lake Michigan when she was four.

In the throes of the experience she struggled with an initial terror. Her fear then turned to another response—she let go of struggling, yielded, and accepted her fate. She said, "I moved to a place of deep peace and calm. I was amazed to actually *see* a little minnow in the water in front of me and a floating piece of seaweed, then a shaft of light shining down through the water. Then I felt myself being violently snatched out of the lake by a man, my next-door neighbor, actually, who must have seen me drop out of sight."

We finished this evocative session by discussing how this repressed experience, the feelings of suffocation, and her inability to make a commitment with a man fit together with her Saturn/Pluto conjunction in the seventh. The woman recovered a new and valuable piece of information about why she felt the way she did about men. Since the workshop, the woman has continued to work with Bob. He has used further bodywork, art therapy techniques, and dreamwork to help her integrate her suffocation experience and overcome the problems connected with it.

Experiential astrology and psychotherapy in combination offer an exciting array of techniques and concepts for exploring the psyche. Both have something unique to offer. And, with Pluto now in Sagittarius, it would be no surprise to find more people interested in a synthesis of approaches that could lead them to a heightened understanding of their charts and themselves.

5

BIRTHING VENUS WITHIN:
A PLANETARY EXAMPLE

The Soul is born in beauty and feeds on beauty, requires beauty for its life.

—James Hillman

She arrives at dawn on a rose and blue morning—this blissfully naked maiden with the face and form that authenticate the divinity of Beauty. Blessed by the flower-laden breath of the nymph Chloris, her fragile shell vessel is wafted by the exhalation of Zephyr the Wind, gliding on a carpet of sea foam that shimmers toward the shore. The gaze of her eyes stirs our souls with a flicker of desire and heightened possibility. Her first step onto the earth will signal the birth of *Humanitas*, that element in humankind that comes closest to the divine. The *Horai*, the personified hours of the day, offer her a cornflower and a daisy-embroidered cloak, symbols of the moment when humanity has its first true awareness of the order of nature and of the seasons, the eternal return of the zodiac. With the birth of the divine Venus comes the *naissance* of the first moment of humanity worthy of the name. Her birth is our becoming—Humanity!

This image of the *Birth of Venus*, painted by Botticelli in 1478, has become so familiar—decorating everything from placemats to software packages—that it may be in danger of surrendering all meaning. Its message flies in the face of the postmodern ironic devaluation of all things beautiful and affirming of human good. A feminist critique might note that it is a depiction of the feminine by men, even of the *anima*, or soul in male consciousness, to Jungians. My aim here, however, is to reclaim *Birth of Venus* for women—to use its imagery and its inspiration to explore the many gifts that Venus, Goddess of Love and Beauty, offers, especially to women.

My interest in exploring the topic so thoroughly springs from a personal experience. Venus almost always shows up unexpected and unannounced, but rarely unaccompanied—her son Eros is seldom far behind. And when they arrive together, it is with the force of a hurricane. This happened to me seven years ago. When transiting Pluto conjoined my Jupiter in Scorpio, opposed to my Mars in Taurus, Venus placed in my path a young and incredibly beautiful man, the perfect "animus male," who seemed to fulfill in every detail the image of my divine lover. I was soon catapulted into a state that anyone who has ever loved can well imagine—swept up into a divine exultation and joy—but also cast down into confusion, fear, and guilt at the betrayer I had become, for I was, and remain, a married woman. Matters unfolded and finally unraveled, as they tend to, but not without leaving me with the knowledge that I had been *initiated* into the many mysteries of the Goddess of Love in forms both sacred and profane, transient and enduring.

With such an initiation comes both a need and an obligation to know more and to share what is known. One result of this search to know and to teach myself led to my facilitating four "Love and Sexuality" groups for women in Chicago over the last three years. Each group met for eight consecutive Friday nights, the night ruled by Venus. Together we created a safe, inviting, healing, and fun-filled environment for exploring our sensual and erotic lives. What a sense of relief we felt to be able to talk intimately with other women about what most mattered in our lives, yet was often unspoken, even unspeakable—about love and its erotic aspect of desire. Though the dark side of love was acknowledged, these were not therapy groups focused on our pain and woundedness, but more like *celebration* groups that honored the Goddess as she appeared in our lives and sought to open each of us to the joys of a more loving, sensual, and erotic life.

Two of these groups were astrologically oriented. We began our time together by looking at our horoscopes, zeroing in on the four elements and on our aspects to Venus and Mars to see what they could tell us about our own experiences of love and passion—about our personal concepts of love and beauty, about the qualities of desire and what gives us pleasure—in short, what *turns us on*. For example, in experiencing and understanding Venus as expressed through the element of earth, we learned a bit of sexual anatomy and physiology, related some of our own experience with orgasm, and shared tips on finding the famous "G-spot." And we reawakened our senses by indulging ourselves in champagne, rose water, and chocolate, and by treating our bodies to the delights of the Japanese baths. For Venus in the element of air, we watched educational videos—*Secrets of Sacred Sex,*[1] *Fire on the Mountain,*[2] and Annie Sprinkle's, *Sluts and Goddesses,*[3] in which the formidable former porn star, now a sex therapist and performing artist, demonstrates a seven-minute orgasm! And we had a candid conversation with a friend who was formerly a high-class prostitute. For Venus in the element of water, we chanted a yogic mantra to help heal and open our hearts, and each of us created a sacred space in her home in which to explore our erotic energy and our feelings. For Venus in the element of fire, we practiced a tantric technique to stimulate and free up our erotic energy, and its daily practice brought encouraging results, including reports of a noticeable and pleasurable erotic charge that lingered throughout the day. Two of the groups concluded with a wildly exuberant Slut-Goddess dance, complete with our own Slut and Goddess names, costumes, and identities— among them, Slither and Hera, Barbarella and She Walks in Beauty, Whiphand and Sophia. Yes, we had fun! Yes, we each became more aware of the many dimensions of Venus, from profane to sacred, an awareness that informs the journey of Venus through each of the signs.

In addition to these groups on love and sexuality, I have developed my understanding of the many permutations of Venus for a series of lectures and workshops, given at various astrology conferences around the world, on the topic, "Birthing Venus Within," using Botticelli's painting and the attendant myth as a starting point for an experiential process which aims to *bring Venus alive!* I take from both the groups and the workshops described below, giving practical methods for drawing down the exquisite pleasures of Venus, for deepening our understanding of Her as an aspect of Soul, and for raising our sights to encompass Her highest expressions. Though women have been the primary focus of these efforts, and I speak to them most directly in what follows, I hope that male readers will stay with us to see what the women in their lives are experiencing as well as to apply, with just a bit of translation, the insights of Venus to their own lives.

To set the scene, I will summarize the myth behind the *Birth of Venus*, as described in Hesiod's *Theogony*:[4] At the beginning of all things Mother Earth (as *prima materia*) emerged from Chaos and bore her son Ouranos (Uranus, the "Sky God," the divine masculine made manifest in the first male and first father), as she slept. Gazing down at her from his mountaintop realm, and with a look of love and desire, Ouranos showered his fertile rain upon her secret cleft. Through their divine, ecstatic union she bore the grass, flowers and trees, the beasts and the birds. This same rain made the rivers flow and filled the hollow places with water, so that lakes and seas came into being. But Ouranos also fathered the Titans and the hideous Cyclopes, and then flung these vile sons back into Tartarus (the bowels of the earth). Mother Earth was furious with him for destroying their children, and she persuaded the Titans to attack their father. And so they did, led by Cronos (Saturn), youngest of seven, armed with a flint sickle. (The rebirth of the masculine demands that the old king must die for the new one to be crowned.) Especially shocking is the way Cronos carried out his task—he castrated his father as he slept and flung the god's severed testicles into the sea. Ouranos's dark primal blood, his testicles, and his potent sperm fell to the depths and were taken up by the fecund womb of the feminine. From this brutal violation of a universal taboo, the "foam-born" Venus was created, and forevermore have love and anguish been entwined. Yet, too, from this cosmic event sprang the enduring connection of human nature with the divine through love. This is the scene that Botticelli bids us enter—the precise moment that the divine Venus, as a cosmological and spiritual archetype, takes flesh as Humanitas and accepts the governance of the seasons and the order of nature that are comprised by the zodiac. Like the duality of the heavens and the earth, this goddess has a double nature, appearing both as Venus Pandemos, who allows love and beauty to be perceived, imagined, and felt on earth, and as Venus Urania, the heavenly Venus, who lives out the highest expression of her nature in the Cosmic Mind, without the limitations or imperfections of matter.

As astrologers we can relate the qualities of Venus Pandemos with the first six of the zodiacal signs, Aries through Virgo, and those of Venus Urania with the last six signs, Libra through Pisces. We may also look to the movement of Venus *through* the signs as a model for her evolving manifestation, progressing from the realm of the body to that of the soul and then the spirit. The first four signs, Aries through Cancer, symbolize love's descent into the senses and the body; the second four, Leo through Scorpio, envision love in the domain of imagination and memory—the reflective, interiorizing process that creates the middle ground of soul. The final quartet of signs, Sagittarius through Pisces, elevate love through contemplation and spiritual practice, to the realm of spirit and back to the divine. This is the same Plato-inspired insight described by Marsilio Ficino, "There is one continuous attraction, beginning with

God, going to the world, and ending at last in God, an attraction which returns to the same place where it began as though in a kind of circle."5

Venus through the Signs

Venus in Aries (Lighting Your Fire)

The journey through the signs will begin with Venus' entry at zero degrees of Aries, the least developed of her expressions. At its worst, Venus in Aries might call up the moment that just precedes the scene in *Birth of Venus*, the violent explosion of passion that leads to Venus' conception, thought this is not a typical first association with Venus. Still, she does make her entrance in the Cardinal Fire sign with the passion, intensity, and impulsiveness that we would expect. Here Venus is most closely aligned with her son, Eros, in his capricious and childish, ego-centered guise. Yet even more fundamentally, Venus in Aries is the basic energy of life itself, the essence that animates all beings, and the drive that leads to reproduction of the species and the evolution of life in its many forms. Venus in Aries "plays with fire," and so that is what I will invite you to do, as I have invited others in my workshops, by teaching you a simple but profoundly effective Tantra technique that first came to my attention in a tiny, hard to find book by Margo Woods, *Masturbation, Tantra, and Self-Love*.[6] But first, let's give a greatly simplified introduction to Tantra. What is it? Tantra is an Eastern ancient tradition that interweaves spiritual teachings with devotional and ritual practices, frequently with a sexual reference. Tantric philosophy sees the world as coming into being through the divine union of *Shakti* and *Shiva*—respectively, the female principle (dynamism, nature, creation, matter) and the male principle (stasis, awareness, consciousness). Sometimes frankly sexual, but often not, Tantric practices embrace the coupling of male and female as a union with the divine, with ecstasy the goal—the total release of the soul into the divine. "The single most significant aspect of Tantrism is Goddess Worship,"[7] in an Eastern form, to be sure, but born of the same archetypal source as our Greco-Roman Venus. David Frawley observes, in *Tantric Yoga and the Wisdom Goddesses*, that:

> Traditional Tantra gives reverence to the Cosmic Feminine in all her forms.... The Goddess possesses all forms of Beauty, including that of the world of Nature, up to the highest beauty, which is pure consciousness.... While sexual beauty is one aspect of her delight...the purpose of Tantra is to bring us in contact with the reality of the Goddess directly within ourselves, whereby we can experience her ultimate Beauty in our own minds... The Goddess is the bliss of Being, and we can never be content unless we realize this joy within our own hearts."[8]

Traditional Tantra has many and varied forms, and writings on the subject are often esoteric and complicated; Frawley's book, cited above, is an exception and good modern review. Tantra also has also recently emerged in a somewhat Westernized expression, compete with workshops and accessible books. My favorite of these is *The Art of Sexual Ecstasy* by Margo Anand—its fine illustrations and range of practical techniques have made it an ideal "textbook" for the women's groups I lead. But the method I got from Margo Woods' book is the one I have most often taught and used, and the one that most clearly catches the spirit of Venus in Aries. Woods' instruction, given to her by her Tantra teacher, is:

> "to make love to yourself, to masturbate and to stop at the point just before orgasm, put your attention in your heart, and let the energy go up to the heart." The exact point to stop was the point where you know that one more stroke will make you come. "After each rush of energy to the heart... resume masturbating, repeating the cycle, until there seems to be no energy, or you feel like stopping.

There is no prohibition against orgasm, only the requirement to delay it, letting the energy go to the heart first...." He told me to do this exercise every day for three months. I did, and it has become part of my life ever since.[9]

And part of my life, too, so that I and those I've taught can testify to its efficacy. However, don't let the injunction to do this every day for three months scare you off. Though many of us had a hard time finding the time to do it consistently, *every* woman who used this technique got results. Even one week of the practice was so encouraging and the results so pleasurable that we were inclined to keep it up. Many of the women felt a new sense of pleasure in their bodies and a heightened sense of attractiveness. Several women had wonderfully erotic dreams. So, to experience the fire of Venus in Aries, the first step in our evolutionary journey with Venus around the zodiac, try this technique yourself and see if you too don't experience one of these delicious results.

Venus in Taurus (Enlivening Your Senses)

Now that Aries has given a jump start of energy, let's move on to the earthy Venus in Taurus to awaken our senses and deepen our capacity for pleasure and intimacy. Unless you are one of the few remaining farmers, or a forest ranger, you are likely to live in an urban environment that dulls the senses. When you and I smell, it can often be the smells of pollution; when we taste, our palettes are dulled with foods that are gassed, waxed, and devitalized, and we can hardly hear above the electromechanical buzz that is the city. And how else do we know the beauty of the world, if not through finely tuned senses? Venus in Taurus invites us to do so. Venus manifests through all five of the senses, and there is much to gain by discovering how she appears in each. Suggestion: try a sensory-awakening experience with Venus. First, choose a sense—hearing, seeing, tasting, touching, or smelling—and then imagine Venus through the houses of the zodiac. For instance, if your Venus were in the twelfth house (A Neptune-Pisces sort of energy), what would it smell like? Perhaps it would be like roses or other soft floral scents, while a Venus in the ninth (much like Jupiter and Sagittarius) might have a soothing sandalwood aroma. Or a woody, earthy, musky scent might signal the arrival of Venus in the second. To go beyond imagination to experience, try putting a dab of the appropriate fragrance on your wrists before you go to sleep. As you get a whiff of this essence in your semi-awake state, you will be sweetly aware of its fragrance. Or you can burn incenses or heat aromatic oils to create the appropriate experience. New Age magazines often feature ads for zodiacally-based incenses—you may want to go so far as to buy a complete set of twelve to compare your Venus scent with the others.

Taste is the sense closest to smell, and in fact the subtleties of taste beyond the basic sweet, sour, salt, and bitter owe more to the nose than to the tongue. But whatever the means, taste is a gateway to the goddess. Is your Venus in the third (Mercury-Gemini)? Spend a night out at a Spanish *tapas* bar and order a half-dozen of the little appetizers that give this cuisine its name. The variety of sensory inputs—from pungent leafy greens to tomato-and-herb scented meats to spicy pastas and beans—strikes all the right notes for the many moods of Venus in the third house. Is your Venus in the second (Venus is at home here, as in Taurus)? You might love to order a full complement of luscious desserts and, by turns, let bites of each slowly melt in your mouth. (I still remember a certain chocolate raspberry mousse cake I never actually tasted, from the sensuous description by a classic Venus in the second house type.) Need a final reminder of the relationship of Venus to taste?—it's no accident that the most romantic evenings begin with dinner out!

Hmm, dinner out. Add violins in the background, or your favorite sexy singer and you're in the realm of Taurean Venus as she appears to the sense of sound. You may wish to gather specific pieces of music that evoke associations to your own Venus, as modified by the sign or house she inhabits, and commit to an hour of listening with your full attention. A Venus in Cancer (or in the third) might choose sentimental love songs or children's lullabies; for classical tastes, Debussy's *Clair de Lune* or Chopin's waltzes and nocturnes come to mind. Venus in the second, or Gemini natives might listen to the "literate" music of Robert Schumann, a Libran-seventh house Venus might take delight in the harmonious tone of some "New Age" music. Well, I'm sure you get the idea, and will consult the appropriate chapters for specific suggestions. For instance: for Cancer, look up the musical suggestions listed under the Moon section. And, as for the sense of touch, I could tell you about the differences between Venus in Leo or in Scorpio—but I'll leave that completely to your own imagination!

Venus in Gemini (Communicating Your Love Stories)

In our journey through the signs so far, we have ignited the flames of the masculine, fiery Aries and awakened our senses with feminine Taurus. Now we will seek to join the two through airy Gemini—to form first a connection, then a union of the *spirit* of fire and the *body* of earth. From this synthesis results Intellect (mind, *logos*) as the vehicle for exchange between Gods and humans. Gemini then is our need to communicate—referring both to our connection with others and to the internal dialogue among our own masculine and feminine archetypes.

This phase requires both the telling of, and the listening to, our own stories of love. When we hear other women's narrative of love experiences, we realize that Love moves in mysterious but familiar ways. By witnessing other women's stories, we pick up the threads of our own. And by recounting our own adventures with love, we reveal the delicate embroidery of human effort on the spiritual fabric of life. The universal first emotion at such story-telling appears to be relief—that the persons, places, and things of life's most soulful experiences are not lost to us, but need only attentive listeners to give them life again. Pain often guards the gate to our memories of love. In my women's groups, the recounting of love's visitations comes with many tears—yet always compels a sensitive, compassionate response from the listening women. In one of my groups, a woman shared her story of her encounters in Italy with the first man who knew how to pleasure her and who taught her what her body had always wanted to feel. He was a Croatian artist, on vacation in Rome. She was an art student in Florence, taking in Rome for the weekend. They met (where else!) in an outdoor cafe. Thus began a long-distance romance that lasted almost a year, in which each took turns traveling back and forth between Florence and his home in Yugoslavia. When she moved back to the States, the two still kept contact by letter and occasionally by phone. And then, a few years later, the war in Yugoslavia broke out. She has not heard from him since, though she has made repeated attempts to contact him. Of course she fears her lover is dead, although her intuition tells her that he is alive and well. It was not only the not knowing whether he was still alive, but her helplessness to confirm or deny it that still brought pain. She cried, and we held her, but in just a few minutes the tears were gone. She flashed a brilliant smile at the joyful memories that lay beyond the anguish—and let us draw her out on some of the exquisite pleasures they had known. (Elsewhere[10] I have written about particular ways to extract the gold of joyful memories from the dross of painful ones. Below, in discussing Venus in Virgo, I describe one such method, "Sorting the Seeds.")

Pain doesn't predominate in all love stories, of course, and the retelling of our group's happier memories warmed every heart and even brought peals of laughter. For example, one woman told of the time she had lived in a fashionable part of downtown San Francisco. Her second-floor apartment was on a street that was the Sunday morning "promenade" for wealthy widows on their way to church. One warm spring morning she awoke to find a handsome young man in her bed. Somewhat shyly she told how she had met him in a bar that night and was so struck by his beauty that she had invited him home. On the Sunday morning in question, they began to kiss and to make love again, as the spring breeze wafted in from the open window. The pleasure she was feeling was abruptly cut short, however. As her young German pilot started his spasms of orgasm, he began shouting at the top of his lungs, "I'm coming! I'm coming! I'm coming!" Our storyteller, confirming the definition of embarrassment as "secret pleasure," flushed crimson, but also giggled like a girl, as she told how completely mortified she still is by the image of the startled matrons who were sure to have been passing under her window.

I hope that you can see that a women's "love story group" has much to recommend it—maybe you will start your own. But, if getting together a group of women is too difficult, you can still have this Gemini experience. I suggest that you read the love stories of others—for example, Heloise's "Letters to Abelard," or Simone de Beauvoir's exchange of letters with Jean-Paul Sartre,[11] or even seek out the love stories, including "Psyche and Eros," in Apuleius' *The Golden Ass*.[12] Or start your own journal of "recollections of love."

Venus in Cancer (Creating Your Sacred Space)

Venus is bidden more easily to a place of beauty and sacredness. In astrology, the sign of Cancer conveys our deepest sense of the notion of "place," of home and hearth. A watery sign, Cancer is, symbolically, the womb of mother earth, the container of the birth of all creation, and the process of birthing itself. Here we need to create our own "womb," or sacred space both to connect with the Venus within and to invite yet another aspect of the Goddess herself.

Creating a Sanctuary to Venus in your home will transform the way you encounter this Goddess. Your intention and a few simple steps transforms an ordinary place into a temple that can have a magical influence in your life. If you have space limitations, you can create a sacred space around your bed or a temporary area in your living room, but a permanent altar is best. With such a dedicated space, we can work most easily with the principles of sympathetic magic, creating a charged environment that acts like an attractor for Venusian energies. Your sanctuary becomes your own *talisman*, a magical object that functions much like a self-recharging battery for spiritual power. What enables this undertaking is the *law of correspondences*. By using the appropriate symbols, colors, music, gemstones, herbs, metals, and incenses for Venus, we are attracting "like to like" and, consciously, engaging all five of our senses to awaken Venus within. (Any primer on magical principles will further explain the law of correspondences.)

Start by giving a good cleaning to your space, clearing out all the clutter and unnecessary furniture. A large enough area to stretch out and dance in is ideal. Next, decorate your sacred place to give it a romantic, spiritual atmosphere—a painting, print, or sculpture serves as a central focus; beautiful cloths, scarves, or shawls draped from your windows or on your floor or walls add interest. Soft lights—candles or rheostat lighting, or colored fabric carefully draped over lamps—lend atmosphere. Add beautiful objects conductive to contemplation or celebration—flowers, appropriate incense and scents, bells, drums, or flutes, and tasty delights—fine chocolates, champagne, luscious fruits. Sensuously flowing robes, nightgowns, or silk camisoles complete the mood. Now you are ready for an evening's celebration—with yourself or with a partner.

I will describe my own sacred space as it appears at the moment. It typifies my own Venus in Gemini. There are two central focuses—a three- by four-foot print of Botticelli's *Primavera* on the east wall and underneath that, a bronze-colored replica statue of Botticelli's *Birth of Venus*, resting on a low meditation table draped in pink metallic cloth. Behind the *Venus* is a generous, gold-framed antique mirror, originally from my grandmother's home. A print of a mountain scene, *Mount Capitán*, by German romantic painter Albert Bierstadt, hangs on the south wall. A candelabrum sits on a dresser, a strand of colored Christmas lights surrounds the one window, and an ultraviolet "black light" can be turned on to illuminate the Bierstadt and the ceiling. On the ceiling itself and high on the walls, there is a realistic night sky complete with several thousand stars, visible when "charged up" by the black light—a replica of the starry dome over Crested Butte, Colorado, on August 24, 1994, a particularly magical, even "cosmic" night for my husband and me. As a Venus in Gemini, but a resident in cloudy and light-polluted Chicago, I had longed to sleep under the stars for years. A few dollars, and more than a few dabs of fluorescent paint made the dream come true. We turn on environmental, cosmic, or classical music, crawl under the covers, and get lost in that night sky—the *Cosmos*, with all the comforts of home!

Venus in Leo (Cultivating Self-Love)

At Leo, we enter into the next quartet of signs and travel along the evolutionary path of the four "mediators" between the more personal and self-oriented signs (Aries through Cancer) and the relatively cosmic and divinely-oriented ones (Sagittarius through Pisces). This middle group of signs (Leo, Virgo, Libra, and Scorpio) charts our course from the domain of self-love to the territory of awareness of the love we have for others in our lives. Through the stages constituting these four signs, we introject our encounters with love into the depths of our souls. We are in the stage of "seeing more deeply," pursuing a psychological penetration into the true nature of our own love and its potential to evolve toward the divine love of Pisces.

The starting point for love is the love of self, and our capacity to love others is in direct proportion to our ability to appropriately love ourselves. Appropriate self-love is not "narcissistic"—not the undue admiration of self that places one above others, but the kind of love that recognizes others as loving and lovable beings like ourselves. The process is circular: If we don't love ourselves, we don't find love reflected in the world, and without that reflection we find our capacity for self-love—confidence, self-worth—diminished. Love of self carried into the world and received in turn can, like two mirrors face-to-face, create a seemingly infinite replication of love, which adds to the sum total of love in our lives and in the world.

The body, that unique amalgam of the physical and the spiritual, is the medium within which love is experienced and expressed, so that love of self also means love of one's bodily experience and bodily expression. Loving our own bodies is a difficult task for "some of us all of the time, and all of us some of the time," to paraphrase P.T. Barnum. Digital images of improbably configured women more "beautiful" than ourselves assault us at every turn, making love of our own bodies a competitive sport. Yet, for the next few paragraphs, and for the processes that are described, I suggest that you set aside external images in favor of an experience that occurs within, rather than outside the body, and that is anciently identified with the beauty of embodied spirit—*the act of breathing with awareness.*

It is no coincidence that in many languages the word for *breath* is the same as the one for *spirit* (i.e., *pneuma*, in Greek; *prana*, in Sanskrit), nor that the heart was anciently believed to be the locus of mind. The following yogic technique, the heart gaze, or *Anahata drishti*, draws on both of these bits of wisdom. While sitting in a comfortable meditative position, and with your eyes closed, gently bring your attention to your heart. Imagine that within the deepest center of your heart is a tiny pink rosebud with its petals closed. (The rose is Venus' floral symbol.) As you focus your attention and breathe in deeply, the rosebud begins to grow. Imagine that it is unfolding one petal at a time. With each petal that opens, affirm your willingness to give love—to yourself, to others, and to the world. Find an affirmation that you can say inwardly that feels right to you, "with each petal that opens I am more loving, more lovable," or "my heart is opening to love," or "my heart is blooming with the fragrance of love." As the petals open, and as you near its center, see the petals growing more vibrantly pink, more luminous in light. When the flower fully opens, see yourself within its center, radiant in pink light.

As you gaze at the image of yourself within the center of your heart, affirm this: "As I come to love myself, I come to love the world." Imagine that this love, your love, is flowing out of you, first embracing those close to you in your life and then radiating out into the world. Now, slowly begin to draw that loving energy back from the world, back from the friends that you love and back into the center of your own heart. Slowly, one by one, imagine the rose petals are closing up at the coming of the night. Let your attention rest on the peace and gentleness of that self-contained love.

The heart gaze is especially beneficial when you have a positive transit to your natal or progressed Venus, or when Venus transits the sign of Leo. A Leo friend, Randi (she played Venus in the performance theater described in Chapter 3), just completed a 10-day intensive workshop on Love, during good Venus aspects (Transiting Jupiter was in opposition to her Venus in Cancer and in trine to her Saturn in Virgo). Using techniques like the heart gaze (and many more), she was able to experience ecstasy and extended rapture for the first time in her life. I saw her a few weeks after she finished the course and found her full of love; even more important, I spent an afternoon with her months after the experience—and she was still radiant! The promises she made to herself while *playing* Venus have been fulfilled by her *embodying* Venus.

Venus in Virgo (Sorting the Seeds)

One of Psyche's tasks in Apuleius' "Psyche and Eros" tale is the sorting of a mountain of mixed seeds (the ants aid her).[13] The task involves *service* and *order*, which, along with Psyche's maidenly virtues, make up the familiar signature of the sign Virgo. For this discussion of Venus in Virgo, let's consider *memory* as the arena within which sorting is to be done, with our *erotic* memories as the particular focus. To associate the erotic with the virginal Virgo may surprise you, but Nor Hall reminds us that "the word *virgin* means not "maiden-inviolate, but maiden alone, in herself," and that, rather than being imprisoned in an oversimplified notion of chastity, she "acts according to her own [instinctual] nature; she may give herself to many lovers, but, like the moon, she can never be possessed."[14] Memory joins imagination as a principal means by which images, the raw material of the psyche, are revived and integrated in a process we may call "seed-sorting." The goal of Virgo/Psyche's seed-sorting is *discernment*, the heightened capacity to determine qualitative differences and to choose wisely among different options. Discernment applied to our erotic memories begins with recollection, the conscious recalling of past events and of our feelings about them—and that is where we will begin with a practical, experiential method for doing your own erotic seed-sorting.

Have you ever set about a full recollection and recording of your erotic life? If not, I urge you to do so. Create a chronology of every instance in which you have loved or made love to a man or a woman. Yes, this takes a concentrated effort for some, but you will find that one memory stimulates another, and soon your chronology fills out with details. Memory may be dim of course—are there old letters? Photographs? Can you talk over old times with a friend or parent? To make it somewhat easier, I suggest that you *literally* sort seeds. Reflect on each loving or sexual encounter from your "chronology" above. Using "seeds"—black and white beans—place a white bean in a bowl for every pleasant memory, a black bean for every unpleasant one. If a memory evokes mixed feelings in you, decide what was your first feeling about that memory and go with that. Record the memories and tally the beans at the end, though it's the process that's most important, not the count. One of my women's groups did this at home and brought their bean piles back the next Friday night. Several were astonished to find that they had sorted out a larger pile of white beans than black. This casual survey suggests that many women have had a more positive experience of love than memory first presents. Is it the same for you? It takes only an hour or so to know.

Recollecting can be delicious fun, but it often is a serious, even painful exercise. Few of us have not been wounded by love, or by loveless sex. Memories may be hellish as well as heavenly. One fact has emerged from my own experience and that of other women: Good memories are often concealed behind disturbing ones. Here begins *restructuring*, an alchemical process that separates good memories from bad, experiencing and releasing the pain of recollection, and thus recovering gold from the leaden dross (see also Venus in Scorpio, below). It can be done alone or with a loving partner or friend, but some processes of recollection are so agonizing and difficult that they are best done in psychotherapy. Even at that, I urge you not to neglect the recovery, the celebration, and the savoring of pleasant or even ecstatic moments of your life.

Venus in Libra (Seeing Beauty)

Venus in Libra brings us to the inherent urge to idealize and to lose ourselves in "the other," transcending the boundaries of our isolated egos through union with another. This is especially true of the Neptune in Libra generation, born October 1942 to July 1957, and the Pluto in Libra generation, August 1972 to August 1984 birth dates. With Venus in Libra we have come halfway in our progression of Venus through the signs and arrive at a point that reflects the divine union of Father Sky and Mother Earth. These first moments of harmony and erotic bliss, this merging and desire for one another, is what leads to the birth of all of creation. Libran Venus is all about relationship on a high plain, about balance, the harmonious joining of opposites. It is fitting then that astrologers also see Libra (ruled by Venus herself) as the exemplar of the primary element in attraction: *beauty*. At first glance, this Venus, as she leaves Virgo to enter Libra, still reminds us of Psyche, so ravishing that all are drawn to her, yet so untouched by life that she is shallow, unformed. Beauty must be appreciated in its essence if a true harmony is to be achieved—a task which demands a momentous confrontation.

Recall that in the myth of the birth of Venus, the Goddess is born out of a painful act, the castration of the supreme male force. The birth of Venus has suffering and pain inherent in its original impetus, thus establishing the eternal and inseparable relationship of Venus to Saturn (of Love to Death), for Saturn, as Time, will indeed reclaim all that we love on the physical plane. This mythical truth is as simple as it is devastating: Some portion of beauty belongs irrevocably to youth. The form that beauty takes in youth will at last leave us, and we will experience the leave-taking as a kind of death. Especially in late midlife, our challenge is to know ourselves as beautiful even as we come to realize that we are now "fair" more in the modern sense than in the older meaning of the term. We cannot manage this without feelings, of course—denial, depression, anger, and finally, the acceptance that follows. All our prior work will help us here. But let's not mince words; what peace we achieve in transcending the loss of mere beauty is preparation for that final privation, death itself. Oddly, it may only be when we reach an age at which beauty is fading, and when we have been diligent in our work from Aries to Virgo that we can truly appreciate beauty. Before that, the love of one's own attractiveness may be no more than narcissism, where love indeed becomes a potion, an intoxicant with fateful side effects. But a mature, cultivated self-admiration—self-love—leads first to love of others and then to higher ends. To separate the false beauty from the true requires the discrimination of Virgo; to bring out beauty's full potential demands a fiery passion, and to find the truth in "Beauty is only skin deep" requires a knowledge of the heart and soul that lies deep beneath the surface.

For such knowledge to develop, we need to cultivate a mode of *seeing beyond the surface*—an imaginal practice best exemplified in the painting and poetry of the 19th century Romantics. It begins with the act of imagining the World to have a Soul and to be a place of Beauty, and with the apprehension of that beauty in every object, with every sense, thus fostering an aesthetic sensibility. Interestingly, the root meaning of *aistheses* in Greek is, "taking in" or "breathing in"—a "gasp."[15] So, what I am suggesting is an exercise in breathing in the beauty of the world, and I mean that quite literally. Begin with what you already experience as beautiful—good bets are that gorgeous hunk of a man who lifts his eyes just as you pass him on the street, or that exquisite dream of a woman, unconsciously tossing her long dark hair as she settles in at a nearby table restaurant. Don't stare, but take them in with one swift glance, one quick *inspiration*, "breathing in their energy" as you fix the image, saving it for later consideration. Even though you may never encounter this particular beauty again, you have practiced what the Renaissance magicians have called "drawing in the phantasm," reaching out through the ether to catch an essence given off by the other. When the time is right, extend the practice to other creatures (that horse dancing in the pasture) and objects (roses, the sunset sky) reliable for their beauty, then to the commonplace (a stone, a bowl, a wedge of cheese), and finally to the downright ugly or the virtually unseen—Shakespeare's "toad, ugly and venomous...yet with a jewel in its head," or Blake's "world in a grain of sand." With practice at breathing them in, more and more will become beautiful—including the beholder.

Venus in Scorpio (Recovering Your Gold)

In our zodiacal journey, Venus has traveled well above the horizon—is now seemingly in the clear—when, as Ishtar-Inanna-Persephone, she reaches Scorpio and is cast down again into the depths, to the Underworld, in which she faces many trials, suffers many wounds. So it is with love: always the trial, always the wounding. It is as if Love's flaming arrow first thrusts us up with the force of the blow, then, as it penetrates in and down, carries us with it to the deepest core of the psyche. This penetration, this wounding, releases raw, primitive, instinctual forces of psyche—psychic juices that flow like fresh blood from the severed artery, spurting fiercely into conscious life and affording us only two choices: to flee from the fearsome sight of our own blood or to peer deep into the wound until it becomes clear how to staunch the flow, mend the tear, and begin the healing of love's injury. If we run from love, the pain of isolation follows close behind. If we toughen our skin against love's further intrusion, we succeed only in stopping the flow of life itself. Love's dark misery cannot discharge, love's bright new promise cannot revive, and the soul withers with the gray deterioration of the wound untended. Novalis underlines the point: "Whoever flees pain will love no more. To love is always to feel the opening, to hold the wound always open."[16] This is the choice that keeps the psychic forces flowing, the heart restoring, and the soul healing.

Our terms for describing Venus in Scorpio often circle about the various evocations of the dimension of "depth"—the Underworld, Pluto's realm—and thus we arrive at the "depth psychology" of love as a process. The work here is psychological, soul-focused, relentless in its demands and profound in its effects. The mining and refining of precious metals is the time-worn metaphor for psychological encounter in depth—one that was revivified for me when, while wandering some of Colorado's mountain roads, I suddenly tumbled out of the idyllic landscape into the barren waste of an operating copper mine. My eyes were assaulted, to be sure, by the ugliness of a ravaged landscape, but what remains with me still is the rank odor of the stagnating lakes of chemical waste. The raw materials and by-products of mining and refining, taken psychologically, have a similar *bad smell*, which Jung was to note in regard to the psyche:

> Only a great idealist like Freud could devote a lifetime to such unclean work. It was not he who caused the bad smell, but all of us—we who think ourselves so clean and decent—from sheer ignorance and the grossest self-deception. Thus our psychology, the acquaintance with our own souls, begins in every respect from the most repulsive end, that is to say, with all those things which we do not wish to see.[17]

The organ of the sense of smell is housed deep in the primitive core of the brain, in close proximity to the "limbic structures" that govern short-term memory as well as the emotions[18]—and that may even comprise the mechanism by which unhealed emotional trauma are "stored." These festering wounds must be drained if our bad smells are to depart; Venus-Scorpio establishes the operating theater for this psychic surgery. What is required of us at this Scorpion stage is for each to acknowledge her own bad smells as they emanate from the memories of our encounters with the actualities of intimate relationship. Has our own behavior toward the lover always been impeccable? Have we never schemed, manipulated, used a lover? Never lied? Never cheated? Have we never allowed ourselves to be deceived, used—abused?—from, as Jung suggests, "sheer ignorance and the grossest self-deception"? Few of us can reply with a definitive *No!* Scorpio's Venus would have us face these facts of our own complicity in Love's darker pursuits.

To acquire the lesson of Venus in Scorpio, revisit the "chronology of love and lovers" you developed for exploring Virgo, above. But this time, as you sort the black beans from the white, reflect upon your own accountability for the consequences of these encounters. Face squarely the pain and harm that may have come from your own limitations, your own human foibles. Be specific about wrongs you may have committed (there are echoes here of the "fearless moral inventory" that constitutes one of the Twelve Steps of Alcoholics Anonymous). Yet don't wallow in guilt or shame—we are all human, after all—but be as generous in self-forgiveness as you are honest in self-criticism. Realize that some of these mistakes were made only once—you learned and did not repeat them—while others have occurred again and again and form a pattern that must be addressed in further self-development. Tend the wounds, mine the gold, and the blessings of Venus in Scorpio will be secured.

We now come to the last four signs, Sagittarius through Pisces, and the manifestation of the higher aspirations of Love.

Venus in Sagittarius (Expanding on Love)

Venus in Sagittarius brings us great friends, warm lovers, and the best of party-going companions. But when *commitment* looks in at the window, Sagittarian Venus may show us the door! Though she is still about connecting, Venus here searches for links among people, things, and ideas that are dynamic, ever-changing, and, perhaps, honored more in principle than in fact. When this energy holds sway in matters of love, pairing off as partners may take a back seat, not because we are driven to experience absolutely everything, as when Aquarius is allied with Venus, but because, well, "Why can't we be friends and just sleep with one another every now and then?" And have other such "friends," too. Or we may find that our most important relationships are with friends, not lovers, and we don't want to mix the two. At this stage Venus wants us to really *understand* love, but from some critical distance. She would have us come to know and to affirm a way of loving that is free from the obsession, the torment, and the frenetic emotionality that too often characterize romantic encounter. She bids us to temper love with wisdom, to recognize that *the love that inflames seldom sustains*. She informs us that love, *in toto*, is much grander and more encompassing than romance alone. To be sure, she means to include the love for children and family and for the animals, the trees, and all of nature—and for the divine as it appears in all—but Sagittarian Venus is most clearly seen in the love that is embodied in *friendship*, and so the self-study that I invite you to undertake is a consideration of your loving friends, in contrast to your lovers.

Take out pen and paper and jot down answers to the following questions:

Who are your current friends—
of the same sex?
of the opposite sex?

How do these friendships differ?

Who is your best friend? Your oldest friend?

What are the qualities that make these friendships what they are?

What, if anything, do you get from these friends that you don't get from a lover?

What do you get from a lover, but not from your friends?

Has a friend ever become a lover? How did this change the relationship?

Has a lover ever become "just a friend?" How was this accomplished?

What does your own experience teach you about whether men and women can be "just friends"?

Who are more important to you, lovers or friends?

Are you a better lover or a better friend?

Are you and your spouse or partner better as lovers? Better as friends?

In looking over your answers to these questions, what wisdom can you extract regarding love and friendship? Consider how you may bring this wisdom to bear on present and future relationships.

Venus in Capricorn (Contemplating Love)

Venus in Capricorn wants to examine loving relationships and experiences to assess their value, even to determine their practical worth. She invites us to a reflective, meditative consideration of our love lives, aiming for higher understanding, yet remaining "close to the data." Under her influence, we free ourselves from superficial concerns and begin the search for greater meaning. Alchemy calls this a process of "distillation," the extraction of the essence of experience, its rarefied substance—in effect, the "spirit of the matter." This process of thoughtful consideration furthers psychic development, integrating love's pains and joys for the soul's enrichment.

Like most of the experiential activities I suggest, the one inspired by Venus in Capricorn has been fully tested in my own "laboratory of love." The suggestion is a simple one: organize your experiences and understandings of love into a scrapbook dedicated to Venus. As I did, you may wish to begin by going through old photos and collecting pictures of yourself at various stages of your evolving beauty—from infant to young girl, to a budding and developing woman, to the present maturing one. Do you have old scrapbooks from your teenage days, the ones in which you kept your old corsages or ticket stubs to the homecoming dance? Are there photographs of your past boyfriends (or girlfriends) or your past lovers stuck away somewhere? Old love letters or songs or poems? Are there images in magazines that depict the image of your divine lover? I spent over six months just searching out and collecting a box full of these. From the beginning I took this as a sacred task (you may not want to take it *quite* so seriously), as if Aphrodite herself had commanded it. Hearing of my project, a friend gave me a beautiful burgundy, hand-tooled leather-bound scrapbook with Botticelli's Three Graces imprinted on the cover. At first, the sixty pages of plastic-covered sheets I bought seemed excessive, but I soon filled them with mementos. Throughout the process, I gave free rein to reminiscence, spending an astonishing hundred hours or so choosing and arranging, while memories tumbled on and on.

I wonder who might be inspired to make a Venus scrapbook of her own. I can't see yours, but I can at least give you a glimpse of mine. It starts with a picture of a delicate peach rose, and a photograph of my radiantly happy parents coming down the aisle on their wedding day; then presents a copy of my astrological chart and the first pictures of me when I was three months old. Next is the tiny Revlon™ doll cocktail dress that, when I was seven, I imagined would be just like the one I would wear when I grew up and danced with a boy. There are photos of me in a bikini on the beach at Acapulco and a love letter from a French man I met there; photos of my husband and me on our wedding day and on our honeymoon; a snapshot of the "anima man" who created such a stir in my life, and an astrological chart of the exact moment of what can only be called a "divine union experience"—it happened completely within my own consciousness. Following that chart are written accounts of three potent Elk Dreams (the Elk governs love medicine in Lakota Sioux shamanic tradition) and a snapshot of one of my women's groups at a male striptease show, along with photos from our own Slut/Goddess dance, including one of me as an ethereal Goddess and another as a *very* earthy Slut—and so much more. My book keeps growing and what a treasure it has become. Some day won't you show me yours?

Venus in Aquarius (Liberating Love)

When Venus enters Aquarius, she casts off all external restraint to become her unencumbered self, Venus Urania. Here she becomes a force of liberation, freeing us from our own self-centered needs and personal preoccupation, and moving us into a new world of connection and relationship. Not only does she impel us toward love of others, but, at her best, compels us to love in a way that is aligned with the creative spirit of the divine. Let's face it, few of us scale these heights, but given a mere glimpse, we are transported in a lightning flash to that archetypal realm beyond sensual, physical existence—to the pure idea of love that resides in the Cosmic Mind. Even when we are halted far below these "peak experiences," Aquarian Venus liberates us from the bondage to convention that traditional society demands regarding love and sexuality. Aquarian love is not about finding, or being, "a girl, just like the girl that married dear old dad," but in experiencing the full range of love's offerings, without regard for orthodox notions regarding race, gender, or mode of expression. And the term "sexual revolution" could be a synonym for Venus in Aquarius. For many of us, this abandonment of the *status quo* is uncomfortable, if not downright disturbing. But even those of us who have no yen to explore the outer bounds of Venus' jurisdiction can still learn from this Aquarian spirit that insists on a dash of spicy chaos in what might otherwise become the bland diet of a too orderly love life.

Nowhere are Aquarian qualities more evident than in the electronic phenomenon we have come to refer to as "cyberspace." As we might expect in the era of Uranus in Aquarius, completely new structures and technologies for sharing ideas and tuning into the collective are being created. On the Internet we have begun to connect with one another, unmediated, and without regard to national boundary, and thus something like a new level of group mind may be evolving. Aquarian Venus is very much in attendance on the 'Net, with an abundance of on-line chat rooms, virtual reality hot tubs, and mailing lists devoted to all imaginable forms of erotic fascination.[19] People are meeting easily who might never have expected one another's existence a decade ago, with the usual mix of outcomes: I have had two recent clients that met their mates "online" and are now happily married, and my psychotherapist husband has had two clients who appeared to be addicted to online pornography.

Others have carried on long-term, erotic relationships that couldn't have existed only a short time ago, because they occur *only* in the medium of electronic communication. A friend with Venus conjunct Uranus in Gemini has had a cybersex partner for over a year. They escape often to their own private "room" where this relationship lives vibrantly in their imaginations and their hearts, and by means of their fast-typing fingers! They take turns deciding where they will meet and choosing the kind of fantasy that will unfold—they "own" five homes together and have imaginal dates that can take them to a romantic dinner on the Left Bank of Paris, to their bungalow retreat in Bali, or to lovemaking in a hot air balloon high over Northern California. Or even to an experience in which the two of them are the sexy half-time entertainment at center court of an NBA basketball game! They both have extensive imaginary wardrobes and vividly describe what they are wearing for each other. And they have developed a whole shorthand of computer commands that have intimate meaning.

Before my friend settled into this monogamous online relationship, she took little naive me on a tour of the Venus-Aquarius hangouts she had discovered. With me riding shotgun, we logged on to a chat room with "group" in its topical description, where, in a display of virtuosity and endurance that an RL (i.e., a "Real Life") body could hardly manage, she made love as a woman to six men, afterwards discovering that there had been two other "women" in the room just watching—who both promptly approached her for an encounter! She gracefully declined in favor of continuing our adventure, which included a visit to a virtual hot tub, a look at IRC (Interactive Relay Chat, which, along with the various virtual gathering places, offers a way to converse with many at once), and a MUD (multi-user dungeon) where our imaginary character was a horse and where, upon entry, we were immediately "fuzzled"—a still mysterious, if not altogether unpleasant experience!

You may not want to know more about this Brave New World, but if you do, you can educate yourself by buying one of the proliferating guides to "net.love" and "net.sex." In it you will find electronic addresses where you can gather for (newsgroup) conversation with other "Little Rascals" or "Kinky Girls"—topics range from alt.amazon.women to z-netz.forum.diskussion.sexualitaet. Mailing lists bring daily messages to your e-mail box, and these too have something for every need or taste. Web sites give you a colorful, sometimes animated, gateways to personal support groups, professional organizations, political action groups, personal ads, photo galleries, and online porn and sex-toy shops—and that just covers the "P's!" The array that is being offered is mind-boggling. These are computer-generated worlds of relationship that go on everyday, twenty-four hours a day, all over the planet.

As we have seen, Venus in the company of Aquarius may not always distinguish the sublime from the ridiculous, but her aim seems to be to give them equal weight as a means to raise all to a higher level. In cyberspace, Hedonism thrives right next door to Puritanism, yet no "ism" has been able to dominate, so that the emergence of a middle way of organizing our erotic natures may be imaginable as the Aquarian "group mind" continues to form with Venus as their group leader. There are two main threats to this possibility: increasing commercialization that seeks to make the 'Net into a giant shopping mall, and the move by the Right to criminalize *all* sexual expression on the grounds that "children must be protected." Here *your* discernment regarding the issues must be brought to bear so that the political process doesn't throw out Venus' baby with Aquarius' bath water.

Venus in Pisces (Surrendering to the Divine)

The zodiac comprises the cycle of eternal return, and at this final sign, Pisces, we return with Venus to the primordial, oceanic world of the feminine, from which she sprang at her nativity. We await here a new birth, a fresh impetus of love in the world, beginning once more at the Spring Equinox, 0° Aries. As a quality of experience, Pisces always returns us to the shoreline, the threshold between image and reality, dream and wakefulness, *gnosis* and ordinary knowledge, and, with Venus as consort, challenges us to know love at its most inclusive, most visionary, and most suffused with the energy of the divine. It is *devotional* love that characterizes the highest expression of Venus in Pisces—a passionate engagement with the "inner beloved," and a practiced discipline in pursuing a blissful union with the divine. Devotional love has blossomed in a number of historical and social contexts—in the "Fideli d'Amore" (faithful to love) literary and artistic movement of Dante's time, in the practices of Bhakti yoga in Eastern traditions, and in the Sufi mysticism of the Middle East, to name a few. "I saw all beings as transfigured into beautiful faces, and as they presented themselves thus to me, their beauty inspired a taste for meditative retreats, secret psalms, practices of devotion and visits to the most eminent among the Sufi shaykhs," says the young boy, Ruzbehan, himself to become a great Sufi Shaykh.[20] By investigating these traditions, we bear witness to the possibility of a conscious, active use of the images and feelings of love to reach a level "that surpatheth all understanding," to use the biblical phrase for a similar idea.

What these traditions teach us as the requirement for this most mystical and subtle expression of love is the act of *surrender* on our part, to the images and experiences governed by the *heart* rather than the deceiving mind. In so doing, we let go of all that separates us from wholeness and fall into the embrace of the divine. Devotional love is a spiritual path as demanding as any Christian monastic or yogic meditative pursuit and is hopeless to encompass in any single practice. But, if you would taste just a bit of the honey of this manner of Piscean love, adopt a practice that I have used on occasion—set aside a minute, an hour, a day—or a lifetime—to repeat this mantra:

Let thy will be my will.
Let thy will be my will.
Let thy will be my will.
Let thy will be my will...

Our passage through the zodiac, with Venus as our guide, is complete, as is the process of suggesting to you what "Birthing Venus Within" might entail. Yet, if astrology teaches us anything, it is that every end is a beginning. And, if experiential astrology has anything to offer, it is that these beginnings may be approached with attention to self-creation through lived experience—intentionally sought, divinely informed, courageously engaged, and heartfully sustained. In his *Commentary on Plato's Symposium*, Marsilio Ficino says that the nature and purpose of human love "is the longing to procreate with a beautiful thing to bring eternal life to mortal things."[21] To me, experiential astrology is just such a "beautiful thing," which invites us all to "procreate," indeed to co-create, in humble partnership with the Goddesses and Gods as they appear in the meaningful coincidence of heaven and the human heart. In so doing, this mere mortal has gained a few glimpses of the eternal. I invite you to do the same.

6

DO IT YOURSELF!

When I can't find words to express what I mean, I get up and dance it.
    —Zorba (Nikos Kazantzakis)

I hope that what you have read so far has whetted your appetite for some direct experience of your own. That's what this chapter is designed to do—to get you started in playing with, and learning from, experiential astrology. The goal is to help you wake up your right brain with visual artistic (Venus/Sun), active (Mars/Sun), and reflective (Moon/Mercury) techniques.

Visual Arts Techniques (Venus/Sun)

Although you'll need paint and other supplies for the activities below, don't think that you need to be an artist to take part. Each of us has an innate sense of color, line, and shape, and even though we may not be trained to create works of art, there is much to learn from the way we arrange things visually. In this section I'll describe four techniques: image boards, birth chart mandalas, masks, and healing images. The first thing you'll want to do is make a resource box of art supplies with as many different types of media as you can find—magazines to use as a source for mandala, image board, or collage images; scissors, glues, tapes, string, construction paper (white and colored), newsprint, posterboards of different sizes; watercolors, magic markers, crayons, pencils, finger paints, tempera paints; an assortment of paint brushes, white, gold, silver, and colored face paints; surgical gauze for maskmaking, cardboard, glitter, sequins, feathers, pipe cleaners, gold, silver, and colored enamels, ropes, and paper straws. (Obviously, it would be expensive to buy everything at once, so you may want to add to your art box a little at a time.)

Using Image Boards to Explore Your Chart

You were introduced to image boards in Chapter 1; now let's talk about them in detail. Making personal image boards of your own planets will give you a new tool for self-study, contemplation, and ritual. These colorful, symbolic picture displays can become a visual extension for your chart, giving you a means to arouse thoughts and feelings and deepen your inner process.

Begin by creating an image board for each of the ten planets in your horoscope. Cut out appropriate pictures, words or phrases from magazines, or draw or paint whatever evokes your planets, their signs, and house positions. For a conjunction of two or three planets make an image board which blends both energies. I have one image board that shows my Sun/Uranus conjunction in the sixth house in Gemini. It's yellow, with a radiant sun, lightning bolts and spiraling galaxies, images of computers, books, words, a television, used plane tickets, weird Aquarian-looking people, an office desk with the word "Serve" above it, a woman deep in thought, the words, "Soothe your nervous system," "Focus your energy," "Breathe," and "Learn to be patient." I use this whenever I need to remind myself of what my Sun/Uranus means to me.

Once you have made your ten planetary image boards, find an open space and place them around you on the floor in the order they appear in your chart. Sit in the center (Ascendant/Descendant, IC/MC axis), facing your midheaven. Now, take up each image board, moving around the circle from planet to planet. Are there any that you're feeling out of touch with now? Which of them feel less accessible? What planets being activated by transits or progressions are affecting your current life circumstances? What planetary energies are giving you problems right now? Which ones help out? What effects have you been noticing? Or ignoring? How are you feeling about them?

Focus your attention on a current problem and note any planets affecting you in a disruptive way. Take out a piece of paper and draw what the problem looks and feels like. If it's a transit of Saturn conjunct your natal Mercury, put those two image boards directly in front of you. Imagine that a specific archetypal image is standing behind each image board. For example, Mercury might be Hermes, the messenger, and Saturn, Father Time, Chronos, or a wise old crone.

Try speaking with these images, allowing yourself to give your own inner archetypes a voice. What do you have to say to Saturn? To Mercury? What does Mercury have to say to Saturn? What do they have to say to you? Ask each what he or she can do to help you feel more balanced. How would they affect each other if these two planets were in trine instead, or in conjunction? In what ways can you *act as if* your difficult conjunction were a trine?

Then focus on the planets that are your greatest strength. Use a piece of paper and a crayon or marker to draw what this current strength looks and feels like. Dialogue with these planets. What do you have to say to each of them? What do they have to say to each other? What do they each have to say to you? How can they come forward and help you to achieve the balance you're seeking? Acknowledge each planet you have interacted with, giving thanks for what they've shown you. Treat them as you would any valued relationship. This may seem like a silly exercise, but experience will prove it isn't. It is a good way to establish a more conscious relationship with your inner voices.

The only limits to the power of astrological archetypes are those imposed by the consciousness using them. Each astrological symbol is a living organic entity within you that is bottomless. By entering into this life-enriching symbol and its mystery consciously, you are interacting, expanding, and deepening your relationship with it. You no longer live out its energy in an unconscious and perhaps compulsive way.

If you're having trouble getting a planet to dialogue with you, this planetary energy is probably the one you are most suppressing from your awareness. If you feel anger or discomfort toward any of them, this too may signal conscious or unconscious suppression. To return to a sense of wholeness, these may be the most crucial ones to learn to relate to.

Using Your Horoscope as a Mandala

The mandala is a universal expression of wholeness that arises from the integration of the human psyche. Natural mandalas appear all around us, in snowflakes, the spiraling galaxies, tree rings, and the annual unfolding of the seasons. In their book, *Mandala*, Jose and Miriam Arguelles speak of the earth itself as a living Mandala, "...a structural matrix through and from which flow a succession of changes, elemental forms, and primal surges, each surpassing the other in an infinite variety of organic structures and impulses, crowned by the supreme attribute of reflective consciousness."[1]

Since time immemorial the mandala has been depicted as a circle with a center-point. The horoscope, also a circle with a centerpoint, is your own personal mandala and can be a living and vibrant tool for contemplation. Symbolically, the centerpoint is the point of intersection through which all life flows. Maintaining contact with the center helps us keep our psychic equilibrium.

To make your birth mandala you'll need a large posterboard, a pencil, magic markers, colored construction paper, magazines, photos of yourself and significant others, and a glue stick. To set a mood, you might want to play some soft, meditative music. Then clear your workspace of distractions and place your posterboard in front of you. Now use your pencil to draw a circle three feet in diameter. Divide the circle into twelve equal, wedge-shaped segments. This gives you the basic form you'll need to make your mandala.

Next, focus your attention on the centerpoint and become aware that this is the focal node through which your life force comes. It is the vital, living part of you, that moves out in ever-widening waves toward the perimeter of the chart. Meditate on this point. Take your time. The more fully you enter into the creative process of the mandala, the more deeply you will enter your chart. Imagine yourself spiraling down into this point. What do you see emerging there? A rose, a star, a black hole, a being of light, a *yantra*, a word? In your mind's eye, see the center of your mandala. Merge with your image, pick up your magic marker, and create it fully.

Now become aware of the planetary forces on the periphery of your attention. Which planet do you notice most? Focus your attention on it. How does this particular planet relate to the center? How does it relate to the others? What colors, words, phrases, and images come to mind? If your Moon is in Virgo you might begin by coloring the house it sits in green. You might draw a large moon and include a photo of a mother and children, or anything that seems to evoke this planetary energy. When you finish, turn your attention to the next one that calls you, until you've represented each planet in the horoscope. Don't think too much about what you're doing. Add whatever feels spontaneous and right.

Try drawing a birth mandala each year near or on your birthday. You will concretely observe your psyche unfolding as it changes through time. It will reveal much to you about the feeling, depth, and direction of your inner process from year to year.

Using Masks to Experience Your Chart

Mask-making can be a fun way to experience your chart in three dimensions. Alone or with a group, masks move you into more intimate contact with the pure planetary archetypes. Mercury in Gemini might wear a fluorescent yellow mask, with pipe cleaner antennas. Scattered across the mask's surface are words and phrases: Study. Learn. Write. Teach. Speak. Move. Travel. Do. "Give me more data." "I love to learn." "When do we go?" And pictures: of books, libraries, universities, bicycles, planes, trains, telephones. Masks like this create a more open channel between astrological archetypes and the psyche. Using them as a kind of shield of invisibility, we can suddenly be free to express ourselves without fear of judgment by others.

To make your planetary mask you'll need these supplies: a handkerchief or barrette to tie back your hair, petroleum jelly, scissors, a bowl of warm water, tissues, towels to protect your clothing; paints, fabric, ribbons, glitter, etc., to decorate your mask, and a roll of plaster gauze (one standard roll will make two masks). Gauze is available at any medical supply store. You'll also need a partner to mold the gauze strips to your face.

First, cut about twenty strips of gauze, two inches wide and about four inches long. You'll also want to cut some smaller strips to work into smaller areas and fill in the gaps. Next, tie back your hair with the handkerchief or barrette, and apply the petroleum jelly to your entire face except eyes and nostrils. Be sure to cover your eyebrows well. (Men with beards will want to coat them generously or your beard will end up in the mask instead of on your face.)

Decide which planet mask you're making and turn on some appropriate music. Then lie back with your head on a towel, get comfortable, and focus on your breathing. Have your partner cover your eyes, nose, and lips with small damp pieces of tissue. Now you are ready for the first layer of gauze. If you have not done this before, remember to keep your face relaxed and neutral. Focus on the nature of the planet you are creating. Breathe. Have your partner dip the gauze strips into a bowl of water and apply them to your face, making sure to smooth them down with their fingers. They should cover your entire face three times, using the smaller strips to mold around your eyes, mouth, and nose. Place the second layer of gauze perpendicular to the first. Then allow the mask to dry for approximately ten minutes. (If it's a humid, rainy day, you'll need to allow more time.) When the plaster has set, pull the mask away from your face gently. As soon as it's fully dry, you can bring your mask to life with paint and other materials.

Variation: If you want your facial expression to be mirrored in your mask (for example, an angry Mars), make the most exaggerated expression you can. You'll need to sustain it until the mask has set—up to ten minutes—so be prepared. These masks are usually more interesting, but take more effort.

Creating a Healing Image for Inner Balance

Another visual approach you might try is to create a healing image of your chart. I have had a group of students do this. One woman with the transits of Uranus/Saturn conjunct in Sagittarius opposing her Moon/Mercury (Gemini) square Neptune (Virgo) drew a forest of trees and green earth. Her healing image helped her ground and balance her highly mutable, nervous energy.

A Pisces physician, who had just completed her first Saturn return, also had transiting Pluto in Scorpio trine her Venus/Mercury in Pisces. She drew the symbols of Pisces and Pluto at the top of her paper, with golden rays pouring down into four fetuses. She said that one fetus represented her new thirty-year cycle, and the other embryos were her patients, whom she wanted to touch with her healing Pluto energy.

Another woman in the midst of Pluto in Scorpio opposite Moon in Taurus drew an elaborate green penetrating spiral that represented her moving into her depths, her contact with her feminine side, whose center became an eye, the "eye of her soul."

To make a healing image, use the same art supplies you used for your birth mandala. Begin with some soft, meditative music. Then place a piece of posterboard, about two feet square, in front of you. Close your eyes and spend a few minutes focusing on your breathing. When you feel relaxed, open your eyes and imagine your chart transposed upon the blank posterboard. Look for a healing image to emerge that represents your chart/life at this moment. When you begin to see it, let it flow through your paint brush or marker onto the posterboard. Keep in touch with its healing, integrating quality as you draw.

Active Techniques (Mars/Sun)

Experiential astrology not only uses the visual arts (Venus/Sun) to experience the horoscope, but the more active form of astrodrama, too. A central principle underlying the holistic therapies is that all of our thoughts and emotions are inextricably interwoven with physical movement. Eastern philosophies have included active practices like yoga, karate, and sacred dance for thousands of years. When it finally began to break with Descartes' dualism, Western thought also affirmed the unity of mind and body. Psychological theorist Wilhelm Reich hypothesized that memories and emotions are stored in the muscles[2] as well as the brain. Biochemist and body therapist Ida Rolf found that pressures on particular muscles evoked memories, sensations, and emotions.[3] More recent research supporting the idea of a mind-body wholeness has evolved into the field of biofeedback.[4]

If we are to fully realize astrology's potential, we need to use our bodies to learn about our psyches. So let's get right to it. Try this: Turn on some lively, pleasant music that is easy to move to. Stand up and slowly begin to move to the music. Dance. Turn. Bend. How does Venus move? *Be* Venus.

Now play more aggressive Marsian music. Feel Mars in your body. Respond to it by dancing energetically. Be *Mars*. Shake yourself up. Get your heart pounding. Get moving! Now turn on some ethereal Neptunian music. Settle into its rhythms, returning to slow, flowing movements. Do you feel how Venus and Neptune are similar? Both are flowing, easy, soft energy. Can you see why astrologers call Neptune the "higher octave" of Venus?

Now that you've got your body up and moving, take out your natal chart and put it in front of you. Choose one of your planets to express. Is it your Mars in Gemini? Moon in Pisces? Venus in Leo? Go through your music collection and find something that captures the feeling of the planet. (Commonly available music for each planet is listed in the respective chapter for each planet and the corresponding sign or signs.) Play a selection for your Mars in Gemini. How does it aspect the other planets? How would contact with them affect Mars' movement? If there's a trine from Jupiter, your movements may become grander, more expansive, more sweeping. Is Mars square your Saturn? That might limit your movement, or cause it to be more staccato and jerky.

With a little research you can gather your own collection of planetary music. Then, when you are feeling the frustration of a transiting Saturn conjunct your Mars, you can put on Mars/Saturn music, dance it out, and release the blocked energy. Whenever I feel the effect of the scattered, nervous energy of my Sun/Uranus in Gemini I turn on "Dynamic Meditation" Music from the Shree Rajneesh Ashram.[5] Its insistent, driving rhythms get me moving and shaking my body, discharging excess mental build-up. I always feel relieved and more centered afterwards. If I am feeling a little blue and "Saturnized," I'll turn on "Fanfare for the Common Man" by Aaron Copland and dance with big sweeping movements to counter Saturn with Jupiter.

Try these dance forms for your planets in their signs:

> Aries—direct, definite, hard-pounding, forward movement.
> Taurus—rooted to one place on the earth and crouched low. Move slowly, methodically, lazily.
> Gemini—quick, butterfly movements, lightly touching here, there, everywhere. Use your arms, hands, facial expressions.
> Cancer—rhythmic swaying, rocking, curling over into a fetal position, or on the floor feeling like a small child.
> Leo—grand, dramatic gestures, regal bearing and movement.
> Virgo—meticulous attention to your small movements.
> Libra—movements of balance and grace.
> Scorpio—hips and pelvis gliding in slow, sensual circles, moving your hands over your body sensuously.
> Sagittarius—movements that direct the body upwards, stretching up, climbing higher.
> Capricorn—concise, authoritarian, sure, efficient, grounded movement.
> Aquarius—"gathering in" movement which includes others, move as a group.
> Pisces—flowing, willowy, tumbleweed movement.

If you love to dance and be physical, turn on some rhythmic, flowing Venusian music, and move from planet to planet, dancing out your horoscope! Try this at least once. It will make you more conscious of the different types of energy within you.

Reflective Techniques

The reflective (Moon/Mercury) techniques constitute another class of experiential methods you can use on your own. To get started on these, try keeping a transit diary, a dream/transit journal or a reflective/writing journal. Here's what a typical transit journal entry might look like:

Transit Diary (March 18)

> Transiting Mars square Natal Saturn—Thought my boss was going to drive me nuts today! Had a big blow-up with him when I gave him the status report on

the project. He kept interrupting me to ask for totally unimportant details. The meeting took twice as long as it should have. I was so angry at him I slammed down a glass, badly cutting my finger. God, I felt so out of control and reactive.

Do you know what occurred when Mars last squared your Saturn? Or what happened when Jupiter last opposed your Venus? Are you consciously aware of the movement of the transiting planets in your life, especially those of Mars, Jupiter, and Saturn?

If you don't know the answers to these questions, keep a notebook to record your transits and the experiences you have. (This is a fine tool for beginning astrologers.) It will help you to be more conscious of how planetary cycles are operating, and to learn what effects transits produce in your life.

A transit diary will also reveal two important things: which planetary energies manifest in a consistent way in your chart (for me, it's the planet Mars when in contact with my Sun/Uranus—consistently unexpected accidents), and when they are likely to be strongest. With planets that retrograde (all but the Sun and Moon), when will the transit fire most intensely? Is the strongest effect on the first, second, or third pass? For example, closely watch the forward and retrograde phases of Saturn in aspect to your natal planet. When does it manifest the strongest? This is an important key to the pattern of intensity of *all* of the retrograde planets.

Keeping a daily diary of all the transits affecting you can get to feel Virgoan very quickly, so if you get overwhelmed, try this abbreviated version. Buy a thick, lined, spiral-bound notebook, and divide it into twelve monthly sections, labeled for easy reference. Leave the first three to four pages blank for noticed effects of the long-term transits (Uranus, Neptune, Pluto) you experience during the month. Start your diary by spending time once a week reflecting on the outer transits of Pluto, Uranus, and Neptune. In what ways are you are noticing their effects in your life? Write down active transits in the lefthand column, allowing a third to a half page of blank space to write in during the month. This way, you need only to read through the first few pages of every month to see the effects of the slow-moving transits.

Then focus on the three more perceivable transits of Saturn, Jupiter, Mars. In the second section of each month keep a daily diary with dates and transit listings on the lefthand side. List the transits in order of strength—all Saturn, Jupiter, and Mars transits that apply. Write down to the right of the listing what you observe occurring in your life that corresponds to the transit.

The transits of the Moon, Mercury, Sun, and Venus last from a few hours to few days. Sometimes they will be the trigger for the more powerful transits. Keep your eye on them and simply list these transits and experiences below the entries for Saturn, Jupiter, and Mars. If you keep a record of the faster-moving planets for four months you will get a feeling for how they operate. The transits of the Moon may last only a few hours. To fine-tune your awareness of the Moon, pay attention to the days that the moon transits your natal planets during a two-month period. Keeping a transit diary takes some discipline, but you'll find that your efforts definitely pay off. You will learn to more accurately anticipate your upcoming transits, and you can more consciously prepare yourself for them.

Keeping a Dream/Transit Journal

Last night I had a dream that someone put a dog choker around my neck. I went into a panic as the chain squeezed off my breath. I clawed at my throat desperately trying to get air into my lungs. (Transiting Saturn opposing my Sun/Uranus)

There is an intimate link between the messages of your dreams and your experiences in daily life. In fact, many events in your conscious world can be foretold by listening to what your dreams tell you. Teachers of the yogic sciences go so far as to say that a symbol that appears in your dream-state will manifest in the conscious, waking world within seventy-two hours.

Because there is a direct link between your conscious experiences and your transits, it stands to reason there is a relationship between your dreams and the transits as well. Keeping a dream journal in conjunction with a transit diary can demonstrate this connection. I've kept a dream/transit journal on and off for twenty years. Many times this practice has given me important information about my inner process that I probably would have missed had I not kept a record.

When you keep a dream/transit diary you will notice two things. First, that active transits do correspond to your dream symbols, and second, that those dream symbols *can* manifest in your waking life.

Here are some examples from my current journal:

When transiting Venus opposed my Saturn, I dreamt I was robbed. Three days later, I received a bad check. Under a Pluto station point I had very disturbing dreams. During this time I was emotionally and spiritually supporting a friend whose father was dying. With the transiting Moon in my twelfth house, I had a dream that I visited a prison where the prisoners were kept confined to a swimming pool. The following weekend on a trip out of town with my husband, an enormous thunderstorm hit, flooding many roads. We drove in a maze for over three hours, trying to find a way around the flooding. With transiting Mars conjunct my Jupiter at Christmas, I dreamt I was downhill skiing, pushing for speed, riding the edge of the fall line down the mountain in perfect control. On Christmas morning, I got new skis and bindings.

Many people say they don't remember their dreams. If you want to remember your dreams you must train your unconscious to do so. Every night before going to sleep plant an auto-suggestive seed, "I will remember my dreams vividly." Then just drift off to sleep normally. It may take a week or two, but your dreams will start coming through.

As soon as you wake, stay focused in your dream state, without opening your eyes. Remember as much as you can. Immediately, roll to the side of your bed and without distraction record your dream, in present tense if you can, in your dream journal. Don't edit, just spontaneously write. Read it through and write down any first responses you have as to its meaning. Underline the key elements in the dream. Is the dream speaking about a specific issue in your life now? Take out your daily ephemeris. Are there any transits during this week that correspond to the dream symbols? Write them beside the dream. Pay particular attention under the planetary station points. By keeping aware of the symbols in your dreams occurring over a two-week period, you will begin to see a parallel between your transits and your experiences in your waking state. You will soon discover that your unconscious is speaking more loudly than you knew.

Contemplating the Horoscope

"Know thyself" is an essential dictum that has survived the ages and come down to us from the temple inscriptions at Delphi in Greece. The horoscope offers us a method for knowing ourselves that is based on a dynamic blueprint of our conscious and unconscious realms. Through deep study and contemplation of our horoscope we gain self-knowledge.

Self-knowledge is crucial if we are using astrology as a tool to help others, since we can only go as far with others as we have gone ourselves. A good way to accomplish this is to keep a reflective writing journal. With this journal you can contemplate and study aspects of your self/chart, dialogue with yourself and record your innermost thoughts and feelings. The journal page will become a living mirror for seeing yourself more clearly.

In a spiral-bound notebook (or other durable diary), write a question, selected from the list below, that has particular interest for you now. Close your eyes and reflect on the question. What feelings, images, words come to mind? Are there any physical sensations you notice? Write/draw your responses. When you have written or drawn your answer, study the indicated planet in your birth chart. What aspects, sign, house position does it have in your natal chart? If this is a question more relevant to how you feel now, study your progressions and transits. Do they correspond to how you are feeling?

Questions for Reflection:

The Sun
How do I appear to others?

What facets of myself do I see?

What is my purpose?

What aspects of myself am I not consciously using?

In what ways can I further develop or express my fuller being?

What was my father like?

What messages did he give me?

Did he consider himself successful?

What were his shortcomings, strengths?

The Moon
How do I feel right now?

How do I nurture myself?

What does the little child in me feel like now? What are its needs?

Who/what around me do I turn to when I need support and encouragement?

The Moon/Sun
What do my inner and outer selves look and feel like now? (Draw what they look like to you.)

Make two lists. List all your Moon, feminine, yin qualities. Then, list all your Sun, masculine, yang qualities. Is one stronger than the other? (What aspects/sign/house position do your Moon and Sun have?)

Mercury

What adjectives describe my style of communicating?

What favorite words do I use a lot?

What parts of my body do I use when I speak?

When I walk into a party with people I don't know, what do I usually do?

What new ideas do I presently want to learn about?

Do I enjoy writing? What kind of writing (letters, essays, articles)? What adjectives describe my style? What do I need to work on and improve?

Venus

What are the things/people I love most?

What do I love about myself?

What do I allow myself to indulge in to excess?

Is there anyone I am envious of? Why?

Mars

For what I am willing to exert my energy and make an effort?

What are my favorite physical activities?

For what cause am I willing to *take action*?

What makes me angry? What qualities in other people make me angry?

What do I do when I get angry?

Jupiter

What are my talents and skills?

What are my positive personality traits?

What have been my most important achievements?

In what areas do I feel confident in my knowledge and expertise?

What are my current potentials?

What areas of my life are smoothly unfolding and offer me promise?

What aspirations do I have for my life in the next five years?

What current beliefs do I have?

What words symbolize my philosophy of life now?

Saturn

What are my greatest strengths?

What are my particular responsibilities right now?

What attitude do I have toward them?

What are the traits I fear, judge, dislike about myself?

What are the traits I fear, judge, dislike in others?

In what areas of my life do I feel secure and stable?

What am I currently struggling with? Is it from within or without? What does the struggle look like? Name it.

Can I see a way to solve my problem? What can I do differently that might make the situation change for the better?

Uranus

Against what ideas/people have I rebelled in my life?

Are there things I like that others consider strange?

What groups am I involved with?

Am I actively involved or on the periphery?

Neptune

What areas of my life do I suspect I am not seeing clearly?

Am I holding any illusions now about my life or anyone in it?

To what am I addicted? Does it have repercussions in my life or the lives of others?

Pluto

Are there any problems in my life that I am suppressing or that are crying out to be transformed?

What resources do I have within/without to help me change?

Is there anything/anyone I intensely hate? Why?

Is there anyone in my life I still need to learn to forgive?

Is there something I have done for which I still need to learn to forgive myself?

Any one of these approaches will give you a wealth of ways to reflect upon yourself in the mirror of astrology. And most importantly, you will be learning from experience, your best teacher.

7

ASTRODRAMA: PLAYING WITH OTHERS

In the Heaven in Indra, there is said to be a network of pearls, so arranged, that if you look at one you see all the others reflected in it.
—Hindu Sutra

It is Ellen's turn for the group to act out her chart, astrodrama-style. She wants a better understanding of her fixed T-square of Mercury opposite Uranus square Neptune. Confused and anxious, she sits in the center of the room, witnessing the struggle between the three planets. Her Mercury begins to lecture her Uranus, "You're always pushing at me. Hurry up! Let's get going! Got to get these twenty things done today. Let me *relax*. I'm tired of trying to get a million things done. Hurrying up makes me nervous and flustered." Turning to the Neptune square she complains, "And you! Always so wishy-washy. You *never* take a stand. Always letting Uranus run over you. She gives you so many options that you just sit there stunned, like you're in some kind of fog! Do something, will you! Then Neptune responds dreamily, "Oh, well, doing's not so important anyway. Dreaming is. I *do* sometimes help you escape. We go off on some nice journeys, don't we? Remember that great idea we had to move to Corpus Christi and open a hotdog stand? Wow! that would've been great, hanging out on the beach." Uranus interrupts, "Yeah, you're really off in Never Never Land. No sense of reality. If you had your way, you'd never let us get anything done. You confuse the issues and dilute our action. You're a *drag*." Neptune responds, "And you're abusive. You never see my sensitivity, and sometimes I *do* give you good ideas, you know. And you *are* a know-it-all, always trying to lord it over me. I just don't know what to do about you anymore."

The energy in the room was intense, scattered, and chaotic, with three strident voices contending in this nonstop tug of war. You could see the frustration in Ellen's eyes as she tried to listen to the voices of Mercury, Uranus, and Neptune. Spontaneously, her Sun in Capricorn in the fourth house (standing behind her) placed her hands on Ellen's shoulders and reassured her, "It doesn't matter how they confuse and frustrate you. You've got *me*, Sun in Capricorn—Strong and Capable. I'll see you through anything your T-square can dish out. We'll deal with them when we need to. When Uranus acts up and scatters your mind, remember to come back to me to ground you and get organized before we go off half-cocked. And when Neptune moves in with her dreamy ideas, we'll listen to her, let her inspire us, even escape from reality sometimes, but we'll keep tabs on all the grand illusions and confusion she brings. Use me as your balancing force when Uranus or Neptune has your mind going crazy. I'll be there—always." Within minutes the energies in the room calmed down and came into balance, giving Ellen the reassurance that she could deal effectively with her difficult planetary combination.

Astrodrama: How to Do It

What you have been observing is astrodrama, a technique within the wider field of experiential astrology which presents the horoscope in dramatic form. Charts literally come alive, giving participants the opportunity to encounter and work with their energies directly. From one person to groups of twenty-five or more, astrodrama is an exciting and fun way to explore your psychic energies.

When you and a friend get together to talk about charts, try doing improvisational skits. Set up an imaginary set of circumstances for the two of you to interact in. Acting skill is not important. Just take a deep breath and give it a try.

Begin by standing up, stretching, and getting the Leo in your soul moving! Here are some examples to help you and your friend begin. After you've tried these, create your own scenarios:

Imagine that you and your friend have decided to take a vacation together. One of you is a strong Sagittarius, the other a strong Pisces. What's your process in deciding where to go? Or suppose that you are teenaged girlfriends on a trip to New York City for the first time. This is your first shopping day. One of you has a Venus in Pisces, the other's Venus is in Leo. What happens? What if one has a Venus in Virgo, the other in Gemini? Try a polarity of Venus in Aquarius with a Venus in Leo, or Venus in Virgo with Venus in Pisces.

You and your colleague are about to present a paper before a major professional body. He has Mercury in Virgo, you have Mercury in Sagittarius. How are you likely to be preparing five minutes before the presentation? You and your friend are downhill skiing. He has a good Jupiter transit, you a Saturn square. How do you go about choosing which run to take? You and your husband are figuring out your bank statement under Mercury retrograde. You have Mercury in Virgo, he has Mercury in Pisces. What happens?

You are about to go into your teacher's office for your final grades. You have transiting Saturn square your Sun. Act this out, then replay the skit with a Jupiter conjunct your Sun. You've just had a "fender bender" and are getting out of your car to inspect damages. You have Mars in Libra. The guy who hit you has a Mars in Aries, or Virgo, or Pisces. Try each variation.

For some nonverbal improvs try these: You are a Taurus lion stalking a Gemini gazelle. What happens? You and your friend are puppies; one was born a Taurus, the other a Gemini. You are four-year-old playmates at the beach. One of you has Sun in Leo, the other Sun in Virgo. How do you play together?

Try being Saturn conjunct the Sun, Saturn trine the Moon, Jupiter conjunct the Sun, Jupiter trine the Moon, Mars square the Sun, Mercury conjunct Jupiter, Mercury conjunct Saturn, Mercury square Neptune, Mercury trine Uranus, Mercury opposite Pluto, Mars conjunct the Moon in Virgo, Mars conjunct Venus, Venus conjunct the Moon in Cancer, Venus conjunct Saturn in Scorpio, Venus conjunct Jupiter in Scorpio, Mars conjunct Jupiter in Sagittarius, Mars in Leo square Saturn in Taurus.

Attempt some generational aspects: Saturn conjunct Uranus in Taurus, Saturn conjunct Uranus in Gemini, Saturn conjunct Pluto in Leo, Saturn in Leo sextile Neptune in Libra, Saturn conjunct Neptune in Libra, Saturn in Libra square Uranus in Cancer.

If there are three of you, take turns choosing some aspect in each chart to work on. Let's say one of you has a Moon in Aries square her Mercury in Capricorn that she wants to know more about. Without prior discussion of the aspect, divide the roles of the Moon and Mercury between you. The person whose aspect it is can just observe. Begin by setting the scene in which the two of you will interact. For example, suppose you are a married couple sitting at home. One of you decides it would be fun to go to the movies. How would the Moon in Aries square a Mercury in Capricorn react? Or discuss the aspect beforehand with your Moon in Aries friend, asking her to explain how she experiences this aspect in her life. Then one of you role-plays the Moon in Aries. The woman whose aspect it is might portray her own Mercury in Capricorn, while the third friend observes. This gives her the opportunity to feel and experience her Mercury. When you're finished, switch roles. What was each role like for her? Did she learn anything new? Did she see more clearly how these two psychic components oppose each other? What did you feel when playing her Moon? Her Mercury? What did the observer notice about the process? Can you all brainstorm ways in which she might better deal with this square? Have any new insights emerged? If you and your friends have some experience with astrodrama, you might want to include the houses as well. For example, portray her Moon in Aries in the second house square her Mercury in Capricorn in the eleventh.

If you have a slightly larger group—five or six people—try combinations of aspects, such as T-squares, i.e., the Moon in Aries square Mercury in Capricorn with Neptune in Libra making an opposition to the Moon and square to Mercury. What does this psychic pattern feel like? Then, add the Moon in Aries trine Jupiter/Pluto conjunct in Leo. How does this change the pattern?

Do you have a group of ten or more? Then try the reenactment of your whole natal chart. This is when astrology truly comes *alive*. My first experiences with astrodrama in a group setting occurred in the fall of 1981 at Esalen Institute in Big Sur, California. As a community workshop leader, I taught an astrology class three times weekly for a group of residents who were both students of astrology and frequent participants in Gestalt encounter groups. It was a perfect group to work with. They were informed about astrology, knew how to work in a group, and were open to new ideas. From these experiences at Esalen grew the reenactment of the full natal chart.

The Living Horoscope

The basic form of the "Living Horoscope" is described below. A more advanced form, using a Jungian mandala and Jung's concepts of the personal and collective unconscious, will be described briefly at the end of this chapter.

If you are working with a larger group, you'll probably want to "warm up" to each other first. Start with a few ice-breaking exercises. When you feel loose and relaxed, choose planets. Don't worry too much about who should play what energy, just choose and begin. When all of the planets have been assigned, you're ready to improvise some simple aspects. Begin by calling out aspects that group members would like to see. Someone may want to see their Jupiter in Cancer trine Mercury in Scorpio, or their Sun conjunct Uranus in Virgo. When an aspect is called out, the two planets should take a moment to compare notes, then use their planetary characters to portray the essence of the aspect. When the group is comfortable with one another, you're ready to enact full charts. To do full charts with a group of ten to twelve, try using this basic form below. It is adaptable, and yet it provides a simple structure within which to play.

Outline of the Living Horoscope—Basic Form

There are three kinds of roles:

The "Director" is the person whose chart you are enacting. He or she takes the lead in designing the astrodrama.

The "Planets" are, of course, the Sun through Pluto, assigned by the director to group members who have the ability to best portray the particular planetary energy.

The "Facilitator" supports the actions of the director by intervening when necessary to focus the drama. His or her relatively detached perspective allows the participants to stay "in role" while matters of overall structure and process are attended to. (As you can see, a group size of twelve—ten Planets plus the Facilitator and Director—is ideal.)

The basic format for a Living Horoscope is as follows:

1. Chart Analysis

Begin the process by placing the natal chart of the person whose drama you're performing in front of the group. (A blackboard is a handy aid.) The Director then leads the group through his or her chart, identifying the key aspects, elemental modalities, etc. If the Director is not knowledgeable about astrology, he or she may use the group as a resource to find the aspects and discuss them.

2. Assigning Planets

The Director then chooses group members to play the Planets. She may want a particular person to play her Saturn. Or she might want the participants to choose which roles they want to play. Sometimes a group member may feel that he or she has a special insight into a particular Planet in the Director's chart, or he or she may want to experience themselves in a particular role.

3. Establishing a Goal

Once the Planets have been assigned, the next step is to find the focus, or goal for the drama. Concentrating on a particular aspectual pattern or theme in the chart is a good choice. Does the Director want to focus on his grand square, his relationship with his lover, his parents? (A beginning astrodrama group needs a focus for their energy. Without it dramas can flounder. As groups gain experience, they'll find that structure becomes less and less necessary. Groups that are especially attuned to each other can create beautifully meditative and spontaneous work.)

To give an example of how the whole process works, we'll suppose that our Director is a woman who wants to better understand her relationship with men. See Figure 3, "Director's Chart," for the horoscope of our Director, who was born on August 12, 1948.

DIRECTOR'S CHART

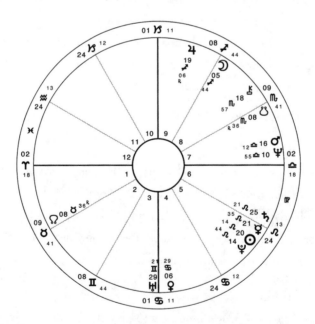

This woman has never been married, wants a relationship very much, and has a historic pattern of attracting a good relationship followed by an abusive one. (Twice these abusive relationships involved alcoholic men.) The group enacting her chart might want to focus on the relationship aspects and signs of her Sun, Mars, Venus, Saturn, 5th, 7th, and 8th houses, and anything else pertinent to understanding the pattern of relationships. How do the participants assess her particular relationship struggle? Where are the points of constructive release?

4. Role-Playing Order

As the brief discussion proceeds, the Facilitator should begin to devise (and display for all to see) a logical order in which the aspects in this particular chart will be enacted. For example, in this case it may be most natural to start with the Director's struggle with the powerful and controlling Sun/Mercury/Saturn conjunction, proceeding to the passive/aggressive Mars/Neptune square idealistic/dependent Venus, and ending with the configuration's points of constructive resolve—the stimulating effects of Mercury /Saturn sextile Uranus, and effects of its idealistic trine to Jupiter, Mars/Neptune sextile Pluto.

5. Planet Preparation

When the group has agreed to the order in which to proceed, the Planets should divide into the aspect groups and *briefly* discuss how they might enact the aspect. (This is to suggest a sketchy idea or sense of direction which will spontaneously unfold in the drama.) Although beginning groups or especially complex patterns may require more time, make this phase as brief as possible, since you want the action to flow from the situation. (Performances planned too carefully in advance often seem stilted.) And add a few extra minutes if you are using costumes or props.

Colorful costumes and ingenious props add an exciting visual element, so if you have them, by all means use them. You can't help but get into the spirit of Mars when you rustle around in a cluttered costume box and find a red satin cape, a helmet, and a sword. To portray Venus in Aquarius, how about a punk wig and yellow, star-shaped, glittery sunglasses? A ball and chain would be perfect for Saturn. For Uranus, almost anything with glitz and garish color will do. Props can also give you a starting point in creating a role. I remember an actress who got her first understanding of what Neptune was really about by swirling 'round and 'round in a dress of filmy scarves. Another portrayed the Moon in Virgo as a finicky mother dressing her baby doll.

6. Setting the Stage

When everyone feels that they have a general sense of how they will portray their Planet, "set the stage." Position the Planets of the natal chart around the Director. Place the Director in the center of her chart facing her midheaven (tenth house cusp). To her left should be all the Planets in zodiacal order that are in her twelfth, first, and second houses; behind her back any Planets in the third, fourth, and fifth houses; to her right, all Planets in the sixth, seventh, eighth, etc.

7. The Drama

A. *Introduction of Planets*

Now that everyone has taken a place you are ready to begin the action. (You might want to take a minute for the Planets to "center" in their planetary energy.) Starting with the ascendant, move from house to house, counterclockwise, letting the Planets briefly introduce themselves. "I am your Mercury in Leo. I am dramatic, think big, and love my ideas. I help you to create and create and create! The others say I'm too egotistic, but it seems to me when I'm having a good time so does everyone else." Move around the circle giving these brief ten- to twenty-second introductions until all ten Planets have spoken.

B. *Role Playing, Interventions*

Then let the drama unfold in the agreed upon sequence. In our example, the Sun/Mercury/Saturn in Leo will come forward first, speak, and interact. When they're finished, the Mars/Neptune in Libra takes center stage. And then the Venus in Cancer adds to the action. These are all the aspects which combine to create problems for the Director. Then move into the resolution phase of the drama—the Mercury/Saturn sextile Uranus, Mercury/Saturn trine Jupiter, Mars/Neptune sextile Pluto.

When the drama described above was actually performed, it was revealed that this woman idealized men (Father's influence), even though she had repressed her feeling that her business executive father was too busy and self-absorbed to give her love. Her longing for a soulmate blinded her to the actual man in front of her. She confused the men in her life with her own at first overbearing, then dependent and compliant behaviors. Her points of constructive resolve showed that she needed to find a *balance* between her desire to rush into relationships (impulsive Fire), and the need to take the time to see through her projections. By satisfying both her dependent Cancer nature and the controlling/demanding Leo with a balanced approach, she could relieve the desperate quality of her desire for a relationship.

In your own astrodramas, as in the one we have just described, the order of events may change as the drama unfolds. The "chemistry" of the Planets working together will give the performance a rhythm of its own. If an alternate sequence seems more suitable, feel free to make changes. For example, a Planet may spontaneously intervene because he or she intuitively knows what to do or say. The Facilitator or Director may want to intervene, perhaps by further drawing out a particular aspect, or the Director may want to assume one of the planetary roles. The trick is to have some sense of structure *and* to allow for the spontaneous "dancing" of the chart while the drama is moving.

There are many ways to vary the basic routine and make a better astrodrama. If a group is doing your own chart, you might choose to passively observe your Planets to learn what insights ten other minds have to offer you, or might dialogue directly with one or more. You might want to assume the role of your Venus. What does she feel like? How does your Venus respond to your Uranus square in Leo? After a minute you might want to change roles and play out, for example, your Uranus in square to your Venus in Taurus. It's up to you, as you gain experience, to arrive at your own best results in an astrodrama. You should also be able to rely on your Facilitator to help you make flexible choices. A good Facilitator maintains an overview of the drama, monitoring both the Director and the Planets, and, where helpful, will intervene to direct the action. Facilitators should remember to trust their intuitions while respecting the Director's experience. (Intervention for Facilitators is covered in Chapter 12, "Facilitating Groups: Tips, Techniques, and Skill Building.")

8. Making Closure

A Living Horoscope can be an absorbing experience for everyone. Taking time to wind down, separate from the drama, and find closure is essential. At this point, the Director is likely to be emotionally stirred, the energy of the chart is "in the air," and the individuals playing the Planets are engaged. As a group, look for ways to bring the astrodrama to that point of psychological ease that we call closure. How can the group sum up, offer further resolution, and support the Director? This consists of a final strong affirmative speech by a key Planet, a spontaneous gathering of the Planets around the Director with a gentle touch, a moment of silence, or a rousing cheer. Or it could be the gentle "rocking" of the Director in the group's arms, or a soft chanting of her name. Be creative in making sure that closure is not neglected.

9. Feedback

Feedback is the reflective stage of the astrodrama, when all can share the observations and understandings that amplify the teachings of experience. At times, this can be as enlightening as the drama itself. Still fresh from the performance, participants make comments with such immediacy and directness that they have potent impact. Begin by letting the Director share her feelings. What struck her most? What new insights did she learn from her chart? Did any Planets hit their portrayal "right on the head"? Then follow with any insights or interesting experiences the Planets may have had: "My gut instinct told me you are now having a lot of trouble with my planetary energy, but you're not saying so." Or, "When I went after Mercury to confront her, I got the feeling that was something you would never do, but very much want to be able to do. Is that true?" And, "When we closed with chanting your name, tears came to my eyes. What we did with your chart really touched my heart."

The Facilitator may also make observations about the process itself: "What I noticed was how dominant Saturn was. As soon as he let up, the chart's energy began to move more harmoniously. What do you imagine might happen in your daily life if you let up on your Saturn's need to be in control? Or, "The drama felt lethargic and uninspired until Mars responded by gathering up those other Planets and activating them to get moving. Do you observe your Mars kick in after you've had a period of no action? How does it usually do it?" Another example: "What struck me most was just how much support you do get from your Moon." And another: "That was a powerful piece of work. I suspect that now we're all deeply moved. Does everyone feel this way? Maybe we should take a break from the dramas and deal with what's happening in the group now."

I suggest that you start out with the basic form of astrodrama that we have described above. Then, as you and your group get more experienced, you might want to try some variations suggested below or invent your own.

Suggested Variations of the Living Horoscopes

Meditative Astrodrama

If a group has already had some experience with astrodrama, they may wish to try working with the meditative form. Here's how it's done: Have the group sit in a circle in the order they appear in the Director's natal chart. Ask each planet to examine the Director's chart, observing their contacts with the other planets. Reflect on how these contacts affect your planet. Then, if you are facilitating, ask the group to close their eyes and focus their attention on their breathing. As they breathe deeply, ask them to tune into the planet they are portraying, and guide them in their imagination, through space, to where their planet spins in the solar system. What do they notice about the planet as they approach? Ask them to imagine that the Lord of their Planet has come out to meet them. What does that entity look like? What feelings, vibrations are emanating from the Planet Lord? Have them sit down facing the Lord and note their impressions. What does the Planet itself have to say? What might the Planet speak directly to the Director? What might the other Planets in aspect say to the Lord of Your Planet? Using this as a focus for meditation, let the group spend fifteen minutes to one-half hour communing with the Planet. Then slowly bring the group back into the room. When they're ready to open their eyes, ask them to share what they learned. Insights which come from this kind of deep experience can be eerily perceptive and touch the Director in exactly the right place. You might also ask the Planets to get up and role-play what the Lord of the Planet said, or have the group enact the drama as a Lord of their own Planet.

Variation—Art Astrodrama

After the group has meditated upon the chart, try an art astrodrama. Have a large sheet of construction paper around the chart at the place of each Planet. Ask your members to draw what they feel expresses their meditative experience. If there is a conjunction, have both Planets draw. Then ask each Planet to move to every other Planet they have contact with by aspect in the chart, and draw that relationship in some way on a separate aspected Planet's paper. Be sure to have enough art supplies available— magic markers, crayons, paints, etc. The first time I tried this art astrodrama, the

Director was an art teacher. She was thrilled with the results and pleased to take her "astro-art" home with her.

Variation—Nonverbal Astrodrama

This is a fine way to do an astrodrama for a highly verbal, or "airy" chart. They're always talking about their aspects, so they'll get great value from a totally nonverbal communication. You might even ask them to get up and play nonverbally an important Planet in their chart.

Astrodrama and Jung's Model of the Psyche

My own growing edge with the astrodrama process has been in finding ways to use astrodrama in relation to Jungian psychology. Since the Fall of 1988 I have been working with a group in Chicago to further develop these ideas. To describe this fully would take too much space, but here's an idea of the basic direction we've taken.

I am now using three different mandala forms, based on Jung's model of the psyche. Instead of working with the circle as simply the natal chart, I'm incorporating Jung's ideas as well. The simplest form divides the circle into two parts, a conscious and an unconscious half, and works with the idea of polarity, the relationship of the Sun/Moon within—or how one has found that relationship in the external world through Father/Mother or in love relationships (I/Thou). Once the Director chooses the focus, then the group examines all aspects of the chart from the selected solar/lunar perspective and enacts the polarities in astrodrama fashion. For instance, if the Director wants to work with his or her parental relationships, we focus on the chart in

JUNG'S MODEL OF THE PSYCHE

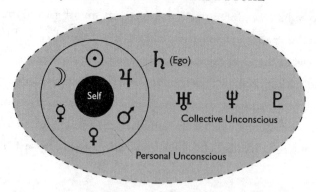

light of the tenth and fourth house influences. Or if he or she wants to work on personal relationships, we highlight the I/Thou (first and seventh house) emphasis.

The second form divides the chart into three circles, representing the three levels of the psyche—conscious, personal unconscious, and collective unconscious. The inner circle represents the center of the Self and all conscious awareness; the second circle stands for the personal unconscious and the planets—the Sun, Moon, Mercury, Venus, and Mars, with Saturn representing the ego and bridge between the second and outer circle. The outer circle represents the collective unconscious and the planetary realm of Uranus, Neptune, and Pluto. The third form works with all the Jungian archetypes within the collective unconscious—the Self, persona, anima, animus, and shadow—as they manifest in their astrological forms. The possibilities for this new model seem endless, and the Chicago group has had some rich experiences as pioneers of this new territory.

I hope you can see from the preceding examples and insights what the various forms of astrodrama may have to offer you. Spending just one day with your "Living Horoscope" can inform, stimulate, and even plant the seeds of transformation. A regular investment of time and effort with the same group brings even more reward. As a group member you can activate hidden parts of your psyche, can experience the poignancy of being an intimate part of another's cosmic drama, and can move toward living out your own chart in all its richness and complexity. Why not give it a try?

HEALING WITH THE POWER OF IMAGES

What to others a trifle appears
Fills me with smiles or tears
For double the vision my eyes do see
And a double vision is always with me
With my inward Eye 'tis an old Man grey
With my outward a thistle across my way.
—William Blake

Imagery has been used in healing since the first shamans appeared in early tribal societies. Their ritual work had direct effect on their patients by inducing altered states of consciousness conducive to self-healing. Indeed, the entire history of Western medicine is rich with examples of image used as a healing tool. (In early medical schools, the gift of imagination was more highly regarded than either surgery or pharmacy. Aristotle, Galen, and Hippocrates, fathers of Western medicine, used imagery for both diagnosis and therapy.[1]) A priestess of the dream incubation temples of Asclepius prescribed successful remedies for patients by listening to their dreams. Hundreds of these healing temples were established, based on the premise that visions and dreams contained seeds of knowledge about emotional, psychic, and physical health. The ancient use of imagery in healing is now being rediscovered in medicine, psychotherapy, and the arts. Similarly, imagery has emerged in astrology as a powerful medium for healing and teaching.

Using Images with Clients

Once, while consulting with a female client, I noticed that a distinctive image kept arising in my mind during the course of the session. There were two figures in the image: One was a waifish, vulnerable-looking girl of about four; the other was a fearsome, half-clad male warrior. Neither figure seemed to pay attention to the existence of the other. When I described the two individuals to my client, she saw that they precisely represented two aspects of her character that she had never before quite recognized. In retrospect it was easy to see that the images were prefigured in the chart. Her Moon in Pisces and Cancer rising were constantly threatened by four planets in Aries—Sun, Uranus, Mars, and Mercury in the tenth house. With this information, I suggested she try to find ways for the two images to communicate with each other. How might the young girl within feel more confident and empowered in the presence of the warrior? How could the warrior within acknowledge the existence of this shy little one, learn to be patient, gentle, and nurturing toward her? I also suggested that, in the next six months, she draw these figures in a series of images aimed at understanding their nature and relationship. She learned a great deal from the experiment.

Several years ago I consulted with a male client who had transiting Pluto in Scorpio conjunct his Sun/Mercury, and transiting Uranus in Sagittarius opposite his Saturn in Gemini, trine Jupiter in Leo. We discussed his current problem: An acknowledged love-hate relationship with his father, for whom he also worked, now manifesting as an intense tug of war (the Saturn/Uranus opposition) over the client's innovative ideas—ideas that his father freely ignored. The younger man struggled with this "no win" situation, while at the same time understanding his father from a more philosophical perspective (Uranus trine Jupiter). The story, and a glance at the client's chart, called up for me the image of a porpoise swimming in a strong and turbulent current, while above, a lightning storm crackled in the air. The client and I talked at length about this symbol of his inner state. On reflection he recognized that as a porpoise (Scorpio), he was in his natural element (Water), and was able to swim easily through the currents. Even though the lightning could upset him and stimulate some unpredictable "adrenal rushes," he could dive and surface at will and would therefore prevail. He left my office much relieved.

Some of you who have examined your thought processes while working with clients will recognize that images like this have come to you, too. But you may not have yet taken the more difficult step of realizing how valuable they can be when shared with the client. When I first began consulting in 1974 and became aware of these images, I refused to share them, writing them off as a distraction. The first time I took a chance and did share, both my client and I were amazed at the richness of meaning that emerged, and I've made full use of these pictures in my mind ever since.

Coming to accept the use of images in my consultation had a curious effect on me. Until then I had been strongly oriented toward my rational left brain (Sun/Uranus conjunct in Gemini) and took no note of visual images. Astrology, for me, was the usual: read, think, talk, talk, talk—with only the occasional spontaneous image for spice. By 1979 I had become increasingly uneasy about my work, feeling that my approach to it had become dry, uninspired, mechanical. Astrology no longer fulfilled me, and this was especially painful since I had so enthusiastically devoted myself to it a few years before. Now I was bored and disillusioned.

Struggling to find a reason for my apathy and frustration, I stopped reading charts for a year. Turning to other interests, I entered the Facilitator Training Program at the Oasis Center in Chicago. Learning skills in group process, encounter, Gestalt, and psychodrama, I spent a year in intense interaction with twelve other seekers, not in my role as an astrologer, but just as a human being. I never once asked for anyone's birth date! This experience was of incalculable value. I became aware of deep feelings, sensitivities, and capacities. I was able to experience and reintegrate the feminine, intuitive, imaginative side of myself that, before, I hardly knew existed. And I learned much about the power of experience and of the image as opposed to the word.

As young children we are natural visual thinkers, in touch with the imaginative, symbolic realms. But those abilities are soon suppressed. Albert Einstein, an admitted visual thinker, failed a primary grade. Obviously his "failure" had more to do with the expectations of his teachers than his own inability. Speaking of right-brain processes, the source of visual thinking, one writer states:

"Because we operate in such a sequential-seeming world and because the logical thought of the left hemisphere is so honored in our culture, we gradually damp out, devalue, and disregard the input of our right hemispheres. It's not that we stop using it altogether; it just becomes less and less available to us because of established patterns."[2]

Astrologers need to remember the role of the image in stimulating the right brain and should take note that at least one brain researcher has identified the right brain with some aspects of the unconscious mind described by depth psychologists.[3] A well-chosen image strengthens our work with clients. You will find it especially useful in conveying the meaning of the outer planets.

Images for a Saturn Return

Suppose you have a client who is about to experience her Saturn return. How would you explain this process to her? You might say that it is a time of trial and major restructuring, confinement, and the falling away of old patterns and relationships. But how much more descriptive it would be to begin with the metaphor of a baby chick in its shell. You say to your client, "As the chick gets bigger, it begins to push against its shell. What once represented security is becoming confining. What was once her snug little envelope of safety is becoming a prison. As she pushes out and strains against the confinement, she breaks free. Finally she pecks her little beak through the shell and begins to be aware of the space beyond her world, the greater world. She struggles through the shell, creating more and more space, until finally she emerges into a whole new life." You remind your client that, just like the baby chick's struggle with its shell, the process of transformation in our own lives is exhausting, and that after such an effort, she will need to relax, catch a breath, and survey the surroundings before moving on. Your client can't fail to understand such a vivid image.

To further the process, pursue the client's feelings about the experience as expressed in the image. Write those feelings down on a piece of paper and elicit responses. Which feeling is most problematic now? What resources can be mobilized? What can be done to change the situation? You might even get an agreement that the client will take certain actions to improve the situation. Together you can arrive at a deeper understanding of what needs to be done.

Another image for a client with a Saturn return might be the tearing away of an old foundation and the pouring of a new one. Stress the importance of dismantling old, outworn assumptions so that your consultee can build a stronger foundation for use in the next thirty years. Just as a new foundation is still soft and malleable, so are the new patterns he or she is establishing. I keep a twenty-five-pound bag of potter's clay in my office closet. Sometimes, when I'm describing this transformation, I'll hand a client a ball of soft clay, which offers a palpable symbol of this stage of life. By physically handling the clay, the client has a compelling sense of the opportunity that this time of uncertainty holds.

I'll suggest a final illustration for the Saturn return: Visualize a great machine with whirring, grinding gears. The return, especially if Saturn retrogrades and repeats its pass again, places the individual between the cogs, caught between two giant forces, not yet free of the one wheel and faced with going through the crunch to board the other—no longer able to fit into the old life, but not yet equipped for the new. They are sure to feel "stuck in the works" until the transition is complete.

Images for Saturn Transits

If someone comes to you who has a Saturn station point influencing the chart, try likening it to leaving a hot iron on a pair of good pants. Or, use the familiar kitchen metaphor of the feeling of being on the back burner to describe a retrograde transiting Saturn. As the transit goes direct and moves toward an aspect, it makes you feel like you're being put on the bigger and hotter front burner. You might also suggest that Saturn aspects may feel like the experience of rowing a boat to shore when the tide is coming out. The closer you get to shore, the more difficult it gets to row. Your oars begin to get stuck in the wet sand bottom, making it difficult to move forward. Eventually the boat gets stuck in the sand, and you need to find another way to solve your problem. Getting out of your situation and trying a new approach may be what's needed.

A metaphor that I particularly like for a Saturn transit is the dual nature of the carbon element. Under usual circumstances we know it as a chunk of coal. But where it has lain under enormous pressure for thousands and thousands of years, it becomes a fine diamond, harder and more valued than any other gem material. Buddhism uses this metaphor to describe the "adamantine diamond self" arrived at after lifetimes of spiritual advancement.

Anecdotes may be thought of as an image or extended metaphor, or as a short story in its shortest form. For an impatient fiery client with Saturn transits, you might want to relate an anecdote that gives the message of patience. Tell the story of the little boy who is given a seed to plant. He goes out, digs a hole in the earth, plants it, waters it, and sits down to watch it grow. After a day with no results, he goes out that night and digs up the seed. Angry and frustrated, he complains that the seed is dead and that all his effort has come to nought. It takes his wise old grandfather to explain that growth must happen in its own time. If a young child is undergoing a difficult Saturn transit, you might even make the story real by giving him/her a seed to plant and nurture. The child will soon learn that patience brings reward.

To be the complete astrologer, build up your own catalog of appropriate stories. Pay particular attention to your own experiences under transits. Parables and traditional tales can be revealing, but there's nothing like the immediacy of a personal account. When you have a client with a similar transit, use a personal experience to explain it. This is healing, for it creates a sense of shared experience. Clients will be encouraged that someone else understands what they are now feeling, and so might have useful advice.

Images for Uranus Transits

Uranus evokes a very different set of images. The most obvious is the lightning bolt coming out of the blue and striking with a searing jolt. Invariably, when a client has a Uranus transit, I'll draw a series of lightning bolts surrounding a head. (Assuming we all have a number of clients who are visual thinkers, you'll find it extremely useful to have a sheet of paper beside the chart as you do the session. Use it to "doodle" while making a specific point, drawing the person's attention to the visual imagery of their experience. For visual thinkers this doodle may have more impact than words.)

The image of Jack and the beanstalk is good for anyone struggling with restrictive, habitual Saturn patterns in the face of the restless urgency of Uranus transits. Jack was offered a handful of magic seeds of unknown worth for his valuable cow. By accepting the bean seeds he took a risk, moved into the unknown, and in the end received the hen who laid golden eggs. This tale can help you convey the possible rewards of taking a risk to someone who is clearly clinging to an outmoded pattern—like staying in an unfulfilling job, or living too long with parents—out of fear of the unfamiliar. The power of Uranus can be harnessed to create healthy new alternatives.

My favorite anecdote for Uranus is a true story. Several years ago the Ringling Brothers Barnum and Bailey Circus came to Chicago. Channel Twenty, a local TV station, did an interview with the Circus' animal trainer. The trainer arrived at the station on a Sunday afternoon for the interview accompanied by his trained bear on a leash! Well, Channel Twenty's studio is in the heart of downtown Chicago on top of a well-known office building. The trainer and the bear got into the elevator and rode up to the top floor. As the trainer was getting off the elevator, the bear got startled and reared back, breaking his leash just as the elevator doors closed! The bear, by himself, was automatically brought back down in the elevator to the lobby where people were waiting. Want to know what a Uranus transit feels like? Those who were waiting when the doors opened can tell you! And any client who hears this story will get the point.

Recall with your client what it was like to be a kid in a Halloween fun house, both the chills and the thrills. You don't want to go down the hallway, because you know you'll be surprised. If you only knew when, you wouldn't be so scared. Is it around this corner? No, maybe this one. No, now, EEEEKK! Your heart pounds. Your palms sweat. Now, *that's* Uranus. Or take your client, in imagination, for a ride on a super-duper roller coaster for the first time. They don't know where to expect the dips, quick turns, and loops. The whole first ride is like a Uranus transit. If they still haven't gotten the point, end your flight of fancy with a fireworks display. You never know where to look next. You wait in anticipation, and are thrilled with spectacular colorful explosions. The creativity and breakthroughs possible with Uranus transits can be just as spectacular.

Images for Neptune Transits

The planet Neptune brings a very different kind of image to mind. When under the influence of Neptune, we never seem to quite know what's going on. It's fuzzy, confusing, like scuba diving in a murky sea. Getting excited only makes things worse, fogging your mask with panicky breath. You must feel your way along, keeping your attention on what is just before you, so as not to get lost in the craggy caves. You might continue this analogy with your client by stressing the need to keep his or her focus close at hand. Stick with day-to-day planning for achievable successes, rather than thrashing about blindly and taking the chance of staying lost at sea.

Try this in your consultations: Neptune is like a walk in the country as evening is approaching. As you walk on the path and climb a rise, there is no mist. Your vision is clear. When the path dips down you sink into a misty fog. Descending, the fog is thicker. You have little awareness of the countryside around you. Sometimes you look down and can't see your feet, let alone the path. This is what it feels like when the Neptune transit is at its peak. Then, by moving slowly, step by step, you ascend to rise above the fog, into the starry night.

You might compare Neptune to wearing a pair of glasses with the wrong prescription. It's difficult to adjust your perspective and make sense of the blurry images in front of you. Or liken it to being in a corridor of many mirrors. I remember a time when I went into a woman's restroom with mirrors on all sides. I pushed here and there to no avail. Then I began to move my hands up and down along the cracks where the mirrors came together. First I was amused, then embarrassed, disoriented, and a bit panicked. Finally, another woman came out of the hidden door. I hadn't anticipated experiencing all those emotional changes just to use the bathroom.

When we drive a car down the highway and want to change lanes, we look into our rearview mirror, then check the side mirror. But we also lean forward slightly to check if anyone's driving in our blind spot. Share with your clients that Neptune is like the blind spot. To proceed safely, we must always make the assumption that we have one, and check it before deciding to move.

Neptune is like a going to a film in a theater. We enter into a fantasy world for two hours, swept away by the march of images taking place before our eyes. We know that this is fantasy, but while we're in it, we are so entranced that it is our reality for the moment. The comparison of a movie to a Neptune experience may help your client to perhaps pay closer attention to the balance between reality and illusion.

Images for Pluto Transits

Pluto, being the most long-term, profound, and cathartic of planetary influences, evokes strong imagery. Clients with Pluto transits find deep identification with these images, and can use them to help themselves cope with, understand, and transmute these complex and deep processes.

I keep two Pluto images close at hand in my consulting room. One is a photo of an erupting volcano from a range of one hundred feet. Red molten lava spewing from the cone fills nearly the entire frame. What many clients don't initially notice is that in the lower right corner a man is standing near the rim in an asbestos suit, with goggles and hat, and his arms flung high above his head. I have never seen the Pluto experience so accurately or poignantly captured. When clients are able to see the whole picture they spontaneously point to the man, and say, "That's me! That's exactly how I feel right now!" This realization leads easily into other feelings they are experiencing. I remind them that the source of the explosion is deep beneath the surface, several miles down. The lava has probably been percolating for years, causing the volcano to build up explosive force. As we pursue the roots of this suppression, we often locate painful experiences in early childhood.

To follow up with the same client, I might then show a second picture of a volcano, this one taken from a more distant viewpoint. The exploding center has quieted down. It is spewing slightly, still an open wound, but much less destructive. The lava is flowing out in wide slow circles, burning and transforming the earth below. We'll then continue our analogy with a discussion of the kind of change that takes place within weeks of the big explosion. The earth, revitalized by the rich lava and ash, springs to life in abundance. I may tell my client about a friend who lived near Mt. St. Helens both before and after it erupted. Afterward, his garden produced the biggest, fastest growing, and most delicious-tasting fruits and vegetables he'd ever had! The explosion brought the soil back to vibrant life.

Another favorite story is about a man who lived in a dilapidated one-room cottage. He scratched out a living by raising vegetables on the surrounding land. One day a stranger (perhaps Pluto incarnate) passed his humble dwelling. "You are not living in a one-room shack at all, but in a rich and prosperous castle," the stranger proclaimed. Naturally, the man shook his head in disbelief. Anyone with eyes can see this is the house of a poor man. But slowly, with the stranger's guidance, and much hard work, the man began to discover that there were parts of his house that he had forgotten. First he found one hidden room, then another, and another, until a huge beautiful home revealed itself. The man became the owner of a one-thousand room palace, the same dwelling that he had mistaken for a hut.

The transforming power of Pluto is also taught in the trite but still useful metaphor of the caterpillar who turns into a butterfly. From the dark, enclosed cocoon, the ugly worm begins his metamorphosis, transforming into a beautiful, winged creature. Clients won't fail to get the message that an individual can completely change form, transmuting dark and ugly memories, emotions, and circumstances into a life of great beauty and value.

Another useful image portrays the unconscious mind as a lightless and neglected basement. When you open the door and peer down the creaky stairs, it is dark, full of spider webs, creepy crawly things, and God forbid, *worse*? The horror of horrors lives down there! You certainly don't want to go down, but you know you must. So, you go. On the way down you may meet spiders and get cobwebs in your hair. But, as you get your bearings and adjust your vision to the dark, you find that it's not as scary as you thought. Maybe you have to wrestle with a demon, but as you keep strengthening yourself, cleaning up the unspeakable, you come to see that the fear was hiding something—something of great value. All this time there has been a hidden treasure chest in your unexplored basement.

Describe the Pluto process as that of a lumpy carpet. The lumpy carpet metaphor is good for Libra types who are good at focusing on their ideal, while stuffing the more difficult realizations under the carpet and ignoring them. It represents all you have brushed aside, ignored, and not honestly dealt with. For Libra types this is especially true of their pattern of relating. When a Pluto transit comes along, they realize they have a lumpy carpet. For the living room to be really clean, they must lift up the carpet and sweep up the hidden dust.

You might use this conventional image: Pluto is the Phoenix rising out of the ashes of destruction. Here you might distinguish between the four classic Plutonian symbols—the Scorpion, the Eagle, the Phoenix, and the Dove. Or describe Pluto as a two-part drama: death *and* rebirth. Most of us are so focused on what is leaving our life, what is painful and is dying, that we can't see further. Pluto does have an Act II, the phase of rebirthing. Remind clients how important it is not to judge their experience until they have seen the full two-act drama.

I can share one image of Pluto with special conviction—that a harsh Pluto transit is like being out in a hurricane, with only two choices: allow yourself to be blown away by the great forces around you, or learn to stand against the storm. The example is special to me because it resonates with a personal experience I sometimes share with clients. In 1982, my father died quickly from cancer of the throat. During the five days it took him to die, I went through every conceivable human emotion—fear, frustration, elation, confusion, deep calm, devouring rage, sadness, joy, and wonder. When I reflect on those painful days, I remember that it felt precisely like an emotional hurricane. The intensity of the experience was exacerbated by the disintegration of two other important male relationships in my life on the same night my father died—one with a teacher and the other with a lover. (Transiting Saturn/Pluto in Libra in the ninth house, square my progressed Sun in the seventh) Leading up to that night, I had also isolated myself to the extent that I had just barely enough emotional support to sustain me. Every time I felt deep pain that seemed beyond bearing, someone would come along and give me just the lift I needed to help me stand up again. This went on for weeks. It was wrenching, but in the process, I learned to psychically survive. And as difficult and painful as those months were, in time I came to see the hidden treasure. It took an intensive psychic blow to expose it.

Like me, you have stories to tell, replete with images that shine through the lens of your own experience. Man is the only creature that tells stories. But men and women are the only creatures that paint pictures, too, and thus the communicable image defines us as human as much as does the word. Share your stories, your images, and your humanity.

BALANCING YOUR DIFFICULT TRANSITS

*Superstitious awe of astrology makes one an automaton, slavishly
dependent on mechanical guidance. The wise man defeats his planets—
which is to say, his past—by transferring his allegiance from the creation to the Creator.*

—Swami Sri Yukteswar

Light-dark, hot-cold, active-passive, yin-yang, good-evil: All are examples of the fundamental pairing of opposites into which all experience can be divided. In Hindu thought,
the Sanskrit term *Dvanda* refers to this dualistic reality, and includes the notion that
the universe itself comes into being through this division. These ideas had great influence on Carl Jung's developing theories of mind: "Just as all energy proceeds from opposition, so the psyche too possesses its inner polarity, this being the indispensable
prerequisite for its aliveness.... That an ego was possible at all appears to spring from the
fact that all opposites seek to achieve a state of balance."[1] As to the significance of this
fact, Jung simply states: "Nothing so promotes the growth of consciousness as this inner
confrontation of opposites."[2] Though their sources and methods might be quite different, both Jung and various Eastern spiritual disciplines intend to resolve the tensions
between opposites and promote a balanced unity of consciousness.

Astrologers know that a principal source of imbalance is the endless permutation
of planets and signs described by the astrological chart. Responding to these, we can
feel out of control, overwhelmed, at a loss as to how to deal with the instability they
introduce. Because our squares and oppositions—and some conjunctions—symbolize
what we have not yet mastered and integrated, they are the aspects that will cause us
the most imbalance when stimulated by a progression or transit. For the average individual the most noticeable psychic triggers are squares, oppositions, and conjunctions

of Mars, Saturn, and Jupiter. The most profound and long-term are the transits of Uranus, Neptune, and Pluto.

This chapter will focus on practical ways to help you, or a friend or client, through these particularly difficult learning periods. Many of the methods arise from a common sense application of principles derived from the astrological symbolism itself; others draw upon a particular branch of Eastern knowledge called Kriya Yoga, that includes astrological concepts in its formulation. *All* have met the test of my own personal experience: They work!

Kriya Yoga and Astrology

It is of course impossible to convey the depth and richness of a tradition like Kriya Yoga in a brief chapter. Evidence for yoga as a system of spiritual training extends as far back as 2000 B.C.[3] "Classical" yoga, enshrined in Patanjali's *Yoga Sutras,* is the most common form, although starting from 1000 B.C. at least eighty types are known.[4] In the narrow sense, Kriya Yoga is a system of breathing techniques that allow "the Breath to be stilled and thereby dissolve the mind, intellect and ego in order to achieve the egoless state of pure Consciousness."[5] More broadly, Kriya Yoga is a spiritual path that may include philosophical teachings and additional yogic practices. As Paramahansa Yogananda, who, as a disciple of Lahiri Mahasay, brought Kriya to the West, notes: "Kriya is an ancient science. Lahiri Mahasay received it from his great guru, Babaji, who rediscovered and clarified the technique after it had been lost in the Dark Ages.[6] "The yogic techniques described below originate in Kriya Yoga as transmitted through the lineage from Yogananda to Shellyji to Goswami Kriyananda of Chicago, to many students, including myself. (Note: For more about Kriya Yoga, read Paramahansa Yogananda's *Autobiography of a Yogi* and Swami Satyeswarananda's *Lahiri Mahasay: The Father of Kriya Yoga*. However, Kriya can best be learned through direct teaching. In the USA, contact the Temple of Kriya Yoga, 2414 North Kedzie, Chicago, IL 60647; the Self Realization Fellowship Church, 3880 San Rafael Avenue, Los Angeles, California 90065; or the Kriya Yoga Center, 1201 Fern Street, N.W., Washington DC 20012. Do not expect these centers to be identical in their teachings, especially as to the extent to which they employ astrological principles.)

According to Yogananda, "The *Kriya Yogi* mentally directs his life energy to revolve, upward and downward, around the six spinal centers...which correspond to the astral signs of the zodiac, the symbolic Cosmic Man."[7] And, further: "The astral system of a human being, with six (twelve by polarity) inner constellations revolving around the sun of the omniscient spiritual eye is interrelated with the physical sun and the twelve zodiacal signs."[8] These spinal centers are the *chakras*, literally "wheel" in Sanskrit, conceived of as vortexes of energy or as force fields composed of different wavelengths, vibrational rates, or colors which, when stimulated, produce various states of consciousness.

Kriya Yoga identifies the chakras with zodiacal and planetary energies; the pattern of their arrangement corresponds to the natal chart, and they are seen to be affected by the planetary transits. Note that the planets are arrayed from the base of the spine (Saturn chakra) to the Moon and Sun centers in the head, and that the three lower chakras share locations, Uranus with Saturn, Neptune with Jupiter, and Pluto with Mars. (The latter is, of course, a revision of the ancient system—both astrology and Kriya continue to grow!) The zodiacal signs correspond to this placement by appearing in order around the spine. Keep this "model" in mind as you consider the yogic balancing techniques below.

Distilled from my dozen years of study of Kriya Yoga, these are three basic methods of balancing astrological influences as they manifest in the chakras:

1. We may seek to counterbalance them by endeavoring to activate the energies of a higher (or otherwise appropriate) chakra, directly or through use of ritual, thus counteracting the effects of lower chakra activity.

2. We may elect to experience the influences. The experiencing may be largely conscious—identifying with a higher chakra and from this perspective accepting the problem as part of life—or the experiencing may reach into the unconscious mind, intensifying the energies of the chakra and leading to emotional release and understanding.

3. We may choose to transmute the problem by using spiritual techniques to bring about fundamental change, activating the entire chakra system in a holistic solution.

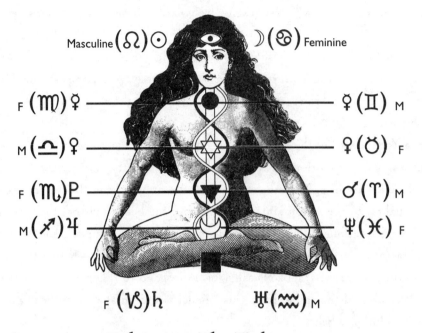

Balancing: The Techniques

Since transits of the outer planets are especially difficult and long-lasting, much of the rest of this chapter will teach techniques for their mastery. Direct counterbalancing procedures are the most accessible and will be abundantly provided. Experiencing methods get so much attention in Chapters 4 through 7 that they need only brief treatment here. Although the transmuting techniques are, in some ways, the most interesting, I will often refer to them only tangentially, since, as Yogananda says, "Because of certain ancient yogic injunctions, I may not give a full explanation in a book intended for the general public."[9]

Counterbalancing Saturn with Jupiter

Let's begin with Saturn. Saturn in a difficult aspect tends to stimulate a state of consciousness that constricts and squeezes, creating limits to our movement and growth. This is the "I can't" state of consciousness that sees the worst, most negative, and doubtful aspects of life. Because Saturn invokes a repressive energy, it can spawn a chronic state of inactivity, lethargy, and depression. In general, to counterbalance

Saturn, move one chakra above to Jupiter. Live and act from the Jupiter state of being. Give yourself a gift of the Jupiter energies. Acknowledge the *good in* your life. What is harmonious, giving you reason for confidence, and satisfaction? What are your blessings? Look in the mirror and affirm the good in you and in your life.

Use the affirmation, "Every day, in every way, I am growing better and better" as a mantra. (It worked for Anton Mesmer and his followers in the nineteenth century— why not for us now?) Write it on paper and tape it to your bathroom mirror. See it. Say it. Say it again and again during the day. Realign the mind.

Look around you to find the sources of Jupiter energy at hand. Use them. Spend time with optimistic and supportive friends. Stay away from any chronically negative ones—you don't need someone's else's troubles right now. Ask yourself who around you makes you feel good. If a series of Saturn transits is approaching, start strengthening relationships with friends, who can help you through more difficult, lonely times.

With Saturn you may at times feel doubtful or lack confidence. If these feelings drag on, search your collection for Jupiterian music and play it loud until you remember how it feels to be fully self-assured. My own favorite for bringing about this mood shift is a set of rousing trumpet fanfares. Sometimes I'll plug in my "Walkman" and soak up those brassy melodies while striding about the house or through the neighborhood.

Saturn begs for a dose of Jupiterian humor. Stop taking yourself and your problem so seriously. Tell a joke. Read a funny book. Take a humor workshop. Go out to (or rent) a hilarious movie—*Blazing Saddles*, *Four Weddings and a Funeral*, or *A Fish Called Wanda* can tickle your funny bone and help you laugh those (Saturn) blues away.

Saturn cries "ME! ME! ME!" Under its influence you are self-absorbed, even egocentric. You dwell on your problems, your failures, your disappointments: "*Mea culpa, mea maxima culpa.*" Under Jupiter you would have found it easy to be expansive, attentive to others, generous; but now is when you need to dispel Saturn's isolation by consciously and intentionally turning outward to do a good turn for someone else. Make an effort to serve. By extending outside yourself, you can break the intense "ME" focus.

Here is a yogic technique for counterbalancing (perhaps even, to some degree, transmuting) Saturn: The *Om Nama Shivaya* mantra. (Pronunciation: "O" is long, "a" is as in "Father", "i" is short.) *Shiva* symbolizes the divine principle of Death that dissolves and destroys all the imbalances and negativities within. The mantra can be translated as "Oh, auspicious Lord, to you I bow." It is chanted repeatedly in a bubbly, brisk, joyful manner, with alternate repetitions ending with first an upward lilt, then a downward inflection. Give this mantra a try. If the several thousand-year history of the chant, as well as my own experience, are any guide, you will feel lifted from the Saturnian depths by its use.

Counterbalancing Saturn with Mars

The Saturn state of consciousness is no stranger in this day of the sedentary lifestyle. At times we all have felt depressed, uninspired, and heavy. But haven't you noticed how different you feel when you've managed to lug yourself out the front door for a run or a go at rollerskating? You return feeling energized, having increased your circulation and metabolism, and you're not nearly so weighed down. You feel better because you have literally broken your chronic "woe is me" stream of consciousness and moved into Mars, mobilizing that chakra and its attendant state of being. Saturn nails you to the floor; Mars pries you loose and pushes you out the door. So: Move! Act! Exercise! Get *physical*! and Saturn will retreat. Or use the Marsian energy in less direct ways: Eat hot spicy foods like Indian curries, Italian and Mexican pepper dishes, Japanese wasabi mustard, hot Thai or Szechuan Chinese foods. They stimulate your system and, in terms of our yogic model, move energy from the base of your spine up to the solar plexus.

Use Mars to elicit an awareness of your courage, rather than dwelling on the fear that Saturn stimulates. Music, this time Marsian in tone, is a help. Who can feel fearful while dancing, as I have, to Wagner's, "Ride of the Valkyries"? Just listening helps, but movement magnifies the effect.

Saturn yields to Mars, but also to Venus and beyond. But I'll leave the specifics of those approaches to your own inventiveness. Also remember that counterbalancing may be accomplished by the use of ritual. These methods deserve special attention and are covered in Chapter 11.

Experiencing Saturn

Experiencing, in the context of this chapter, may be largely conscious, or relatively unconscious in its focus. The first instance involves a shift of *perspective* from a lower chakra to a higher one, so that the ego may act accordingly. Note, for example, Mahatma Gandhi's state of mind and his actions, when, early in his struggle for racial justice he was bodily thrown from a South African train, far from Pretoria. "I did not know where my luggage was, nor did I dare to inquire of anybody, lest I might be insulted and assaulted once again. Sleep was out of the question. Doubt took possession of my mind. Late at night, I came to the conclusion that to run back to India would be cowardly. I must accomplish what I had undertaken. I must reach Pretoria without minding insults and even assaults. Pretoria was my goal."[10] This "enobling" of the problem one faces by viewing it in light of the higher good constitutes conscious experiencing. For Gandhi, this kind of test of character and self-respect would become common, and thus lead him to the principle of "satyagraha…the force born of Truth and non-violence."[11]

When Saturn bears down upon us we may get some relief by realizing (some might say rationalizing) that without its endless challenge there would be no incentive for character building or accomplishment. So, in the midst of your next struggle try the path of noble acceptance. Allow yourself to experience Saturn and pause to reflect upon the gift it bestows.

Both counterbalancing and experiencing as described so far rely upon ego's exercise of will to change either the environment or one's conscious response to it. When instead we yield fully to the experience of the moment, amplifying its intensity and allowing feelings and unconscious elements to emerge, we enter a new level of experiencing. At one extreme this way of operating gives us no more than a good cry followed by acceptance; at the other, the change is so profound as to approach the "transmuting" spiritual techniques. A personal example of experiencing Saturn: When my dad was sick with what was to be his final illness, I took a few hours away from the hospital to go out with a girlfriend. We wanted to see a movie, and as we were passing a theater a parking place opened up right in front. I pulled in, thinking, "This must be fate." The film turned out to be *Sophie's Choice*, laden with a full portion of Saturn's death and despair. My friend and I both cried throughout the film. But coming out of the theater afterwards I felt so much relief. I had moved into pain that I had been avoiding, had spent a few miserable hours being in its grasp, and had cried it out. If you do this, be sure to bring along a *good* friend!

You have already encountered experiential techniques in earlier chapters, so they won't be repeated. Refer back, especially to Chapters 4, 5, 6, and 7. Saturn aspects may provoke you to seek out a guide for in-depth experiencing, especially when we bear in mind that Saturn may stimulate unresolved issues with Father or other past authority figures. Psychotherapy or an intensive group experience may be in order. But such drastic measures are not always required. Other ways to manage Saturn while experiencing it are just to "burn it off" by working extra hard, or by using its evocation of structure to provoke you to get things in order. There is much that can be accomplished under a difficult Saturn, though you won't find it easy or fast work. Be patient and keep on striving. The reward will come later.

Counterbalancing Uranus with Saturn

Saturn brings order, Uranus dwells in chaos. Saturn enjoys structure, Uranus delights in formlessness. Saturn is the patron of constraint, control, and oppression. Uranus is the high priest of impulse, unpredictability, and therefore the possibility of freedom. Polar opposites, these two are inextricably linked, and they are so represented in the chakra model, at the base level. When in balance in the human soul, they are like a harmonious chord that underlies the melodic flow of life. When out of balance, on the one side they impose the morbid tones of the funeral dirge, and on the other, a mad cacophony. Applying each to the other, we can achieve that harmony. Let's first concentrate on counterbalancing Uranus with Saturn.

When under the influence of a Uranus transit, make a conscious effort to introduce Saturn's self-control. Take your time when considering a radical action. Impulsive decisions can tear apart life structures, so proceed carefully and methodically. Don't ignore the old saying: Count to ten—or ten thousand—before making a rash move. And stay grounded. Use any of the grounding techniques suggested below for counterbalancing Neptune. By "earthing" yourself you will anchor more of the erratic, frenetic, scattered energy, giving yourself more control and peace of mind. Also make this a time to create order around you. Spring or not, consider spring cleaning your home. Reorganize your office or workspace. As you see order in your outer world, it helps you to restore order in your inner one.

Without Uranus there is no impulse to change. Without Saturn change leads to disintegration rather than growth. With too much Saturn, too long applied, change can be explosive. The balanced use of Saturn with Uranus implies *planning*. Look ahead to your Uranus transits and plan how to incorporate their influence long before they hit. Methodically compile a list of what has begun to feel restrictive. These are the areas in which to establish goals for change in structure and routine, bringing in fresh action and direction. Your Uranian friends won't be a help in this process. Prefer instead your more Saturnian, calming and responsible friends rather than the frenetic, unpredictable ones who will only distract you from your task. Plan now, party later.

Counterbalancing Uranus: Other Ways

Planning for Uranus may also include laying out a plan for counterbalancing by evoking the other chakras or by experiencing or transmuting approaches. For example, to prevent the buildup of pressure, choose, before the main thrust of the transit, to activate Mars by beginning an exercise program. But guard against extremes since Uranus can backfire and cause injury through accident.

In another manifestation of its character, Uranus can cause feelings of alienation. Because the inner level has a lightning storm going on, unanticipated and disconcerting feelings and quick changes of mood can separate us from those whose lives seem to be going on as usual. The antidote? Place yourself in the consciousness of the Jupiter chakra. Join a group, workshop, or networking organization that is oriented toward self-help, growth, and change in order to give yourself more regular contact with others. Or put out a call to friends and family you've lost touch with.

Some ideas are especially compatible with Uranus. Use the auspices of the Mercury chakra to pursue activities with Uranian content. Learn specific new techniques and skills, for instance, computer programming. Or tackle a complex astrology idea now. Investigate systems new to you, such as Harmonic or Uranian astrology.

Experiencing and Transmuting Uranus

There is a place, of course, for allowing Uranus to spring forth in full measure in one's life and actions. Here's a bit of strange but useful advice, which can be attributed, I think, to singer Willie Nelson: "You've gotta get crazy to be sane." Chaotic dancing (arms and legs akimbo, with no apparent plan or pattern) to oddly rhythmed or discordant music (some jazz and rock, mostly punk and New Wave) is an outlet for that hyped-up Uranian feeling. A "chaotic meditation" has been taught by Rajneesh and his followers; music for this practice, which may be one component in a transmuting approach, is available ("Music of Shree Rajneesh Ashram," Lucerne Valley, California, Geetam Rajneesh Sannyas Ashram, 1979). If you are involved in a spiritual program which includes meditation as a tool for personal transformation, you may already have noticed that meditation during a Uranus transit can be disrupted—but persistence brings reward.

Counterbalancing Neptune

Saturn makes reality known and certain. Uranus strips away the comforting illusion of predictability. Neptune calls reality itself into question, offering the disturbing suggestion that reality itself is an illusion. Neptune has a major impact at the level of perception. Under an unfavorable Neptune, clarity is banished, and we are left with a kind of "fuzzy discernment" that makes it nearly impossible to distinguish what is relevant from what is merely fascinating. To be sure, Neptune leads us on, but too often into dark pathways and blind alleys. Like Jupiter, with whom it is paired in the chakra system, Neptune expands consciousness, but where in Jupiter the expansion leads to integration into a larger whole, in Neptune the expansion is without boundaries and ends in dissolution.

We would not want to do without Neptune's gift of lofty dreams and ideals, but to keep the dream from becoming a delusion, we must keep our footing in ordinary reality. Let Mercury advise. Think: Is this idea realistic? Or am I kidding myself? Am I seeing the truth, or am I seduced by a grand illusion? With Neptune about, don't rely on just your own counsel. Reason out matters with a clear-thinking friend. Your major decisions at this time are particularly vulnerable to confusion. Postpone them if possible, or make short-term contracts rather than long ones, and build in an escape clause. That way, when clarity returns, you still have options.

Neptune in difficult aspect to Venus or Mars can be particularly troublesome for your love life, since you are prone to over-idealization, seeing a soulmate in any rascal who comes along. Let any new relationship that comes into your life now prove itself before you rent the hall and order the flowers. Assume that there is something you are not seeing. As to friends, take care not to draw in needy, dependent people who may take advantage of you.

With Neptune, planning ahead is especially difficult. It is as if you are driving along on a dark, lonely road, the way ahead hidden by dense fog. To get through you must keep your eyes fixed on that white line and follow it home. Similarly, to counter Neptune you must attend to matters close at hand. Focus on keeping your day-to-day routines. Take one day at a time. Set little goals you can accomplish and feel good about, thus using Saturn to best advantage.

Note that the Lotus Position of the meditator in our Chakra Diagram (page 121) places her on a firm base, solidly connected to the earth. Contact with the earth, grounding, is especially important for counterbalancing the effects of Neptune. Here is a list of simple ways to get grounded:

1. Stand and walk barefoot on the earth.
2. Take a shower (especially good after working with someone else's disturbed psychic energy).
3. Eat grounding foods—particularly red meats and grains.
4. Stay away from all drugs and spacey, confused people.
5. While standing barefoot on the earth, imagine that you are a tree trunk with roots deep in the earth. Imagine the roots expanding in thick, strong shoots deeper and deeper. Allow whatever makes you confused and unfocused to enter the roots, flowing down deep to where it is absorbed by the earth.
6. Spend time with your earthy friends.
7. If you have outdoor space, planting and caring for a garden is an excellent ongoing means for grounding. If you live in the city, tend to the plants in your apartment.
8. Take regular breaks and go away to the country. Contemplate the earth—look at it, walk on it, lie on it.

Experiencing and Transmuting Neptune

If you've attended to practical matters and set aside time for Neptune, just floating along with its dreamy meanderings can be a delight. I remember a Neptunian day when my husband and I sat from dawn to deep starry night just watching a day go by in a high mountain meadow. Daydreams had equal footing with the natural beauty around us and yielded a "Rocky Mountain high" to remember. When you know a Neptune effect is coming, look for ways to experience its positive qualities. Revive your neglected practice of meditation. Make a special effort to recover dreams. Allow yourself to escape in a positive sense through inspirational reading—Lama Govinda's documentation of his trip to Tibet, *The Way of the White Clouds*,[12] or Peter Matthiessen's *The Snow Leopard*,[13] or John Neihardt's *Black Elk Speaks*[14] would be good choices.

Issues that arise in the deeply afflicted Neptune aspects may yield only to transmuting approaches. I am never surprised to find alcoholism or drug abuse, gambling, food abuse, or relationship addiction in charts with hard Neptune aspects. "Just say no!" is good advice, but an injunction is seldom enough to even faze an addiction, once begun. For alcoholism and other addictions, only one approach has brought recovery to millions: Alcoholics Anonymous and its affiliated "Twelve Step" programs. This must be so because AA is a complete spiritual program, aimed not at alleviating symptoms but at transmuting the energy that provides the impulse to indulge, transforming the life of the sufferer at physical, mental, emotional, and spiritual levels. Eastern spiritual systems are not a substitute for AA—if that is what you need, then by all means go there—but they do offer various means of self-transformation that offer freedom from attachment, compulsion, and suffering. In Kriya Yoga, for example, there are meditations that carry the breath from chakra to chakra, integrating their energies, and discharging the burden of karma. Their goal is complete Liberation and Absolute Knowledge beyond the reach of any Neptunian illusion.

Counterbalancing Pluto

Form, dispersion, chaos, re-formation: all substance, all energy, all being, cycle in the endless chain of Death and Rebirth. And the hand of Pluto guides every turn of the wheel. Every ego is born and will die, only to be born again, even within the boundaries of a single lifetime. Drawing on countless experiences with patients, pioneer in LSD psychotherapy Stanislav Grof describes the quintessential Pluto experience:

> Paradoxically, while only a small step from an experience of phenomenal liberation, the individual has a feeling of impending catastrophe of enormous proportions. This frequently results in a desperate and determined struggle to stop the process.... [The] transition...involves a sense of annihilation on all levels—physical destruction, emotional disaster, intellectual and philosophical defeat, ultimate moral failure, and absolute damnation of transcendental proportions. This experience of ego death seems

to entail an instant merciless destruction of all previous reference points in the life of the individual.[15]

Mercifully, every Pluto transit does not plunge us into these depths—but the potential is always there. Even at lesser intensity, Pluto stirs deep emotion. It uncovers all you have hidden, secreted away in your unconscious, and demands that you come to terms with your inner nature. Pluto is worthy of respect, even fear, but remember that like Kali, the Hindu goddess of destruction, Pluto destroys only to re-create. Essential to managing the difficult Pluto aspect is that you acknowledge your need for fundamental change. Thus, counterbalancing techniques are not the ultimate answer, but since in Pluto's grasp we are likely to petition for any form of relief, I should at least offer what has proved of some use.

The Saturnian grounding techniques offered above for Neptune seem to help drain away Pluto's excess energy. Try them. Since our physiological system is stirred and heated to excess with Pluto, also try to enlist Saturn by eating cooling foods. Stay away from heavy meats and spices that stimulate the Mars/Pluto chakra. And consider fasting—settling your digestive system may bring some relief from the turmoil.

When Pluto visits, we are seldom easy company for others. Our feelings are so deep and so intense that we have much trouble conveying them. And we are as likely to lash out as to plead for understanding. So, just when we are most in need of support, we seem least likely to get it. This is the time to draw upon that source of love within. Stimulate your Venus chakra. By intensely focusing on love, gentleness, and compassion for yourself and others, you can rob Pluto of some of its force. Love yourself. Find ways to be good to yourself and give yourself pleasure. Eat a favorite dish. By all means, if there's a hot tub around, lounge in it. If you are lonely, get on the phone to those you love and tell them that you care—love is the gift that always returns to the giver. Honor your need for warmth and touch—wrap up in a blanket or your old winter coat and sit by the fire. Or get a weekly massage from someone with a loving nature.

Self-love often requires forgiveness of yourself and others. Yoga offers a "Forgiveness Mantra" that I have often used to lighten Pluto's load: *"Hai Ram, Jai Ram, Jai, Jai Ram. (Hai* as in "hay," *Jai* as in "sky"; the "a" in *Ram* is like "Father.") When Gandhi was assassinated, these were the last words he spoke. In essence he was saying, "I forgive this act." For your own self-forgiveness, chant the mantra in a steady monotone, allowing the sound to entrance you. Continue the chant for an hour or more if needed; your feelings will guide the decision. On especially intense days, you may silently continue the chant throughout the day, continuously releasing anger, frustration, and self-doubt, and opening up to the peace and love of Venus. I've found no better tool for counterbalancing Pluto.

Experiencing and Transmuting Pluto

Pluto penetrates into every level of mind, shifting and breaking up calcified layers of consciousness. Thus Pluto aspects signal optimum times for efforts at self-transformation. You will benefit especially from metaphysical study or spiritual practice such as yoga, tantra, self-hypnosis, meditation, past-life regression, and from psychological work such as Jungian dream analysis, psychodrama, Reichian release bodywork or Bioenergetics, rolfing or other mind-body therapy. With a qualified guide you might try this simple but powerful method. Sit comfortably; turn your attention inward. Begin to breathe deeply and with each breath repeat to yourself, "I'm afraid" (or "sad" or "angry," if these are a better match for your mood). As you continue to breathe and repeat the phrase, you are likely to notice the emergence of feelings, perhaps associated with images or memories from the past. Don't censor these, but allow them to come to some expression: curl into a ball, strike a pillow, or cry. Fair warning! Don't try this on your own, unless you are very sure of your ability to tolerate strong feeling.

Methods that give an external form to the emerging Pluto archetype may also be of use. You may, for example, wish to make a mask of your "dark side." Try to find a way to represent each of your inner demons on the mask, then place it on your altar with flowers and candles and meditate upon it. (See Chapter 11 for a more complete description of such a ritual.) Honor the power of the dark side within you. It will be interesting to discover how you perceive the mask and respond to its symbolism. For some, just seeing the inner life in concrete form helps to bring a sense of control. Pluto can then become more personal and less threatening.

When Pluto stimulates your chart, your desires push you strongly, and you are likely to overwhelm yourself with far too much activity. This suggests three solutions: Simplify. Simplify. Simplify. Let the back-to-basics influence of Saturn lead you to a more manageable course of action. Set aside some of the complicated issues and focus only on the most pressing ones. Keep your attention on the task at hand, and you will engender more accomplishment and less struggle. If you find that you can't even recall the benefits of simplicity, take a lesson from Winnie the Pooh[16]: Once when a particularly nasty Pluto transit had me in a spin, my husband bought me the complete set of books about the charming Teddy Bear. Affectionately, Bob inscribed the books as "Something to complete your education." And that they did! Pooh counters the comic complications of his life with Rabbit and Tigger, Kanga and Roo, with such simplicity and wonder that I could not help but see how to apply that to my own life as well. Take an afternoon off from your next Plutonian episode, and read *Winnie*. You too can learn to be a "Bear of little Brain."

FACILITATING GROUPS: TIPS, TECHNIQUES, AND SKILL BUILDING

Although many experiential astrology methods are suitable for individual use, others require well-run groups for their success. In this chapter, I will try to condense my years of group experience into a brief but useful guide. If you are a beginner, you will appreciate the attention I give to the basics of group process and design. If you are an old hand at leading groups, you may still find useful hints and tips, especially when I adapt familiar principles to the particular requirements of experiential astrology groups.

G. I. Gurdjieff reminds us that each of us has a definite repertoire of roles which we play in our day-to-day lives, with a particular role for each circumstance we normally find ourselves in—sometimes one or two for our family, another one or two at work, and another role with our friends. We are not one person, but six, seven or more. At different times we find ourselves so enmeshed in one of the roles we play that we completely identify with it.[1]

When we create an environment which puts us in slightly different circumstances, like a group, we have difficulty finding suitable roles and momentarily become ourselves. Outside of our repertoire, we feel uncomfortable. Gurdjieff believed that only by experiencing this discomfort can we truly experience ourselves. A group setting helps to eliminate the oppression of our "dominant perceptions" and allows us to experience other possibilities within us.

Being with others in a group exposes us to other points of view, helping us to see that we all have similar problems and experiences. We see in each other's situations something of our own—some attitude, response, behavior, or reaction we share. By contacting, acknowledging, and accepting another's humanity, we are encouraged to accept our own.

Working together in a group helps individuals achieve a new sense of participation and an ability to act in their lives. By participating in the moment, we experience ourselves outside our usual roles, and in so doing, come to see that we are capable of being as self-initiating and dynamic as we want to be.

Starting a Group: The Preliminaries

If you want to form a group to try out experiential methods, whether it be for an afternoon, a full day, or ongoing, some basic considerations will help you to design a more effective group experience. First, consider logistics. How large will the group be? Do members know each other? If they do, less time will be needed for "ice-breaking." Is the workspace for the group adequate? This can be critical. The more comfortable the environment, the more conducive it will be to active participation. A large, well-lighted room, part carpeted and part finished floor, with mirrors and cushions, will give you the most flexibility. Movement and expression can't be encouraged in a crowded room.

How long will the group meet? If you are planning a one-day group, know that group energy will be highest two to three hours into the process and lowest in the period right after lunch. Plan the key activity of the day in the peak period and choose quiet time or physical activity after lunch.

Find out what enriching resources you have available (costumes, art supplies, participants with acting or group experience, or counseling, music, or dance skills). These can add enormously to the group's experience.

What is the group's astrological skill level (basic, intermediate, or advanced)? Initially you will find it better not to mix all three levels into a single group. Too much difference in skill level can make it more difficult to satisfy everyone's needs. Intermediate and advanced students work well together, but beginners often feel overwhelmed. Once when I inadvertently made this mistake, I found myself overcompensating for those who were just getting started, while not really giving more advanced students the detail they needed—and they let me know it!

Getting Started

Once you have considered logistics, clarify your own goals for the group. Is it most important that the process encourage a meditative inner focus? Sharing? Emotional catharsis? Play? Your goals will determine the particular quality and tone the group will have. (A goal of encouraging catharsis will create a very different group experience from one aimed at having fun with astrology.) Schedule your group whenever the transits most support your intention. For example if a meditative experience is your goal, schedule the group when there's a Mercury trine Neptune. A cathartic goal might call for a Pluto station, or full moon in Scorpio. If your goal is fun, do it with a Jupiter sextile Mercury/Mars.

An overall goal should be that the experience for participants be a positive one, especially in a serious astrodrama. I suggest you begin in a positive tone. Indicate the resources that the Director has to balance out more problematic aspects. Having explored these resources, then move to more tender parts of the psyche. Once you have created an atmosphere of possibility, it is safe to turn to the more painful issues. From the beginning, aim toward a conclusion of the experience that will leave the Director with a sense of positive accomplishment.

In any group, be flexible and ready to modify your objectives. Because you can't know the exact response any group will have to these experiences, suspend your own expectations and be open to changing your plan. By adjusting the event to suit the situation, you can better respond to the particular energies of your group.

Be clear in your instructions. Confusion on anyone's part will dampen the effect, and even undermine the exercise. If the exercise does not proceed in the way you planned, or the group missed the point, admit it. There's no shame in repeating instructions. The group will appreciate the clarification.

Have the group wear comfortable, unrestricted clothing to encourage movement and a relaxed tone. And, by all means be innovative! Use these ideas as a springboard for your own creating!

Making it Safe

By far the single most critical task for the Facilitator of a successful group experience is creating a safe environment. Group members must feel as though they can safely share their feelings without fear of judgment or criticism. If this neutrality doesn't exist, there will be conscious or unconscious resistance to the process and your goals will probably not be realized. To be successful, you must first create an environment of trust. One of the best ways to accomplish this is to begin slowly. Ease the group into feeling comfortable with each other. Start with warm-ups, ice-breaking exercises, and some simple body stretches. Then, as people begin to loosen up, add more movement. When you invite people to stretch their bodies, you are inviting them to stretch their discomforts and resistances too. Some groups will require more time to move through this warm-up phase, so have a number of fun, stimulating exercises ready to use if you need them.

To maintain trust and group rapport, always ensure that participants can decline any particular exercise without being made to feel uncomfortable. Experience has shown that if a person approaches what is for them a danger point, they will instinctively stop, absorb what they have learned, and reconstruct their defenses. If this is respected, you shouldn't have a problem. Especially important: Don't forget to take risks yourself. If the group notices that you are being adventurous and stretching yourself, it gives them permission as well. Your attitude can set the tone. You should also give attention to deciding what role you want to play in relation to the group. Leading a group using the traditional teaching format of one active/twenty passive members is usually less successful than "facilitating" or guiding the group to create for itself. In this way, the focus shifts from you to the group.

Group Dynamics

Throughout the 1970s, groups came into special prominence as a means to allow more people to have access to psychological help at lower cost than individual therapy. Thus it became recognized that group members are a great resource to one another as "psychological helpers," and a wealth of knowledge began to accumulate concerning ways of maximizing that help. By drawing on that body of knowledge you can make your own groups effective and can encourage the supportive, nurturing energies that give this kind of experience the most impact. Much of what follows is taken from my training and experience in group facilitation.

Feelings

Experiential groups should provide a direct encounter with feelings. Through direct experience we get more deeply in touch with these important emotional responses. Much neurotic behavior stems from a desperate desire to avoid the emotions. For some of us, the intellect has provided a kind of "interference" which separates us from our feelings. I am not discounting the value of reasoning and discussion, but rather emphasizing the value of our neglected emotional life. By evening out the disparity between the two modes of experience, we are able to view our world from a more three-dimensional perspective.

Since the emotions released in experiential processes can be powerful, it is important to maintain the pace of events in a group activity. Keep talk to a minimum directly after an experience to prevent the diffusion of energy. If group members immediately begin talking it may be because they have touched an area which is sensitive for them. Changing the subject just pushes it back into the unconscious where it needn't be expressed.

After an experience, it is also important to allow the group to "come down" gradually. Because each experience stimulates us in different ways, you'll want to allow time for digesting and quiet reflecting. By establishing a rhythm between action and reflection, you honor the natural interchange between inner and outer experience. This produces a more complete healing event.

If the group is strong in the Air element, focusing on feelings will be even more important. A group like this will tend to stay in their heads and want to "talk about" feelings rather than express them. Several years ago, I had an experience like this with a strong "Air" group. To help them gain access to their right-brain, feeling sides, I asked them to perform their astrodramas nonverbally. Although this was very difficult for them, it proved to be a valuable intervention.

Structure and Timing

Too much or too little structure will stifle group creativity. If a group is too structured it will feel repressed and controlled, unable to be spontaneous and expressive. If there is too little structure, a group might suffer from dissipated energy. Or it can get bogged down in a competitive bid for control among members. Learning and keeping this balance is something experience will teach you.

The average attention span for adults is twenty minutes, so be sure to vary the rhythm of your processes. Mixing individual exercises with a large group exercise, dyads, and small group exercises, keeps the group interested. For example, alternate a left-brain exercise with a right-brain one, or utilize the four modes of consciousness referred to by Jung, alternating a sensing experience with a mental, or intuitive one.

Feedback

Throughout the group, teach and model the giving of accurate *feedback*. The information recorded and shared by others can be as enlightening as one's own living out of a powerful moment, adding shape to the experience. Many of us do not give adequate information to one another about the impact of the other's behavior on us. We are either too "polite" and give no feedback, or give it in a way that's too general or too accusatory. "You never say anything," we complain, or, "You're just as bossy as your Mother." Neither of these gets good results! Learn to be direct and specific, labeling the particular behavior that affected you, the feeling it elicited, and the interpretations you made: "When you didn't stop and listen to me, I felt angry and hurt, because it seemed that my needs weren't important to you." In an experiential group, as anywhere in life, bruised feelings can surely occur; they can best be dealt with by accurate, caring, mutual feedback.

"*Primum non nocere.*" (First, do no harm.)

Among therapists there is a rule of thumb: Do not tear down what you are not ready and able to rebuild. As a Facilitator, know clearly your capabilities and your limits. Experiential astrology sometimes stirs up powerful unconscious energies, so if you do not feel qualified or confident to take the therapist role, don't. If you're sensing that you have approached your limit, move slowly, or better yet, back off. Be especially careful when you recognize "resistance." Behind resistance is some kind of fear. Jung might say resistance signals contact with an unconscious "complex." Here, symbolically, is where the volcano lies. If you are skilled you can probe it further. If not, do not force the issue. Doing so may have serious consequences.

Working deeply with others takes sensitivity and skill. In my experience, you will only be able to take a group as deeply as you have gone yourself. If you are really serious about working at this level of intensity with others, get into therapy about your own issues. Or join a class in group facilitation, psychodrama, psychosynthesis, or Gestalt. By traveling through your own depths you will develop the experience necessary to work deeply with others.

If you are already qualified to work in this way, your skills will allow the group to go deep beneath the surface and transform troublesome psychic and emotional energies. But, again, know your limits. Particularly in a group that meets only a time or two. If someone wants to work deeply, make sure they have a follow-up resource to go to in the event that uncomfortable feelings continue to unfold. If a participant is currently seeing a therapist, insist that they have his or her permission before proceeding.

Outline for Experiential Groups

Here is a basic outline I sometimes use for experiential groups. Use it as a starting point, then amend it to suit your situation.

1. Introductions

Tell the group about yourself, your interest in experiential methods, and some of your experiences with them. Remember, the first ten minutes of any encounter, whether one to one or in a group, are the most critical; they "set the tone" for all that follows.

A. Ask the group to take turns introducing themselves. Have each give their Sun, Moon, and Ascendant. Do they have experience in this kind of group? What drew them to participate? What do they expect? (This is important. There will always be hidden agendas but it's helpful to know what the conscious expectations are.) Do they have any skills they would be willing to share which may be an asset to the group? (Acting, dancing, extensive group experience, counseling, massage, etc.)

B. Group mix—As group members introduce themselves, ask one person to record the Sun, Moon, and Ascendant of each individual. After introductions, tally up the results and discuss the "Group Mix." (Astrologers will recognize this as characterizing only the general tone of the group, since other chart variables are not considered.) This helps groups recognize what characteristics they share as a group, and how they are likely to respond to the group experience.

Knowing and acknowledging the elemental mix of a group allows you to tailor a creative group experience for a particular group of individuals. For instance, if a group is strong in Fire, you might add more physical exercises to stimulate their enthusiasm. Or it may be appropriate to monitor that energy and, at some point, ground them with some sensing experiences. If the group has a predominance of Air, be sure they don't habitually "talk about." Nonverbal or highly physical exercises and astrodramas may be helpful.

If the group is strong in Water, they will tend to be more in touch with their feelings. If this group is scheduled near a full moon in Water, expect much emotional releasing. To break up this emotional atmosphere, try some energetic Marsian dancing.

C. After introductions, let the group know what you have planned for the day, so they understand what to expect. For example, "We'll be doing improv dyads until noon, with one ten minute break in between. Then we'll take one hour for lunch, followed by an afternoon session with two full astrodramas. We'll end the day with thirty minutes for group feedback and sharing, closing at 5:00 P.M."

2. Stretching, Warm-Ups, and Ice-Breaking

Begin with slow stretches, movement, and dancing. Follow this with several ice-breaking exercises that slowly build comfort and trust in you and the rest of the group. Increase the level of interaction from experience to experience, moving from one-to-ones to small groups of three or four and, finally, to exercises involving the entire group.

3. Process

What process you use depends upon your goal and the particular group you are working with. If your goal is to teach the basics to a group of beginners, you might begin by focusing on the four elements, describing their differences. Then, add an exercise for each element, like the ones described in Chapter 4. Or you might spend one evening covering the five personal planets, complete with an experience of each planet's appropriate music and movement. For variety, you might have the group cut pictures out of magazines to make image boards of the planets.

Or introduce the concept of duality by teaching the dual planets—the Sun/Moon, Venus/Mars, Jupiter/Saturn. A friend who teaches astrology in Chicago spends one class on each planet. She's so excited about experiential astrology that she dresses in the costume of the "planet of the week," and conducts the entire class in planetary character! For Mars, she's boisterous and energetic, for Venus, soft and sweet!

If the group is more experienced, schedule a Jupiter night where everyone comes dressed as Jupiter and spends the evening sharing insights on the aspects and transits of each individual's Jupiter. Plan the event when Jupiter is strong by transit. For an evening of activity schedule the group during a transit of Jupiter conjunct Mars. An evening of art might coincide with a Jupiter trine Venus. For meditating on Jupiter, try this when Jupiter is in harmonious aspect to Neptune. Your options with experiential astrology are endless!

4. Closure

It's important to allow time at the end of the session for the group to share feelings, give feedback, and say good-bye. Without closure, some may walk away still feeling the effect of the experiences of the day. A closing exercise helps the group to end in a focused manner.

Learning how to skillfully facilitate astrodrama groups will take some time to learn. Hopefully this chapter has given you a good running start.

Astrodrama: Interventions

In Chapter 7, I mentioned that you'll often want to intervene in group astrodramas. Here are some of the ways of intervening that I have found useful:

Freeze!

Sometimes the spontaneous unfolding of astrodramas stimulates the planets to interact and talk with each other all at once. When chaos ensues, shout, "Freeze!" Everyone will stop suddenly and be silent. While the action is stopped, ask the Director what they'd most like to see at the moment. Or as Facilitator you might make the suggestion, "Why doesn't everyone be quiet except the T-square. Let's start there and move into its contact with Jupiter."

"Freeze!" can also be useful to stop the action if you see the Director is being overly affected by what is going on. This gives you a way to check in with them to see if they need to do something or if the action is stimulating something and the focus needs to be shifted.

Doubling

This technique is borrowed directly from psychodrama. A double is a person who walks beside the Director and adds ideas or feelings that the Director may not be expressing. There are usually two doubles, one to support, the other to tear down. For example, suppose the Director is under the simultaneous influence of a square from both Saturn and Uranus. He knows that staying in his current job is killing him but feels paralyzed to move. Here is where the doubles come in. Have one person double as his Saturn in this situation; the other doubles as his Uranus. Place an imaginary straight line outside the chart circle and ask the Director to walk back and forth along it. The doubles walk with him. One voices the perspective of the Saturn square, "Stay safe. Stay with what you know. Yeah, it's boring, but it is secure." Then have the Uranus voice his opinion, "You can't stay any longer. If you do I'll scream. You'll die in this job if you don't move now." The Director then responds to each of these as if they were his inner voices. Is there a way to work with both of these energies now? Have the Director walk again and this time let each double interact with the Director to help him find solutions to their parts of the problem.

Another example: Let's consider another Director who has concerns about his upcoming Pluto opposite the Moon. Have one person double the negative quality of Pluto in opposition, while the other expresses the positive outcomes and possibilities of the opposition. By playing out the opposition in advance, the Director not only touches his fear of this transit but gets a preview of the possible opportunities that await him as well. Frequent use of these doubles can allow him to more consciously use and attune himself to the positive side of Pluto.

The last intervention to mention here is an astrological version of Fritz Perls' *Gestalt* intervention of the Top Dog/Underdog, which is helpful when a conflict of polarity appears.[2] It is important to remember that polarities not only oppose one another; they also seek out and attract each other. These inner polar conflicts must be integrated in order to give the psyche a sense of wholeness. Perls equated the Top Dog with the Freudian superego and characterized it as the dictator and judge who tells us what to do, criticizes, and belittles us. The other role, Underdog, is the little, seemingly less powerful, passive one. Perls held that the Underdog usually won through sabotage, postponement, and evasion. To find a resolution between the two halves, a dialogue can be set up between them. To use this technique, move two chairs into the chart circle. (Let's say the Director has recognized a conflict in her Saturn/Venus natal square which has manifested as a desire to get married. In spite of this desire, she always sabotages and rejects relationships as soon as she knows she has met "Mr. Right.") To begin the process, the Director assumes both roles and takes turns sitting in the Top Dog, then Underdog chair. A typical dialogue might run like this: Top Dog (Saturn) says all men are weak and irresponsible, with a fatal flaw. Underdog (Venus) recognizes her dependency, wanting a man to take care of her, but is surprised by her coolness when she meets a suitable partner. The Facilitator asks if the Top Dog reminds her of someone. She discovers it is her father. The dialogue shifts to one between her father and herself. Through this exchange, she comes to realize that although her father always treated her like a princess, he managed to undermine her relationships with her boyfriends by degrading them. She sees how she subconsciously agreed with him, and that his interfering attitude lives within her.

Resolution to conflict can also be approached without the metaphor of Top Dog and Underdog. Simply ask the Director confronted with an inner conflict to sit down and express both sides of his feelings. Have him move back and forth, from one chair to the other, until something begins to break through and make itself known. Then, develop the dialogue according to what is revealed.

PART 11

PLANETS AND SIGNS

THE SUN AND LEO

Beginning with the following treatment of the Sun and Leo, each of the remaining chapters first introduces, then extensively discusses a planet and their meaningfully related sign or signs. I've provided films that illustrate each astrological symbol, as well as musical selections that can be used to evoke as well as to understand the appropriate energy. Finally, I've given numerous detailed exercises for bringing the planet or sign to full experiential expression. My aim is to place all the tools of experiential astrology in your hands.

The Sun symbolizes the active, energizing principle. It is the "spotlight" or true source of light through which planetary energies are synthesized and integrated—what Jung calls the "Self." It represents the urge in each of us to express our total self-identity, and to grow into our full potential.

The Sun/Leo is linked to consciousness, light, day, fatherhood, and will. It is the principle which is expressed in mythology as the Hero. The journey of the Hero is expressed through the symbols and associated images of the natal chart.

Individuals with strong Sun/Leo energy can be vibrant, dramatic, and vital. If afflicted the Sun/Leo personality may demand center stage and the constant admiration of others. Those with little Sun/Leo energy may be hesitant to take a risk or to express themselves to others.

The following exercises may bring contradictory feelings to the surface for someone who has a strong extroverted-introverted theme, such as Leo/Gemini/Aries planets on the top half of their chart, and Virgo/Scorpio rising with planets below.

The Sun—An Experience of Self (The Hero's Journey)
The myth of the hero can deeply teach us about the principle and process of the solar

energy within our psyches. The journey can be done in either active or passive ways. As a more active experience, re-create the drama by asking the group to choose and enact the various roles in the Hero's journey. You might be the narrator of the basic story while they embellish and improvise. Or perhaps each individual can act out for himself or herself the Hero role as the story is told.

Or try the Hero's journey in a somewhat less active form, perhaps relating the story as a guided imagery exercise, and allowing an opportunity for the group to draw at various stages of the story. (Have newsprint and crayons, magic markers, etc. beside each person.) Proceed as follows: Ask the group to lie down and get comfortable. Turn down the lights. Have the members focus on their breathing, guiding them to breathe more deeply, more slowly. Once the group has reached a place of deep relaxation, begin to tell the Hero's story. As you will see, there are several key stages of the journey of the Hero. Stop at each stage and ask each individual to draw the feelings and images they are experiencing. How does the Hero's journey relate to their current life? This process will open up much to share and talk about when the experience is over.

The Story of the Hero's Journey

To more fully understand the myth of the Hero, read Joseph Campbell's *The Hero with a Thousand Faces*. Here's a bare outline of the themes of the story: The Hero had two yearnings—first, to discover the details of his birth so that then he may learn his True Purpose, and second, to find his Beloved (his other half) so that he could become whole. These two urges were the call to his adventure. This call brings "the awakening of the self" which lifts the curtain on a mystery, a moment of spiritual passage in which the old life is outgrown and shed. No longer content with the old ideals, values, or emotional patterns, the Hero is urged across the first threshold. With his destiny to guide him, he enters a zone of power which has a guardian of the threshold. The threshold stands for the limits of the hero's present life, both what holds him back and what helps contain him. Beyond is darkness and the unknown. The regions of the unknown contain all the projections of his unconscious content.

The passage of the magical threshold does not come through conquering the guardian, but in the Hero's being swallowed into the unknown and appearing to have died. Once passing the threshold, the Hero moves into a lucid landscape, where he must survive a series of tests and trials. The Hero is usually aided by helpers that he

met before his entrance, or he becomes slowly aware that there is a benevolent power supporting him. The Hero's ordeal represents the beginning of a long path of initiatory conquests, with moments of heightened insight. Dragons must be slain again and again, and survival is constantly threatened, yet there are also victories to be had.

Just past his fearsome trials (once his obstacles and demons have been overcome), the Hero meets the Beloved, his mistress, bride, mother, and sister. She is the promise of perfection, the bliss of comfort and nourishment—the archetypal "Good Mother." The image of the Beloved is not simply benign, for it also contains the "Bad Mother," and, as well, the unattainable, absent Mother, the hampering, forbidding Mother, the desired but forbidden Mother, and the clinging, suffocating Mother.

At this stage of the journey, the Hero gains assurance from the helpful Female by whose magic he is protected in a further trial to come: the ego-shattering initiations with Father. Father is the one by whom the young are passed on into the larger world. Just as the mother represented both Good and Bad so now does Father, but with the added element of rivalry.

After meeting his trials from both the Female and Male aspects, the Hero is finally granted a boon. Though his obstacles were many, he has triumphed, and is revealed to be a Superior Man. And he has come to a realization of his original yearnings. As he crossed threshold after threshold, conquering his dragons, he pushed past his limiting horizons onto a wider plain, steadily increasing his consciousness and his spiritual awareness until he finally breaks the sphere of the cosmos and arrives at a realization transcending all experiences of form.

When the Hero's quest has been accomplished, he has yet one more stage of the journey to complete; he must return to his people and community, to humanity. And he must bring them the Gift, the results of his blessing by God and Goddess—the healing and restorative Elixir. Herein lies the central problem of the Hero's return. How can he communicate even the mere shadow of what he has found? How can he convey the secrets of the Dark, the Unknown, the Unconscious? How is he to translate the revelation which shatters the pairs of opposites? Or communicate to people who insist on the reality of the senses alone?

What is the final outcome of the Hero's miraculous passage and return? He, or indeed *she*, for only by convention does the story have a masculine protagonist, is now a whole *Self*, having found that the voyage to the Unknown does not destroy, but enlightens. Thus The myth of the Hero let us experience, directly, the principle of the Sun within us.

What's Good About You?

In a group, pair off and sit facing each other. One person begins as questioner, the other will respond. The questioner asks, "What's good about you?" The person answering gives himself a compliment. (Questioner is silent except to nod his head in agreement.) Questioner asks again, "And what else is good about you?" Process continues until the person answering is out of compliments for himself. Switch roles. Then ask these questions. Was this hard or easy for you? Were you easily able to find compliments to give yourself? Do you have your Sun or Leo in challenging aspect, or difficult transits currently to them?

Memorize a Poem

Memorize a favorite poem, joke, or funny story. Take turns getting up in front of the group and delivering your memorized piece. Pay attention to how you feel as it comes closer to your turn. Are you very nervous, embarrassed, confident, at ease, anxious, or anticipating? Find a word that most describes your prominent feeling before. After your "performance" find a word which most suits your feeling then. Were you relieved, stimulated, energized, etc.? Now go back and see if you can capture a feeling while you were delivering your piece. Compare these three words. Do they reveal a typical process you undergo when you express yourself to others or are the center of attention? Does this experience relate to the aspects to your Sun or Leo in your chart? Group discussion.

Name Chant

Our names are strongly tied to images of self and quality of expression. An extremely powerful experience is to do a name chant. With a group, let each individual take turns sitting in the center of the circle. (In reality, the group is making the symbol of the Sun, with the person the group is focused on having become the central "bindu point.") Ask the group to close their eyes and take a few deep breaths. Now slowly have the group chant the first name of the person in the middle. Ask the group to spontaneously let their voices roll, and crescendo. Listening to your name, hearing it resonate in the circle around you, in you, sounds very ethereal, almost as if angels were calling.

It is a moving experience. (Use this as a closure for an individual's astrodrama or try this in particularly soft and loving tones for someone with a Sun/Saturn transit.)

Tell about a Leo Experience

Tell the group about a Leo experience you have had (lead in a play, presentation at work, TV appearance, leading a group or class, etc.) How did you feel about being the focus of attention. What kind of feedback did you get? How did you evaluate your experience?

Telling Stories

Tell the group about a funny incident from your past.

Tell about a humbling experience from your past. (This may be good for the Leo, "I'm Mr./Ms. Wonderful" character in some of us.)

Take turns reading or telling a fairy tale or story to the group.

Get up and talk about yourself for three minutes.

Whichever variation you choose, evaluate this experience afterward. Was this easy for you to do? Did you feel more comfortable with "script" in front of you or when you were spontaneous? Was there a rush of adrenaline at any time? Does this typify how you generally are in front of groups?

Affirmation

Write down, "Every day in every way I am growing in vitality, self-awareness, and light." Tape it to your bathroom mirror so every morning you see and repeat this affirmation. This will be helpful when the solar energy is being influenced problematically by the outer planets.

Warm Fuzzies

This Transactional Analysis exercise begins by forming a circle with the group and sitting down. One person begins with a small, preferably furry, object in their hands. (This could be a small stuffed animal or sponge ball.) That person looks around the group and finds someone they want to compliment. Say the person's name, throw the "warm fuzzy" to that person and give them a compliment, as sincere and wholeheartedly as possible. (Saying their name will help your compliment make more of an impact.) That person tries to really feel the compliment, then in turn finds someone they want to compliment. Continue playing until everyone has received two or three compliments from the group. Another version of this is to give hugs in place of throwing the "warm fuzzy."

How easy was it to give a compliment? Was it easier to receive one? Did you feel discounted or ignored by any group member? How did that feel?

Another variation of warm fuzzies is to form a circle and take turns standing in the center. Either the group can give compliments directed to the one in the center, or that person can give her/himself three or four compliments. Be as proud, as Leonian as possible!

Those with too little Solar/Leo energy may have more difficulty or discomfort with this exercise. If this happens, you might give this individual a task to do. Have them *notice* when someone gives them a compliment. Have them write the compliments down in a special notebook. This may help them become more aware of getting compliments and their responses to them which may lead to a deeper understanding why they respond to compliments the way they do. This could be a good suggestion to someone with challenging natal Sun/Saturn aspects.

King or Queen

In a group, take turns role-playing being the king or queen. (All of us Pluto in Leos should have no problem with this.) Everyone else be their subjects. Hold court. Hear and decide on cases brought before you by your subjects. Afterwards, did you like being king/queen? Did you think you were fair to your subjects? Were you arbitrary? Dominating? A kind ruler?

Sunbathe

When having difficult Solar transits, particularly from Saturn, spend time lying in the sun. Imagine the health, and vitality of the sun is pouring into and through your body and psyche. Let the Sun heal you, revitalize you.

Birthday Ritual

Because each year your birthday is the time the sun returns to its birthplace, it is an important cycle. Have a solar return chart calculated to know the exact time the sun returns to its natal position. Take the day off and spend the day focused on reviewing/evaluating the last year, especially appreciating what you have accomplished or feel good about. Spend the day expressing yourself, drawing, writing, or doing exactly what you want to do. As the time of your exact solar return approaches, put your chart on an altar and meditate on your Sun sign, how you exalt in expressing yourself, and what positive contacts your sun has to the other planets. Breathe as your sun, bringing in new life, new vitality, and new hope. Or use any meditation technique that focuses particularly on the Sun center, the *Ajna chakra* or point between your eyebrows. Or focus attention on your breath, remembering you are approaching the time of your first breath. Breathe as if each breath were your first. Or light a single candle, symbol of your sun, and meditate/reflect on it. Use the name chant and softly repeat the sound of your own name.

A nice ritual to do for a birthday friend is for a group to get together and do the name chant or take turns saying what it is you love about your birthday friend. Or light a single candle in front of them and all meditate on that person and their life, sending them prosperity, happiness, and peace for the new year. Maybe close your ritual with the birthday person moving around the circle and lighting a candle held by each group member as a symbol of their light joining and touching yours.

A moving experience for a large conference size group is for one candle to be lit symbolizing the collective spirit, inspiration, and aspirations of the theme of the conference and for it to be passed one candle to the next until everyone holds a lighted candle.

MEDITATIONS AND VISUALIZATIONS

Sun Meditation—The "Ball of Light"

Close your eyes. Take some deep full breaths, exhaling any tensions, scattered thoughts or energy. Now *slowly* bring your awareness to the point between your eyebrows—called the Sun center, Ajna chakra, or Third Eye. In the body, this point represents the Sun in your chart. It is the light through which all others are expressed. Focus your awareness on a pencil point of light between your eyebrows. Now slowly intensify this light. Let it become a little larger, a little more intense. Put your full conscious awareness on this light of your existence. Let it become even larger, and more intense. Let it become a ball of light, filling your head with light like a giant light bulb. Now let that light slowly begin to expand out, permeating your throat, chest, arms, hips, butt, legs, and feet. Let your whole body become a ball of light, radiant in the fullness of who you are.

Group "Ball of Light" Meditation

In a group circle, build a ball of light within your head. Now focus the energy of your ball of light into the center of the circle. Merge and blend with the light of those around you, keeping your focus in the center of the circle. Intensify the ball of light. Now expand it to permeate the bodies of everyone, envisioning it expanding to behind your backs. Now slowly expand the light out to touch all of your loved ones. Distance does not matter. Take a moment to visualize your loved ones in the ball of light. Take a moment to feel this. Now pull back the ball of light which has touched all your loved ones, and imagine it once again behind your backs. Intensify the light. Now move it back into the center of the circle. Now move it back into your head. Allow the light to gently fade to the pencil point of light. Allow yourself some moments of quiet reflection and re-orientation back to the room.

Sun/Leo Planet Walk

Visualize yourself as a royal person—the king/queen of the world. Concentrate upon expanding your chest. Inflate your whole body. Imagine that it's grand and something beautiful to behold. Now, confidently extend your normal walking stride, carrying yourself in noble posture. Adjusting your walk will help you to touch the solar/Leo part of your psyche.

SUGGESTED FILMS AND MUSIC

Sun/Leo Films

Go to or rent a movie with a Sun/Leo theme. For example, *The Lion King; Apollo 13; Shine; Evita; Hercules; It's a Wonderful Life; The Color Purple; Zorba The Greek; Breaking Away*.

Suggested Music

"Brass in Pocket" *The Pretenders* (The Pretenders), "Hot Fun in the Summertime" *Sly and the Family Stone Greatest Hits* (Sly and the Family Stone), "Good Day Sunshine" *Revolver* (The Beatles), "Here Comes the Sun" *Abbey Road* (The Beatles), *William Tell Overture* (Gioacchino Rossini), *Firebird Suite* (Igor Stravinsky), *Superman* Soundtrack, "Symphonies for the King's Bed Chamber," "Soldier's Air," and "Fanfares for the Royal Tournament" *The Baroque Trumpet* (Lully), *The Messiah* (Handel).

THE MOON AND CANCER

The Moon symbolizes the passive, receptive, nurturing, feminine faculty of the psyche, the retention of impressions or emotionally charged events of the past that creates our conditioned emotional behavior and patterns. The Moon/Cancer links to the tides, mother, childbirth, family, intuition, images, and fluid conditions, as well as to our cultural and societal archetype of the feminine. This femininity is now reemerging after a period of hiatus, with many being drawn to better understand and integrate it both into their own daily experience and into our culture as a whole.

Individuals with strong Moon/Cancer energy can be nurturing and caring. If afflicted, one may be too easily influenced, vacillate, or may indulge in emotional drama. Those with little Moon/Cancer energy may have difficulty knowing their feelings and tend to be cool emotionally. Those with highly polarized charts, such as Sun/Moon oppositions may experience contradictory feelings, especially at full moons and eclipses.

The current profusion of women's books offers some enlightenment on the aspect of the feminine within our psyche and its emerging role in our culture. To begin to better understand the feminine, try reading some of the excellent books available, especially *The Return of the Goddess,* by Edward C. Whitmont[1], *Descent to the Goddess* by Sylvia Brinton Perera,[2] *She,* by Robert A. Johnson,[3] and *Women's Mysteries*, by Ester Harding.[4]

Because the Moon has to do with the process of reflection, most of the exercises described in Chapter 6, "Do It Yourself!" will be appropriate as Moon exercises. As the Moon symbolizes the unconscious, instinctive realm, dreamwork is also an appropriate technique to more fully understand the Moon. Creative visualizations and guided imagery give added knowledge of the Moon's function. *Creative Visualization*, by Shakti Gawain speaks simply about this process and offers useful instruction.[5]

Here's a tip: Plan to experience your Moon as close to the full moon as possible. The results will have more impact. The best times to reflect and do inner searching are when the Moon is in Water signs, conjunct your fourth house, or transiting through the Water houses, the fourth, eighth, or twelfth houses. For extended research wait until the progressed Moon is in a Water sign, or transiting the Water houses. The best times to do some emotional healing of wounds obtained from your childhood or relationship with Mom is when the Moon is in water, by transit or for an extended time by progression.

Another excellent Moon experience is in Jean Houston's book, *The Possible Human*. In it she describes a two-and-one-half- to three-and-one-half-hour sequence called "Exercises in Evolutionary Memory."[6] It allows us to reexperience the evolutionary unfoldment of life on the planet from being a fish, to reptile, and on, to a modern human and "extended human." Having done this exercise in one of Jean's workshops, I can attest that this experience stimulates a deep bodily knowing as our brain and body respond to these ways of being, antecedent to our human evolution. Refer to Houston's book for another interesting Moon experience: "Recalling the Child."[7]

The Moon and Nurturing

It's healing to take a break from the world to experience a nurturing moment. Several women friends and I meet periodically for a group foot bath. Each of us brings a towel and small kitchen pan for our feet. We simmer up a brew of different soothing herbs—chamomile, lavender, sage, valerian, calendula, and rose petals for twenty minutes. Then mixing the hot herbal brew with cool water until it is a comfortable temperature, we put our feet in and relax. The herbs do their work and this is time put aside for yourself.

You might reflect on your Moon while doing this. How well do you take time to nurture yourself? Get a massage? Linger in an herbal bath? Or get a manicure? How well do you receive? How well do you allow others to give to you? How well do you nurture others?

The Moon symbolizes both water and nurturing, so as a group you might visit your local hot springs or spa. Spending an evening of relaxation while soothing tired

muscles is "being" rather than "doing"—and helping each other to experience the receptive, feminine mode.

Childhood Photo

Bring a childhood photo of yourself to the group. Divide into pairs, sharing about that time of your life. What were the circumstances around the picture? Spend time recalling your memories around this time. Was it a happy time or difficult? Do your memories summon up feelings? If time permits, extend this exploration to include your whole childhood. Was it a happy or difficult time? Can you recall some specific memories? Allow time to let this process unfold as this can be a very intimate, sharing time for both partners.

If you are alone, take out your baby book and reflect on the baby you were. Can you, in your imagination and in your body, experience yourself as that baby again? You might try curling up in a fetal position, or crawling on all fours.

Variation: Bring a picture of your mother. What was she like? What are your earliest memories of her? Was she a good mother to you? How good of a mother are you to yourself? Can you see a relationship between how you were mothered and the way you mother yourself? Reflect on your own Moon and its natal aspects.

Can you recall specific experiences which parallel the specific aspects? For instance, if you have Moon opposite Jupiter, can you remember your mom making sure you've eaten, always giving you treats or desserts? Or did you experience your Moon opposite Saturn as mother forcing you sit at the table until you were completely finished, withholding desserts, or maybe she was not even home to feed you? These reflections can help you understand your Moon relationships.

Rocking

Rocking can be a nurturing group exercise when it's used appropriately. Have one person lie prone. Each group member takes an area of the body: a leg, head, upper torso, etc., places their hands underneath and as a group slowly lifts the person to waist height. Then have them gently rock the person back and forth, up and back. It is important that there be enough people to do this comfortably. It works best when one person takes the head, and two people take the torso. Also, be sure the head is comfortably supported and the rest of the body is kept in alignment. After a few minutes, slowly lower the person until they are lying back on the ground. Be silent. This is a good closing for an individual's full astrodrama as a means of acknowledging and integrating. It can evoke strong feelings. I have seen this work effectively for everyone who has tried it. Don't start off the group with this one, wait until some level of group trust has been established.

Variation: If you have a backyard with trees, string up a hammock. I have a hammock and most days in the summer I'll take a break and rock myself.

Childhood Home

Describe your childhood home. If there were many, choose the one you most liked. Extend this to describe the neighborhood, favorite childhood hangouts, etc.

Where You Grew Up

In a group, take turns briefly describing where you grew up. Extend this to ask, "Where were you in the summer of 1968?," for example. It's interesting to know where the individuals in the group were at the exact same time. Were there any parallels of life experience then with anyone in the group?

Home

Reflect on the home you now live in. Are you happy there? What special features do you like about it? Where is your favorite place? If you are not happy where you live, what kind of home do you want? Good Moon transits to either look for a new home or actually move in is great use of this energy.

Childhood Toy

Bring a childhood toy. Divide into pairs and share memories about the toy. Do you know who gave it to you? Do you remember seeing it for the first time? What social experiences did you have with your toy? Can you recall a specific experience in which it comforted you?

Variation: What was your favorite toy? Describe it fully. You might find more "food for thought" if you have the group each draw their favorite toy. Or you might split up into small groups according to the particular toy, i.e., all those whose favorite toy was a bear, or dog, or frog. Is there a quality about that animal that they exhibit in their personality?

This is Your Life!

As a birthday present for a member in an ongoing group, spend an evening of "This is your Life." Get photos and childhood experiences from their mothers, sisters, brothers, and friends.

Variation: Give a group massage as a birthday present to a friend. Treat them to a facial, herbal bath, etc.

Feminine Issues

A group discussion about feminine issues can expose the emotional patterns and feelings of the individuals in the group. If your intention is to stir up feelings as part of the group process, then choose emotional issues like abortion, women's rights in the workplace, sexual harassment in the workplace, etc. If your intention is to draw the group closer, share your pleasant, funny childhood memories with each other.

Childbirth

Since the Moon represents the function of childbirth and the nurturing of children, another discussion might be to bring up the topic of having or not having children, or have women share their experience of the birth of their own children. In connection with this, you might watch a film of a child's birth and spend time sharing your feelings. Or, if you can, witness the birth of a child.

An extension of this may be to facilitate a process through guided imagery to allow the group to return to the moment of their own birth. Or, if you want a strong Moon experience, you might even bring in a qualified rebirther. (This is a therapeutic method of reexperiencing your birth.)

If you believe in reincarnation, remembering the distant past is also lunar. You might use a past-life regressionist to guide you through a past-life experience.

Women's Issues

Have a "women only" group addressing some of issues of women. Once everybody's feelings on a particular topic are known, then look at the group members charts.

Where is the Moon by sign, house, aspect, and/or transit? Does this reveal something about the kind of feelings, or the manner in which they were expressed?

Time Line Charts

Making Time Line charts is a long-term project for regularly meeting groups interested in learning more about the Moon. Using posterboard, construction paper, or notebooks, have each person construct a time line, beginning with the year of birth and continuing to the present. Leave room for the future, too. Leave more room than you think you will need. Then spend some time recalling and writing down the memories in brief. For example, write down "first rode a bike" under the month during which that occurred for you. You'll be amazed what a wonderful recall tool this is.

One recovered memory will remind you of another, and another—until you have to start squeezing new headlines in. Then bring your time line to the group, and share your new memories. Spend group time looking at the transits of major childhood events. (If your group can meet at the house of a member who has a computer, transits can be done quickly.) This look at past transits can be very enlightening. Many times, fuller insight is gained about a particular experience. For instance, "Ah, I learned to ride my bike when Jupiter was conjunct my Mars in Sagittarius!" or, Saturn was squared my Sun when my fourth grade teacher made me go to summer school!

Autobiography

A further extension of making time line charts is to write an autobiography. This is truly a reflective, lunar experience that will help you to reawaken to your past. So few of us spend time reflecting and digesting our experiences. Writing an autobiography can be a therapeutic and integrating experience.

Pipe Cleaner Time Line

Buy a packet of long pipe cleaners (hobby shops carry these as well as the tobacco shops). Pass one out to each person. Use the pipe cleaner as a symbol of your life. Twist it, bend it to express the progression of your life until now. Use it to express the highs and lows of your life, express major events, etc. Once everyone is finished, share what your life symbol means throughout your life.

Sand Play

A technique offered by Jungian therapy is sand play. In this therapy, participants stimulate early life feelings and memories by returning to the sandbox complete with toys, etc.

Motherpeace Tarot Deck

This is a lovely tool created by Vicki Noble and Karen Vogel to bring about inner healing of the feminine.[8] Their emphasis on love and compassion, circular shape, and empowering images make this tool ideal for tuning into the Moon's energy on a continuing basis.

MEDITATIONS AND VISUALIZATIONS

Cancerian Planet Walk

Visualize yourself as a young child having just learned to walk. Feel the tentative, not quite sure feeling within. Begin to move, exploring your environment. Respond to things around you as if for the first time. Roll, crawl, walk, or fall as you move, being aware of your changing inner feelings from delight, fright, or surprise. This exercise will help you touch the Lunar/Cancer part of your psyche.

Moon Meditation—The Tides

This meditation is especially strong near a full moon in Water signs. An effective way to meditate on the Moon is to play a recording of ocean tides, with only the wash of the waves. First ready your tape recorder and place it next to you. Now close your eyes. Take some deep breaths. Turn on your recording, and slowly begin to imagine that you are lying down in your favorite place near water. *Feel* the sand beneath you. *Feel* the sand under your feet, calves, thighs, butt, back, shoulders, arms, hands, and head. Breathe deeply and allow yourself to drift; allow yourself to follow the process and your feelings in any way it unfolds. When the music ends, allow yourself some moments of quiet reflection and reorientation.

Moon Experience—Moon Grotto

Adapted from Diane Mariechild's *Motherwit*, this is a fine experience for a group of women to do together on a full moon.

Relax, deepen your concentration, and enfold yourself in protection. Begin to move deeply, winding through long passageways, and labyrinths, winding down and down until you come to a body of dark water on which there is a boat tied. Climb into the boat. Now float further down through more passageways, going deeper, deeper. Feel the gentle rocking of the boat, and soothing sound of the water lapping against your little boat. Float until you come to a large grotto. Your boat comes to rest on its shore. Looking up, you see this space is lit by the moon and the moonlight is pouring down from a slender threadlike opening far above you. You know this place is sacred.

Here in this sacred place of magic you meet Sophia, the giver of wisdom. She appears here on every full moon and shares her knowledge with the women who find their way to this place. She is appearing now. Pause for five to ten minutes. Now leave the grotto, winding your way back to the point you started. Remember what you have experienced and carry that knowledge with you. Become aware of your surroundings slowly, feeling refreshed and relaxed.

Mirror Dancing

Turn on music which is flowing and easy to dance to. Begin in pairs. Loosen up your bodies, then have one of the pair raise their hand. That person is the Sun and will lead. The other dancer is the Moon and follows the Sun as exactly as possible. Follow with your feet, legs, body, arms, facial expression. Feel what the Sun is doing. After a time, switch roles. How does it feel to follow? To lead? Was it hard or easy to "shadow" the Sun?

A variation is to have one partner pretend to be a mirror that the other is looking into. Add a dramatic element. "You are hiding in a room and must keep from being discovered. Someone who is searching for you enters. He is standing right in front of you. You must be his reflection to not be discovered. Dramatic embellishing can add more thrills, concentration, and fun.

SUGGESTED FILMS AND MUSIC

Moon/Cancer Films

The Joy Luck Club; Forest Gump; Big Night; Hoop Dreams; Waiting to Exhale; Eat, Drink, Man, Woman; Mother; Martin's Room; Fanny and Alexander; On Golden Pond; Ordinary People; A Trip to Bountiful; Let It Be!

Suggested Music

Secret Garden: Songs From a Secret Garden (Phillips), *Gone Again* (Patti Smith), much of Somebody-Done-Somebody-Wrong country music, *Blue* (LeAnn Rimes), *You Were Meant for Me* (Jewel), *Bodzium,* (Enkal Badu), "Feel Flows" *Surf's Up* (The Beachboys), "Dock of the Bay" *Best of Otis Redding* (Otis Redding), "Hymn to Her" *Get Close* (The Pretenders), "Woman" *Double Fantasy* (John Lennon), "Waltzes and Nocturnes" (Chopin), *Clair de Lune* (Debussy), *Violin Concertos* (Beethoven), *Water Music* (Handel), *Blue Danube* (Strauss), "Stardust" (Nat King Cole), "The Tide is High" *Autoamerican* (Blondie), "Here Comes the Rain Again" *Touch* (The Eurythmics).

13

MERCURY, GEMINI, AND VIRGO

Mercury is the thinking, analyzing function of the human psyche. It is the way we assimilate our experience through dividing, discriminating, and sorting out data. It is how we form connections, become aware of underlying relationships between things, and exchange ideas with others. Mercury serves the dual function of inner communication and communication with the world around us.

In this respect, Virgo represents Mercury's introverted, analytical inner aspect of thinking, while Gemini is the extroverted, outward-seeking aspect of communication. Mercury is one planet which has a dual rulership of both Virgo and Gemini.

Mercury is connected with the Greek Hermes, an androgynous being who possesses the keys of knowledge and carries messages between the Gods and humankind. Mercury is linked to words, the origins of language, all literature, and to all ways and means of communicating and educating through bodies of knowledge.

Individuals with strong Mercury/Gemini energy in their horoscope may have a healthy desire for acquiring knowledge and mental adaptability. If afflicted, one can scatter their mental forces and use their social skills as a defense against deep intimacy. Those with less Mercury/Gemini energy may lack sociability.

Those with strong Mercury/Virgo energy may have excellent analytical skills and are willing to work hard for perfection. If afflicted, one can be incessantly critical of self and others. Those with less Mercury/Virgo energy may lack focus and attention to detail or experience shy, incompetent feelings in some areas of their lives.

Mercury/Gemini Experience
Mercury represents the particular skills and techniques we learn during our lives. Any experience of skill refinement and improvement is a good example of Mercury energy.

A guided imagery called "Skill Rehearsal with a Master Teacher," described in Jean Houston's *The Possible Human*[1] is ideal for this. The exercise allows you to achieve a deeper understanding, improve your motor connections between brain and body, and gain new resourcefulness in the use of your skills. Time: forty-five minutes. This exercise can be pretaped or guided by a facilitator.

Choose a skill you wish to improve. Go through the physical motions of the skill where you are, rehearsing with as much attention to detail as possible. Obviously, it would be easier to practice a tennis swing than swimming the butterfly stroke. Once you have rehearsed, stop, and imagine in your mind's eye that you are doing this activity. Re-create as fully as possible your body's response to this activity. Now go back and forth, acting out the skill, and seeing yourself acting out the skill in your mind/body. Now run around like a three-year-old, twisting, turning, rolling, and jumping until you are exhausted, then lie down.

Listen to these instructions:

> Feel yourself lying alone in the bottom of a little rowboat. You are being carried out into the ocean by gentle waves. You feel relaxed as the waves carry you further and further out. The boat begins going down and around as if you are being carried in a vortex, down and deeper into the ocean. The water does not close in on you. The water rises above you and you go deeper into a tunnel of water. You land on the ocean floor. You discover a door handle which you pull. The door opens and you take a stone stairwell leading to a realm beneath the ocean floor.
>
> You step down, down, down, deeper and deeper. The stairs end and you are in a great cavern filled with stalactites and stalagmites. You find a stone corridor and walk down it. You come to an oak door over which is written "The Room of the Skill." Entering that room, you find yourself in a place completely imbued with the presence and spirit of your skill. In this room is the master of the skill.
>
> The master teacher may speak in words, or teach you through feelings or muscular sensations. The learning will be effective and deep and give you much more confidence. The skilled person within you is emerging and overcoming inhibitions and blocks. You are undergoing very intensive training and learning.

Take five minutes, which will be all the time you need to have this rich lesson with the master teacher.

> Now it is time to leave your master teacher. Thank this being and know that you can return here whenever you want. Before you go, you see a special light streaming down from the ceiling. Stand in the light. It is the light of confirmation

of your skill. Feel the deepening and confirming of your skill throughout your mind and body.

Leave the room, carefully closing the door. Move through the corridor to the cavern and into your little boat. Emerge up and up through the vortex, reversing itself now to bring you up and up to the ocean's surface. You feel your skill continuing to grow within you, permeating your whole being.

As your boat is approaching the shore, you feel excited and want to get out and try your skill. When you touch shore, you are wide awake and full of your skill, and you get up as soon as possible and try it out. Rehearse your skill physically. Now stop and rehearse it in your mind/body. See the image of you performing the activity perfectly. Go back and forth between doing your skill and seeing yourself do it in your mind's eye. Rehearse until you feel the two integrating.

What do you notice about the improvement of your skill?

What do you remember about your master teacher?

I participated in this experience in one of Jean's workshops. Before we started this journey to the master teacher, Jean asked for a volunteer to demonstrate their skill both before and after the visualization. A woman volunteered to play the piano. She was extremely self-conscious, played hesitantly, and made quite a few mistakes. After the visualization, she sat down with a look of sheer joy on her face and played the same piece smoothly and flawlessly.

Mercury Movement

Mercury's action is quick, changeable, mischievous. Put on some Mercurial music, for instance, music from the Talking Heads. Move your body and mime with your hands the conversational rhythm of the music.

Dialogue with a Planet

An important technique of interaction that many of us do not consider is to talk with our own unconscious through our planets. The planets are not abstract symbols; they are living energy within us. Sit down with your natal chart and have an exchange with a planet giving you trouble. Ask yourself one of these questions: On a regular basis, what planetary energies most affect my life? Examine your natal chart and list them in order. What planetary energies are affecting me most right now in my life? Examine your transits. What strong harmonious/problematic aspects are now most evident?

This can be done like a meditation. Take a few deep breaths and begin to focus on the planet you want some answers from. Imagine that a living presence or archetype of that planet is before you. (You might imagine Hermes for Mercury, Aphrodite for Venus, a warrior for Mars, the tarot card of the Fool for Uranus, or the High Priestess for the Moon.)

Visualize that image standing before you. Invite it to sit down to talk with you. Continue to deepen your concentration, flooding yourself with the feeling of that planetary energy before you. Ask these questions one at a time:

If this planet is problematic for you, ask "Why are you giving me such trouble?"

If this planet is clearly helping you, thank it for its help and ask "What else do you have to give me?"

Then ask "What is it you need from me?"

Allow some quiet time for each answer to emerge. Because you are taking the time to interact with your own unconscious, new insights and answers do come.

Memory Games

Because Mercury has to do with the function of ordering data, it can be stimulated by a game, like the following one, that exercises our power of memory. Take a full deck of cards. Spread them out face down. Select a card and turn it over. Select a second. If the numbers match, start a pile for matched cards and take another turn. If they do not, return them face down to their original places, and try to remember what number is where. Time yourself on how long it takes you to remember and match all the pairs. Doing this exercise on a regular basis will show a measure of improvement in your memory.

Another version of the game allows two players to use one deck of cards, scoring one point per card. In a group, you might pair up and see what team can pair up all the cards in the shortest time.

To play this game with a group, gather a number of small objects (about twenty-five) on a board and cover them so they cannot be seen. Uncover the board and show the objects to the group for a brief ten seconds. Cover them again, and ask that each person write down as many objects as they can remember.

Telephone

This well-known children's game is a good Gemini exercise, telling us how clearly and accurately we listen and communicate. Form a circle. Someone begins by whispering in the ear of the person next to them a fairly long descriptive sentence which is challenging for adults. Pass it on around the circle, having the last person speak the sentence they received aloud.

Conceptualize the Sky

The zodiac and planets are part of an astrologer's conceptual model, yet many of us do not keep a daily awareness of where the planets are today. Stop and think. What degree is the Sun in and where is it in relation to you right now? Where is the Moon? What part of its cycle is it in—first quarter, full moon, etc.? Where is Mercury? Mars? Venus? Is it the morning star, or evening star? Where are the other planets?

At night, go out and find the zodiac belt and identify which planets are visible. Which ones are about to rise? Set? Which are on the other side of the earth? Making a daily mental or visual observation of the moving planets around you will keep you more in touch.

Some of us do not have a good mental grasp of the astronomical model we use, nor do we have a good understanding of celestial motion. What is the celestial equator, declination, right ascension, azimuth, planetary nodes, for example? If you don't know the answers to these questions, buy a book on astronomy for astrologers. Frequently, there are classes in astronomy at conferences—take one. Or sign up for a few classes at your local planetarium.

One-Week Event Diary

Keep a written log of astrological observations you make of events around you. If you see a pedestrian angrily shaking a finger at a motorist, write it down with the notation (Mercury/Mars)—or a heavy-set man buying some eclairs in a bakery (Sun/Jupiter/Venus/Neptune), or a child hugging her teddy bear (Moon/Venus), or a funeral procession passing you on the highway (Saturn/Mercury). Relate what you see to the astrological symbols. You'll learn to use astrology more readily in relation to your day-to-day environment.

Cocktail Party

In a group, hold a ten minute "cocktail party" where each of you is the host. Your goal is to make social/ verbal contact with everyone in the room. Was this uncomfortable for you? Did you feel at home in a highly social, communicating environment?

Miming

Form pairs and take turns miming each other's movements. Try to observe carefully and imitate as near perfectly as you can, paying attention to eyes, hands, expressions, etc. A version of this requires that each pair do something together in front of the group. For instance, mime being a pair of puppies, or objects that work in tandem together such as mortar and pestle, hook and eye, two turning pedals on a bike, etc. Have the group guess what you and your partner are imitating.

Strong Mercury people tend to be excessively verbal. Doing nonverbal exercises in which we express ourselves is helpful. With a partner, make statements about everything you have done since waking up. Instead of repeating the statement, your partner uses his or her hands to express the statement silently. Switch roles.

Follow the Leader

Ask the group to line up against one wall in a large space. Turn on some good dance music. Ask them to take turns leading out with a movement or action which everyone tries to mimic exactly as they move across the room to the other side. Continue until each member has led a movement at least once.

Learning to Listen

The consciousness it takes to listen is in itself the discipline that sharpens one's ability to communicate. Sit with a partner you do not know. Take turns telling each other about yourselves. Pay attention to what your partner says and how she says it. Now introduce your partner to the group, mirroring as closely as possible how your partner introduced herself to you.

Relaxation

Both Gemini's and Virgo's primary tool is their thinking function. They have strong tendencies to get carried away in their heads, absorbed with their thought processes and out of touch with their feelings and their bodies.

For Mercurial people, any mental relaxation technique is excellent. They should learn to "dial the mind down," to breathe deeply, and return their awareness to their body. Learning how to just "be" is good for Mercurial types.

My Ideal Trip

Mercury, particularly Gemini, is associated with travel. In your imagination, spend ten minutes creating your ideal trip. Where would you go? How would you get there? How long would you stay? What would you do?

Variations: In a group, have a member lead a guided journey, re-creating their most memorable travel experience.

Get a group together to see slides and photographs of a recent exotic trip taken by someone in the group. Have them tell in vivid detail what the experience was like. Ask each person to imagine as fully as possible what the sights and sounds of the trip were like.

Language

The process of learning a new language is a Mercury experience. Take a class or course of study.

Charades

For an experience of communicating without use of your mouth or words, this is a classic game.

Gibberish

With a partner, spend five minutes in conversation without using any known language. It may be hard to get started, but once you have the hang of this, you can communicate quite explicitly. It's fun and silly.

Siblings

Get together with your brothers and sisters, and ask each to write three paragraphs about your mutual family. First describe your father, then your mother, and finally your early home life. Compare notes. Do you each see them differently? Can you see, in your brother or sister's chart, why they responded the way they did?

Dictionary Game

This is a classic game of words, word mastery, and trickery—all a part of Mercury energy. In a group, hand out slips of paper and pencils. Give each person a turn to trick the others by choosing an obscure word from the dictionary. The object of the game is to make up a definition that sounds like it fits. The real definition is written down by the player who has chosen the word. The fake definitions as well as the real one are gathered and read aloud. Each person then guesses which definition is the dictionary's version. A player scores a point for choosing the right definition or when someone chooses his or her faked one. If no one chooses the correct definition, the player who chose the word stumps the group and scores additional points by taking one point away from each player. This is a game in which you learn new words and sharpen your ability to organize thoughts. It can be challenging if you play with a group of people with strong Gemini/Virgo energy like I do!

Trivial Pursuit™

The board game, "Trivial Pursuit" is an ideal game made for the Gemini/Virgos among us!

Health Profile

Virgo is often connected with our health concerns. Make a health profile of your past to help clarify some of your health patterns.

Several months ago, I ran across my medical file recorded by my family doctor. It documented every illness, accident, complaint, and immunization I have had since birth. By writing down each illness and noting the particular transits at that time, some interesting patterns were revealed to me. For instance, I have had three accidents involving cars, motorcycles, or horses as well as two accidents with kitchen knives under a Mars/Uranus transit, a repeated side effect to a particular drug every time Neptune aspected the ruler of my sixth house, and noticeable weight gain whenever Jupiter squared or opposed my natal Venus over the last nine years. Now knowing this, I may better safeguard myself with similar future transits.

Task of Detail

Observe yourself doing some task which needs attention to detail. It could be a handi craft project, sewing, knitting, woodworking, or cleaning and organizing your office junk drawer. How do you feel while doing the task? Do you feel you did it well? Are you satisfied with the concrete results?

Work Analysis

Spend time examining your current work situation. Are you satisfied with your job? Satisfied with how you are performing? What bothers you about it? What's pleasant about it? Do you enjoy your fellow workers? Who? Why? If something is bothering you about work or co-workers, can you think of something/someone that may help the situation? Can you develop a strategy and plan to deal with it successfully?

MEDITATIONS AND VISUALIZATIONS

Mercury/Gemini Planet Walk

Visualize yourself as a young, curious teenager. Feel the peppy, fresh energy exuding from you. Adjust your walk so it is light and sprightly, almost as if you were just barely keeping on the earth. Express curiosity about many things as you walk down the street, keeping your attention flitting from one object of interest to another.

Mercury/Virgo Planet Walk

Observe yourself walking normally. Can you notice any way in which you can change to make your walk more efficient? Notice the whole process of your walk as minutely and precisely as possible, from small motor responses to where and how your foot carries your weight. How long is your average footstep? Where do you focus your eyes when walking? Now walk in very slow motion. Do you notice anything else about the way you walk?

Mercury Meditation

Storytelling is a Mercurial form of meditation whether you are the teller or listener. The storyteller weaves words to create stories. Stories are designed to make us think and listen. Curl up with a good story.

SUGGESTED FILMS AND MUSIC

Mercury Films

Short Cuts; Absence of Malice; All the President's Men; Altered States; Breathless; Room with a View; House of Games; Diary of Anne Frank.

Suggested Music

Mercury Falling, (Sting), much rap music (for its political, philosophical content), "Coyote" *Hejira* (Joni Mitchell), "Cross-Eyed and Painless" *Remain in Light* (Talking Heads), "Once in a Lifetime" *Remain in Light* (Talking Heads), *Speaking in Tongues* (Talking Heads), "I Feel So Good" (Mose Allison), Songs of Bob Dylan, *Sergeant Pepper's Lonely Hearts Club Band* (The Beatles, especially the lyrics by John Lennon), "Mercury, The Winged Messenger" *The Planets* (Holst).

14

VENUS, TAURUS, AND LIBRA

Venus is the feminine, balancing, and harmonizing function of the psyche. Venus is connected with the more ancient Greek goddess, Aphrodite, the goddess of love and beauty. Venus is the urge to unite the opposites, look for similarities and bring equilibrium. She is linked in a magnetic polarity with Mars, the god of war, which expresses the opposite principle of aggressive action and coercion, exposing differences and creating waves that rock equilibrium.

Venus is linked to all forms of behavior that produce solidarity, coherence, sympathy and peace, everything we value, money, possessions, relationships, intimacy, and our esthetic sense and appreciation of art and beauty.

Venus has sensual and softly erotic attributes, contrary to Mars which is sexual, raw, and primitive. The Renaissance painter Titian depicted this sensuality in his painting, "Venus." Botticelli's "Birth of Venus" is a painting that not only captures her sensual, full nature but paints her arising in a shell born from the sea. This myth of Venus' origin of birth is worth noting since the higher, more refined manifestation of Venus is Neptune, ruler of the sea.

Individuals with strong Venus/Libra energy in their horoscope (by sign, house, and aspect) can be agreeable and cooperative. If afflicted, one may be too passive and idealistic, choosing not to confront the difficult part of any relationship. Those with little Libra energy may be unwilling to work at long-term committed relationships.

Individuals with strong Venus/Taurus energy can be determined to succeed and have a steadying effect on others. If afflicted, one may be acquisitive since their security needs are often directly tied up with possessions, money, or sensual pleasure. Those with less Taurus energy may have little urge to enjoy the pleasures of the world. They may not be very sense-oriented.

Venus—A Sense Experience

Since Venus, especially with Taurus influence is so sense-oriented, here is a group experience for you to feel it. For a touch experience, gather objects such as balloons, clay, Slinkys, magnets, whiffle balls, paper clips, etc. Ask the group to sit in a circle and space themselves close enough to easily pass the objects around. Have them take a few deep breaths to relax the body. Rubbing palms together will stimulate the blood and the tactile sense.

Because we rely so habitually on our sight, these sense experiences are best done with eyes closed to help focus more acute attention on the other senses. Ask that this be done in silence since spontaneous verbal responses may be distracting for others. Begin by passing each object, one at a time, in the same direction around the circle.

Encourage each participant to experiment with the object, brushing it across their cheek, neck, wrists, legs, and feet. What do you imagine this looks like? Smell it. Taste it. Listen to it. Do you notice any sound it is making? Imagine each object to be a special personal object of yours. What kind of feelings do you have with each?

After each object has gone around, place it in the center. When an individual has experienced all the objects, have them open their eyes and sit quietly until everyone is finished. This process is interesting to watch, as facial expressions reveal a variety of feelings—certain objects elicit similar responses of pleasure, dislike. For many, you can observe the "child" come out. In fact, some of these objects will stimulate early childhood memories, especially objects like Slinkys™, jacks, chalk, etc. (If stimulating memory is your goal, this experience could be used as well for a Moon exercise.)

If you want to try this on your own, gather your sense objects in front of you, close your eyes, mix up the objects, and one at a time, immerse yourself in touching, smelling, or tasting.

Or, for a more sensual experience, choose various fabrics—silk, taffeta, velvet, fur, lace, ribbons, etc.

To experience the sense of smell, gather small bags of different fragrant herbs—chamomile, bay leaf, basil, dill, etc. Or a number of different and distinctive perfumes.

To experience the sense of taste, gather different flavors and textures of foods—lemon, marshmallows, grapes, cooked pasta noodles, tobacco, etc. Or taste different kinds of nuts.

Oranges

Bring one orange for each group member. Have each member choose an orange, and sit with it for five minutes, noticing special markings, how it feels, etc. Then put all the oranges in the center, mix them up well and have each member find their orange.

Contact

Our sense of touch is as important to our contact with reality as our sense of sight. For hundreds of years in our culture we have encountered the world primarily through the domination of sight. For many, the world of touch is new territory. Here are ways with which to communicate without words and learn to touch.

Massage

Massage is a healing art. When practiced between friends or lovers, it can be a beautiful way to show love and caring. The essence of massage is the unique way it communicates without words. Most of us are out of touch with our bodies and not paying too much attention to the stresses that build up in us. Massage can be a wonderful gift that helps another get more in touch with their body, release tensions, relax, and receive some nurturing. For more specific information on techniques of massage, try *The Massage Book*, by George Downing.[1]

Contact Games

These are games which bring people into contact through touch. Remember to follow any experience that has to do with touch or intimacy with an adequate amount of process time. This may be stirring for a number of players, stimulating their issues about intimacy, sexuality, or relationships. Be sensitive to this. Contact games in general, are better played after a level of trust has been built in the group.

A Massage Line

Have the group turn in one direction. For five minutes, spend time massaging the back, neck, and head of the person in front of you.

Spoon Touch

One player is blindfolded. He or she takes a wooden spoon in each hand and stands in the center. One player comes and stands in front of the blindfolded player in any position they choose—kneeling, bending, or laying down. The blindfolded player tries to identify who the person is through touching them with spoons.

Sheet Game

Each player puts a sheet over their head. Ask the group to walk around the room in silence and try to identify each other by feeling through the sheet. How do you recognize people? Perhaps by particular physical features? Afterward, ask the group how they felt about feeling others through the sheet? Hesitant? Aggressive? Embarrassed?

Contacting Others

Have everyone close their eyes and begin to move, arms extended. When two people make contact, have them square off facing each other while keeping their eyes closed. Tell them to drop their arms and focus on their feelings. Ask them how they feel about this person after spending a minute sensing each other. Then have them move onto making contact with another in the same manner. After four or five contacts, tell them to sit down, open their eyes and make a list. What words describe the quality of contact with #1? #2?, etc. (Each person might have met up with the same person twice.) Ask if they can now match up their sense experience with the particular individual.

Stand Up

This cooperative game is great for drawing a group together. It results in a whole crowd of struggling, giggling folks. Start with two people sitting back to back, knees bent and elbows linked. Now stand up together! With a little practice and cooperation this will work. Now add one more person and try to stand up. Continue to add people until the whole group is attempting to get up together. (The trick for a large group is to stand up quickly and at precisely the same moment.) If you make it past four people, your group has made a genuine accomplishment!

Pillows

Since Taurus loves comfort, gather a huge amount of pillows. Take turns piling into them, rolling around and under them, surrounding yourself with their "squooshy" soft comfort. What words describe this experience? Do you have any planets in Taurus?

Food Addictions

Venus can represent food addiction, particularly to sugar. Examine your food patterns, especially your use of sugar. How many times a week do you eat dessert? Do you get cravings for it? Do you binge out on a particular food? When? Is this a technique for coping with painful emotions? If change is desirable, read any of the many books now on the market about alcohol addiction. The same strategies can be applied to sugar addictions.

As a group, eat out together. This could be done with an eye toward just enjoying and sharing the food and company. Or go to a restaurant pretending you are all food critics, evaluating the food, decor, and service.

Spend an evening together discussing food. What's your favorite food? Cuisine? Most memorable meal? Most decadent food experience? See if you can come to a group consensus and choose the best restaurant in your city that has the best malted milks, sushi, hamburgers, desserts, coffee, etc.

For an experience in learning taste discrimination, go to a wine tasting. Many larger cities have classes or one-night tastings of particular wine varieties. Did you know that there are over eighty descriptive categories used by wine connoisseurs to discriminate the subtle tastes in wine?

Eating with Mindfulness

With the availability of fast foods and eating on the run, we are more inclined to eat mindlessly, stuffing in food and being mostly unaware of our experience. This exercise can help to regain the sense of pleasure and enjoyment we can experience from eating. Take a piece of bread or your favorite cheese and feel the texture with your hands and fingers. Notice the appearance and color. Smell it. Now taste it, noticing its texture on your tongue, the explosion of taste sensations in your mouth. Savor the taste. Chew slowly, noting the changing flavor and texture sensations in your mouth. Above all, take the time to really eat.

Pleasure

Make a list of your pleasures and delights. What are the things you truly enjoy? Windsurfing on the lake? Dove™ ice cream bars? Swinging in a hammock in Oaxaca,

Mexico? Going to the season premiere at the symphony? Recalling these memories can heighten your senses and sense of pleasure.

Choose one that is most vivid. Visualize this experience deeply as if it were happening now. Return to that moment. Hear it, smell it, let that experience fill your whole body. If appropriate, reach out and bring it close. Or move with it. Enact that pleasure, allowing it to flood your being. You might sing or draw it. Relish this reexperiencing.

My Most Attractive Features

Make a list of your most attractive physical features. Rank them in order. Choose your most attractive feature. (If you are in a group, share this.) Then evaluate this experience. Was it easy for you to come up with features you like? Difficult? Why? If this was difficult, do you have either a natal or transiting Saturn in challenging aspect to Venus? Do your feelings mirror any aspect you may have to your natal Venus?

Clothes Evaluation

People with strong Venus in their horoscopes can be "clothes horses." Take time to go through and evaluate your wardrobe. What don't you like? No longer fits? What are your basic color themes? Have you had "your colors" done? Are you Spring? Winter? Summer? Fall? What accessories do you have? What items do you need to look for to give your wardrobe more versatility?

You might make an appointment with a clothes consultant to have her help you overhaul your wardrobe. Jupiter trine/sextile Venus is a wonderful time to buy your spring wardrobe. If you want to shop and find things you like, do it at this time. You may spend more money than you want, but you will love what you buy. This is a classic time for beautifying or pampering yourself. Get a new hairstyle, cosmetics, massage, or manicure.

Parties!

Venus/Jupiter transits help to make memorable parties and/or celebrations. Try having one when Venus is harmonious to your Jupiter, or better yet, Jupiter to your Venus. With good food, wine, company, and a pleasant environment, this will be one occasion talked about for a long time!

Money Assessment

Money and Venus are intimately connected. How do you feel about your money? Do you budget? Or have you no idea where your money goes? How much money do you need? Want? Have you ever seen a financial planner? Is that a good idea now? Take out a twenty, fifty, or hundred-dollar bill. Talk to your money. (Sounds silly, but it can help you get a clearer idea of your relationship to money.) Or if you want to create more money, make a "money magnet." This is a reasonably large sum of money for you that you cannot spend. Its purpose is to act as an attractor for money. Wrap your stash up in a cloth bag, leather pouch, or silk and keep it in a sacred place. Treat it as a ritual or ceremonial object. See what happens.

Erotica

Venus symbolizes that aspect of our sexuality that is gentle, subtle, inviting, sensual, and feminine. Much of erotic literature (*not* pornography) is Venusian in tone. Erotica dwells on the emotions of relationship, the excitement of romance, and the subtleties of surroundings.

Before Anais Nin's, *Little Birds* and *Delta of Venus*,[2] women had little choice but to read Victorian erotica written by men. Because of this, a dozen years ago Anais Nin encouraged women to write their own erotica. Now, over the past few years, women's erotica has blossomed and is printed by large publishers and mainstream book clubs.

If you want to experience Venusian erotica more intimately, here are other good sources of reading—*Ladies Own Erotica* by the Kensington Ladies' Society,[3] or Lonnie Barbach's *Pleasures* or *Erotic Interludes*[4] are sensitive and well-written books.

Relationships

For most of us, our first significant relationships are with our parents. Write down a list of people who have been your most significant relationships, from birth until this current time. After seeing them written down, go back one at a time and reflect. What quality of feelings does this relationship have? What is your most pleasant memory with this friend? What quality do you most like about them? Don't like? What did and didn't you like about the way you were with them? By doing this reevaluation, you may see a pattern in the way you relate to others.

Art

Art as a creative medium is an expression of Venus. Spend a day at your local art gallery or exhibit opening. Or take a class in art appreciation. Read a book on how to approach and critique art. Or spend time reflecting on one of your favorite artists. Take a class exploring a new creative expression—pottery, still life, photography, dance, or music.

Art Supply Box

This is an indispensable resource for anyone involved in experiential astrology. The more variety of media you have at your fingertips, the better for your spontaneity and inspiration. Get large sheets of construction paper, clay, colored paper, magic markers, colored pencils, crayons, finger paint, temperas, watercolor, glitter, feathers, sequins, plaster cast gauze (for impromptu mask-making), and basics such as glue, scissors, tape, etc. Keep them together and accessible in a large cardboard box. Just knowing you have these resources, you will be inclined to make use of them.

"My Heart Now"

Draw a picture of what your heart looks like now using colors, images, words, or whatever feels right. Study this picture. If so, is there any negative feeling in your heart now? Is this feeling connected to a particular individual? If you want to do something about this, focus on the parts of your heart that are clear, warm, and loving. Imagine that part is expanding slowly into the more negative spaces. Intensify the positive image and feeling. Allow your love to take in the imbalanced energy.

Is there something you want to take into your heart now? Imagine it in front of you. Now see your heart suck it up like a vacuum cleaner, absorbing it inside.

Luxurious Baths

A true manifestation of Venus is to pamper yourself in a special bath. Try a bubble bath or an herbal bath. Some herbs are used for relaxing muscles (sassafras bark, mugwort, burdock root), soothing the body (comfrey, chamomile), and others to stimulate and rejuvenate (lavender, peppermint, nettles). Place a handful of herbs in a pot, bring to a boil and simmer ten to twenty minutes, or fill a muslin bag or tea brewing ball with herbs and drop into tub.

Jeanne Rose's *Herbal Body Book* [5]

Here is a wealth of ideas for natural beauty care for men and women. Ms. Rose includes a glossary of useful herbs, both for health and beauty, facial steaming, natural lotions, shampoos, makeup, conditioning packs, herbal hair dyes, and herbal baths. Get together with a small group of friends and spend the afternoon beautifying.

Lingerie

Nothing makes a woman feel more feminine than lingerie. Just knowing you have pretty lingerie on under your street clothes is psychologically uplifting. If you have Saturn aspecting Venus, a trip to the lingerie store might give you the psychological boost you need.

Goddess Worship

Under Venus/Jupiter/Pluto transits, you can strongly empower yourself with the feminine Goddess energy. If you have a meditation altar or sacred space, create an altar to the Goddess. You might have a statue of Kwan Yin, or mentally envision and embody Ishtar, Inanna, Psyche, Persephone, or Aphrodite. If you have a Jupiter transit that lasts a month, spend that time dwelling on the Goddess energy within you, inviting the Goddess into your consciousness. Bring her out with you into the world. If you have a good Pluto transit to Venus, this year-long positive transit would be the most powerful time for catharsis and in-depth healing of your heart. Use this magical time to deeply heal your heart's wounds from the past, transforming and creating a change of heart.

Work intensely during this time to deepen your contact with your own heart. Then take the strength of that inner love and send love lines out to those you know. Radiate your love lines up and out of the atmosphere and send them radiating around the earth.

A very cathartic group experience, especially at a large conference, is to ask each individual to intensify the love in their heart. Consciously send it out to all those who touched you. Then send it to anyone in the room you may have had difficulty with. Let the power of the group love dissolve that difficulty. Let the barriers and separations dissolve. Ask the group to see their hearts linked up to everyone else's. See one big heart. Imagine the group heart expanding and contracting with each person's breath.

MEDITATIONS AND VISUALIZATIONS

Venus Walk

Venus is reflected in flowing, sensual, and soft movements. Think of the moment you first knew you were in love. Recapture that joy in your body, in your step, and in your smile. Do this while wearing something wonderful.

Venus Meditation

Lie down and get comfortable, preferably on a pile of soft pillows. Turn on some Venus music. Take a few deep breaths. Focus your attention on your heart. With each breath, expand your heart, filling it with love. Expand your heart and your love for a few minutes until your heart feels as big as your body. Now let your heart be a dancing heart. Then after a few minutes, let your heart be still. Breathe deeply and slowly into it. Mentally chant repeatedly, "I will build and preserve all that is meaningful in my life." Spend a few minutes just drifting, absorbing your joy.

Another powerful variation to ask, as you are expanding your heart, "How much bliss can I take in?" As you feel your heart resisting, limiting, breathe into that resistance until you can feel it expand. Keep asking yourself this question, reaching a limit, breathing, and opening. (This is a wonderful meditative process to use in rituals especially utilizing Venus/Jupiter/Pluto/Neptune transits.)

SUGGESTED FILMS AND MUSIC

Venus Films

Heart of the Lion; Sirens; Bitter Moon; The Lovers; Like Water for Chocolate; Il Postino; Sense and Sensibility; Romeo and Juliet; The English Patient; My Best Friend's Wedding; The Pillow Book; E.T.; Black Stallion; Out of Africa; Casablanca; South Pacific; Emmanuelle; Splendor in the Grass.

Suggested Music

Ti Amo, Amore (Pavarotti), *Don Juan de Marco* soundtrack—especially "Have You Ever Loved a Woman," *Sensual Classics*, *Red Shoes Diaries*, *Passion for Guitar*, *Heartdance*

(Robert Encila), *I Ain't Movin'* (Desireé), almost all tango music, "Icarus" (various artists), *Deep Breakfast* (Ray Lynch), "Sailing" (Christopher Cross), "Natural Woman" *The Best of Aretha Franklin* (Aretha Franklin), "Love is All Around" *Greatest Hits* (The Troggs), "There is Love" (Captain and Tennille), "Evergreen" (Barbara Streisand), "Ave Maria" (Schubert), "Jesu, Joy of Man's Desiring" (Bach), "To a Wild Rose" (Liszt), "Angels of Comfort" (Iasos), "On Wings of Song" (Mendelssohn), *Canon in D Major* (Pachebel).

15

MARS AND ARIES

Mars symbolizes the first step in the process of individuation, how we differentiate and separate ourselves from the group and our manner of initiating this process. It is how we act to get things done. Without Mars, little would be accomplished. Mars is the "primitive" root of our instinctual and biological urges, especially our sexual nature. Mars tells us how we are likely to feel about sex, the type of partners we attract, potential conflicts in relationships, as well as how we approach confrontation.

Individuals with strong Mars/Aries energy in the horoscope have a love of action (athletics) and a pioneering spirit which can act with independence and initiative. If afflicted, the frustrated energy can turn to aggression—bad temper, destructiveness, egocentricity, and recklessness. Those with little Marsian energy can lack initiative, self-motivation, self-assertion, and the impetus needed to bring things to fruition.

Mars—NASA Adventure Game [1]

This game is ideal to explore the Aries/Libra polarity, observing independent and cooperative group decision-making processes in a Marsian situation—Survival.

Allow one and one-half to three hours. If the group is large, break it up into smaller groups of five to eight players. Each player should have paper, pencil, and these instructions:

You are members of a space team which had originally planned to meet up with a mother spacecraft on the surface of the moon. As a result of technical difficulties, however, your spacecraft has been forced to land about two hundred miles away from the meeting place. A lot of equipment on board was damaged during landing. Since your survival depends on reaching the mother ship, you have to choose the most vital of the available equipment for making the two-hundred-mile journey. Below, you will find a list of fifteen items that were not damaged. Your task is to arrange them in order of their importance for the journey. Write "1" beside the most important item, "2" beside the second most important item, and so on.

    1 box of matches
    1 tube of food concentrate
    15 yards of nylon rope
    30 yards of parachute rope
    1 portable heater
    2 pistols
    1 box of powdered milk
    2 ten-gallon oxygen cylinders
    1 astronomical chart (moon constellation)
    1 rubber dinghy, automatically inflatable, with bottles of CO_2.
    1 magnetic compass
    5 gallons of water
    signal flares (ignitable in vacuum)
    1 first-aid box with syringes
    1 telecommunication receiver and transmitter with solar batteries

In this exercise, we act out our ability to make decisions under pressure, test the most sensible way of making decisions, and see what difficulties arise in the process.

First, as an individual, work out your own solution to the problem. Then gather with your group and arrive at a joint consensus. This means everyone in the group must agree to the order of the items that would be necessary for survival. Sometimes a full consensus is impossible, but try to design a plan that each member can at least partially accept.

Once the group has arrived at a solution, compare the group's plan to that of the NASA experts who gave the following order:

Oxygen cylinders (fills respiration requirements); water (replenishes loss by sweating); astronomical chart (one of the principal means of finding the right direction); food concentrate (supplies daily food required); telecommunication apparatus (distress signal transmitter for possible communication with mother ship); nylon rope (useful in tying an injured individual onto another, or for help in climbing); first-aid box (oral pills or injection medicine valuable); parachute rope (shelter against sun's rays); rubber dinghy (CO^2 cartridge for self-propulsion across chasms); signal flares (distress call when line of sight possible); pistols (self-propulsion devices could be made from them);

powdered milk (food, mixed with water for drinking); heater (useful only if party landed on the dark side); magnetic compass (probably no magnetized poles, thus useless); matches (little or no use on the moon).

At this point, have each group member reflect on their own charts and how they handled both the individual decision-making and the group process. If you are a strong Aries/Capricorn type, did you decide quickly or attempt to take control? How soon? Did you hold a strong opinion and force your view on the group? If you are more Libran or Virgo in nature, did you abdicate control, not care about control, withdraw, or find yourself easily swayed?

Recognizing current transits can add another dimension of understanding. For instance, with your transiting Neptune square Mars, did you have difficulty deciding what choices were best? Is this influence now affecting your normal "take charge" behavior? How did this affect the group and how is it influencing areas of your life now?

If you are facilitating this group, be aware of the evolving group process. Did members work objectively? Emotionally? Was there a power struggle? If so, how was this handled? How well did the group get along during this process? Who was quiet? Verbal? Pushy? Argumentative? Your observations will serve to help the group further understand its process and experience.

The NASA game opens and stimulates recognition of behavior patterns in everyday life, both as an individual and as a member of a group. Much interaction and insight can result.

Athletics

An obvious way to feel Marsian energy is through sports. Any activity in which you physically exert yourself is Marsian. Any sport in which you test yourself and aim toward higher physical achievements, such as weight lifting or bodybuilding is Marsian.

If you have good transits involving Mars, plan to take a challenging and physically exerting excursion like a twenty mile roller skate, or a hundred-mile bike trip. Or take an obstacle training or survival course.

Adventure!

Most of us know that when we take risks and expose ourselves to challenge, we live fully in each moment. We become more *alive*. Nothing's more exhilarating than traveling to another part of the world and testing yourself physically, mentally, and emotionally with a new experience. Take an adventure! Book a river raft trip down the Colorado. Go scuba diving in Cozumel. Take that long-dreamed-of trip trekking the Himalayas. Many of us have secret longings like this. Don't just long to begin an adventure, *do it!*

Competitive Sports

Mars individuals love to challenge themselves against others, especially in individual sports that pit one person's ability against another—wrestling, tennis, golf, and downhill racing. Observe this sense of competition when engaged in a sport.

Professional Football Games

Few sports express pure, brute, raw Marsian energy as well as football. Get yourself as close to the action as possible. Spend post-game time in the neighborhood sports bar. See how it feels to get rowdy.

Amusement Parks

The excitement and thrills of an amusement park are Marsian. Observe how you approach going on that first ride. What words describe your process? How do you confront risks and challenges?

Emergencies

Have you or anyone in the group ever found themselves in an emergency situation? Have you pulled someone from a burning car, or given CPR to someone having a heart attack? Tell about this experience. Did you act without thinking or was your action calculated? Did you at any time feel fear or danger for yourself? Do you recall experiencing any physical sensations while responding? How did you feel afterwards?

Aries/Libra Pushing

Pair up with someone of comparable physical strength and spend a minute pushing against each other. Then join another pair and take turns being a strength of one pushing against the strength of three. Notice your feelings while you are doing this. Do you like pushing? Do you feel challenged when pushing three others? Or resigned to losing against them?

For a Libra/Aries version of this, get into pairs and take turns being the aggressive one who pushes and then the other who submits. Which role feels more familiar? Which didn't you like? This could reveal something of your male/female elemental split, or about your Libra/Aries contact axis to other planets. It may also reflect current transits.

Anger

Recall the last time you really got angry. Who were you angry at? How did the process unfold? How did you respond? Did you confront the person explosively? In control but direct? Did you have to think about it first? Did you "stuff" your anger? Does your response correspond to the aspects of Mars in your chart? Or was there a fiery square or opposition by transit at the time of your argument?

Observe anger in others and how they express it. What sign do you imagine their Mars is in?

Observing Your Mars

Make a list of your responses to these questions:
What makes you angry?
When and how did you last take a risk?
When and how have been courageous?
For what causes would you crusade?
For what causes would you physically fight?

Marsian Images on Television

Television is loaded with examples of aggressive, macho, tough guys. Turn on any channel and there is bound to be a number of hard-hitting good guy/bad guy story lines.

MEDITATIONS AND VISUALIZATIONS

Mars Planetary Walk

Assertive, aggressive, and direct. Have you recently pushed your way into a subway? Or hurried to beat someone in line? What feelings are associated with this act—uncaring, childish, embarrassed, triumphant? Is this the way you frequently are? Rarely are? Examine Mars in your natal chart.

Mars Meditation

Since Mars relates to action, a moving meditation would be appropriate. To experience Mars in Libra try a T'ai Chi class. T'ai Chi has been practiced for over six hundred years as a meditational technique, health practice, martial art, and is essentially a sacred dance for evoking the life force. The practice of a T'ai Chi form is a series of movement patterns intended to be executed with no excess muscular activity or tension in the center of gravity so that all parts of the body are properly balanced. When done correctly, it generates the life force throughout the entire body and revitalizes one's energy.

SUGGESTED FILMS AND MUSIC

Mars Films

Con Air; Braveheart; The Terminator; Mad Max: Beyond Thunderdome; Raging Bull; Pumping Iron; Rambo; Mona Lisa; Fatal Attraction.

Suggested Music

"Mars" from *The Planets* (Holst), *Drums of Passion* (Olatunji), *The Emerald Forest* soundtrack, *Jagged Little Pill* (Alanis Morisette), "Birds of Fire" (John McLaughlin), *Dynamic Meditation* (Music of Shree Rajneesh Ashram), *Flashdance* soundtrack, "Immigrant Song" *Led Zeppelin III* (Led Zeppelin), "The Ride of the Valkyries" (Wagner), "Pull Up to the Bumper" *Nightclubbing* (Grace Jones), *Music for Bouzouki and Orchestra* (Theodorakis), "Marches Slave" *Symphony No. 5* (Tchaikovsky), *African Sanctus* (David Fanshawe), "Marches" (John Phillip Sousa), *Chariots of Fire* soundtrack, *The Empire Strikes Back* soundtrack, *Oklahoma* soundtrack, "Missionary Man" *Revenge* (The Eurythmics), "I Need a Man" *Savage* (The Eurythmics), *Toccata and Fugue in D Minor* (Bach).

16

JUPITER AND SAGITTARIUS

With Jupiter, we leave behind the forces of the personal realm, our social drives and impulses experienced through the Sun, Moon, Mercury, Venus, and Mars. Jupiter and Saturn are the guardians at the gate of the personal sphere that take us outside the boundaries of our ego and within the influence of the outer planets, the collective unconscious.

Jupiter symbolizes the force that drives us beyond our individual concerns, the hunger for more encompassing states of consciousness. It is the urge to bring the chaos of the unconscious into the light of greater perspective, recognition, and acknowledgment. In so doing, we perceive and understand the meaning of life's experience from a more expansive vantage point. Jupiter is the spiritual urge within ourselves and our society that sustains hope and meaning. Its force arises from an inherent faith in the essential "goodness" of humankind.

Jupiter is linked to our philosophies, belief systems, our sense of justice, and our instincts to heal. It is associated with the Father archetype who inspires his children through his warmth and acceptance. Individuals with strong Jupiter/Sagittarius energy will be philosophical, generous, and helpful. If afflicted, particularly to the Sun or Moon by sign, house, or aspect, one can overrate their own abilities, be an unrealistic "Pollyanna," easily become self-righteous, or hold on blindly to dogma and misconception.

Those with little Jupiter/Sagittarius energy in the horoscope may not feel motivated to refine their more base instincts or to reflect upon their lives.

Jupiter—An Acknowledgment Experience

The greatest of human potentials is our power to acknowledge each other. Our society has concentrated so much on "appearing" successful that those appearances hide the starvation of our inner world, in which meaning wanes and essence is denied. To be acknowledged by another, especially in times of confusion and discouragement, is to be given some sunshine. By simply saying "I see you," we charge the circuits of others and provide the stimulus for renewed hope.

In a group, take turns sitting in pairs for five minutes. What about this person can you truly acknowledge? Variation—each group member takes a turn sitting in the middle to spend a few minutes being acknowledged by others. This can be very uplifting and healing.

Learning to acknowledge oneself can be an even more difficult task. We are so conditioned as a culture through media and other sources to recognize what's not working, inefficient, ineffective, and inept that we don't see how this pervasive Saturn state permeates our everyday life. If each of us were to make a list right now of our qualities and characteristics, I would guess that many of us would list a fault or two near the top. Try making a Jupiter list. Only list positive qualities you can acknowledge in yourself. This is a fine exercise to balance against challenging Saturn transits, which is precisely the time you need to validate yourself. Or if you know someone who is currently experiencing Saturn, make a point to acknowledge them now. Reflect over the last week. Who in your life helped to make your life more pleasant—was it the postal clerk, the cashier at the grocery store, your neighbor, or your spouse? Did you acknowledge their kindness?

Beliefs

Most of us would be amazed at the many unconscious beliefs we hold about ourselves and others. Our beliefs can be like fences, preventing clear judgment and obstructing our vision. Spend time reflecting and listing what you believe about yourself, your life, and about life in general. What beliefs feel most comfortable? Which of these do you believe most deeply? Do you sense that any of these beliefs are limiting you in any way? If you are doing this with a group, spend time sharing your thoughts.

The Mountains

What better way to feel the expanse of Jupiter than cantering on a good horse in the mountains. Under good Jupiter aspects, try taking a two-day pack trip. Under the influence of Jupiter, you'll return more inspired and motivated, envisioning your life from a "higher" perspective.

Friends

Some of us do not distinguish between an acquaintance and one who is truly a friend. What does the word "friend" really mean to you? What qualities do you most value in others? Who around you has those qualities you admire?

Surprise Trip!

Here is a terrific way to manifest Jupiter. Ask a group of close friends who are coupled to a Friday afternoon party. Prior to the party day, you have collected $50 from each couple. Ask that everyone come to the party packed for a weekend trip. Once your party gets rolling, hold a drawing for a surprise getaway. Hand the winning couple plane tickets to some exotic locale and send then off! Win or lose, participating in this event is great Jupiterian fun.

Theme Party

Organize a theme party for your friends. Perhaps a group slumber party or a Southern "Dixie" dinner complete with country ham, corn pudding, and videos of *Gone with the Wind* or *Cat on a Hot Tin Roof*. Ask your guests to come as Rhett Butler and Scarlett O'Hara.

Exaggeration

In a group, or even with just two or three others, select an episode in your recent life to talk about. Instead of relating this experience in a normal manner, really embellish your tale. Exaggerate. Stretch your story it to its limit. See how grand a story you can create.

Famous People

Imagine you are giving a splendid party in a beautiful mansion, complete with opulence, elegance and style. What ten individuals who have existed in history would you invite for an evening of repartee? Why?

The Philosophies of the World

Jupiter symbolizes the spiritual basis, codes of conduct, and values that are adapted by a society to hold the group together. These are the creative forces which merge to form the great religions of the world. Spend time studying one of the holy books of the great world religions—The Bible, The Talmud, The Bhagavad Gita, or The Upanishads. Study one that is not from your own religious background.

People of Other Cultures

To stimulate Jupiter, go to dinner with one of your foreign friends. Hang out at your local university. Or spend the afternoon at an art gallery or museum. Write down how many different nationalities of people you see.

Foreign Films

Foreign film festivals can give you the flavor of Jupiter. Read reviews of the particular directors and screenwriters to more fully appreciate their style and methods.

Foreign Journeys

Along with the spiritual thirst to experience our inner horizons, Jupiter represents the need for a richer life, an enlargement of perspective, a longing to know and participate in the world beyond the horizon. Journeying to foreign countries and exposing ourselves to the different philosophical/religious contexts of other cultures allows us to understand our world from a wider point of view.

Travelogues

Traveling to a foreign country would be the number one choice on many of our lists, but time and money may make it impossible. The next best thing might be to have a secondhand experience of someone else's trip. I recently spent an evening saturated with images, descriptions, and stories of my friend's six-week trek to Nepal. The group asked eager questions. By the end of the evening, we all experienced a vicarious adventure in the Himalayas.

Giveaways

Here is a Native American tradition that is pure Jupiterian. At year's end, gather together a small group of your special friends. Ask each to bring an object that has been important to them and that they want to pass on. It may be a special crystal, book, good luck piece, etc. Spread the gifts on a blanket. Take turns telling the story of why your gift is special to you. Then one by one, select a gift. Observe your feelings as you choose an item, or as your gift is taken. How willingly can you part with something meaningful? Do you experience a subtle bond with the one who takes your gift?

Stretch

So many of us sit in chairs for long periods. Sometimes you can feel your vertebrae squashed down on top of each other. To remedy this constricted state, do a full body stretch. Lie down and image your body getting longer. Start from your toes. Stretch every part of your body. Then let your body move as it tells you to.

Fingerpaint

No other art medium offers a Jupiter experience quite like finger painting. Get yourself a package of large sheets of paper with a shiny, nonporous finish and bright blue finger paint. Lay your paper down on top of newspapers to protect the floor. Open the blue jar, turn on some Jupiterian music, and swirl away. Really feel the sensuous quality of your hands sweeping in large circles on the paper. Imagine that each circle represents a situation in your life that you are feeling good about. Feel it and express it.

MEDITATIONS AND VISUALIZATIONS

Jupiter Walk

Wear loose-fitting clothing that allows your movements to be fluid and flowing. Visualize your body. Imagine that it is growing, expanding out from every pore. Feel your body to be a giant helium balloon. You are barely able to keep your feet on the ground. Try walking down the street, your steps longer and lighter with this expansive feeling.

Jupiter Meditation

Lay down with some ethereal music in the background. Stretch and relax your body. Take a few deep breaths and begin to imagine your breath visually expanding outward. Envision inhaling more space with each breath. Continue your visualization until you are breathing in the sky. Imagine that it has become night. Breathe in the planets in the solar system, the stars in our galaxy, and all the stars in the universe. Breathe in this Jupiter state of awareness.

Abundance/Healing Meditation

An excellent affirmation to neutralize a Saturn state of consciousness is: "Everyday, in every way, I am becoming lighter, more confident, more empowered, and more inspired. " Use it daily, even hourly, if necessary.

SUGGESTED FILMS AND MUSIC

Jupiter Films

Mr. Holland's Opus; Free Willy; Baraka; Apollo 13; Gandhi; And Justice for All; A Thousand Clowns; The Sound of Music; The Robe; The Ten Commandments; Song of the South; Chariots of Fire; Cry Freedom.

Suggested Music

"Dancing with the Gods," from the *Baraka* soundtrack (Milan), *Luminous Ragas* (Steve Gorn), *Dixie Chicken* (Little Feat), "Ode to Joy" (from Beethoven's *Fifth Symphony*), "Fanfare for the Common Man"(Copland), "Jupiter" from *The Planets* (Holst), *Shadowdance* (Shadowfax), "Journey to the Center of the Earth" (John McLaughlin), "Sailing" (Christopher Cross), "Tell All the People" *The Soft Parade* (The Doors), "Wedding March" (Mendelssohn), "Climb Every Mountain" (Rodgers & Hammerstein), "Hallelujah Chorus" from *The Messiah* (Handel), *Sound of Music* (Rodgers & Hammerstein), *Piano Concerto no. 1* (Brahms), *Prelude to the Afternoon of a Faun* (Debussy), *Symphony no. 41* "Jupiter" (Mozart), "Whistle While You Work," from *Snow White*, and "Zipitty-Do-Dah" from *Song of the South* (Disney).

17

SATURN AND CAPRICORN

Saturn (ego) is the gatekeeper between the realms of the personal and collective realms of the psyche. Saturn symbolizes basic form: the structure of the psyche or the body (bones), boundaries, responsibilities, abandonment of old forms (death), and the principle of contraction. Through the force of contraction, one learns to work with limitations, communal values, standards of conduct, and rules to create a stable ground to conduct life with greater security, self-knowledge, and wisdom.

Saturn is associated with the Father/God Yahweh from the Old Testament whose inaccessible, cold and harsh disciplinarian nature demands obedience to his commandments.

Individuals with strong Saturn/Capricorn energy in their horoscope may exhibit self-control, perseverance, and a methodical, steady approach to life. If afflicted, one can be inaccessible, skeptical, or even heartless. Those with little Saturn/Capricorn may not possess staying power, be easily discouraged and controlled by others, and lack a sense of life direction.

Saturn/Capricorn Experience

Since Saturn symbolizes the death of form, an interesting experience for Saturn is enacting the struggle of the chick breaking out of its eggshell. Turn on some appropriate laboring music such as "Saturn" from *The Planets* (Holst). Alone or with a group, allow yourself to relax and begin to feel the music. Imagine you are a baby chick safely curled up in your comfortable and cozy shell. Enjoy the safety of your contained, fully nurturing environment. Now slowly imagine with the intake of nourishment, you are growing bigger. With each breath you grow. You begin to feel the sides of the shell. As you grow bigger, the shell feels more confining. With each breath, the shell brings a stronger feeling of confinement. Pay attention to how you are feeling as you meet these limits. Does it feel like any current situation in your life? Focus on that situation. Keeping in contact with your breath, feel the shell (the situation) become unbearable. You strain, pushing out, struggling to break the boundaries. Somewhere you break through. From that point, allow yourself to wiggle, straining to get out a foot, leg, head. Stay in contact with your feelings as you break through the shell which shatters into pieces around you. You are free, but the effort has exhausted you. Rest. Take time to reflect.

Is there some new feeling or awareness? Has this experience helped move you through your "stuck" place? After reflecting, write down what this was like, or pair up with another group member and share what happened. Discuss these feelings with the entire group.

Boundaries

Experiences of boundaries and limitation elicit a Saturn feeling. If a group member is undergoing a Saturn transit or was born with a difficult natal Saturn that they want to more fully explore, ask them to stand in the center of the group with their arms at their sides. Ask them to begin to take slow, deep breaths, bringing their awareness to their body. Ask the group to move *slowly* in toward the center, encircling the individual. As the circle tightens, remind the individual to keep breathing and to focus on the feelings in their body. Is there constriction anywhere? Are there fears coming up now? Keep them in contact with their emerging feelings. Allow the process to unfold as it needs to, keeping alert and sensitive to their responses. Ask, "Does this feel like a specific circumstance in your life now? Keep up the group "pressure" as long as the individual feels it is appropriate. Ask, "Do you want more pressure?" If you can keep them focused on their breathing and feelings, some important awarenesses may emerge.

A group I was working with in Phoenix did this exercise for a woman who wanted to better understand her natal Saturn in the seventh house. In this case, we added another Saturn element—a body brace, which confined her from her hips to her head. The work elicited strong suffocation feelings and early childhood memories of anger and sadness. This experience was a catalyst for her to break through into new realizations about her seventh house Saturn. (Remember to tread softly with sensitivity and alertness for the individual's process. *That* is the most important element of this experience.)

Variation: Instead of a circle, have the individual get down on all fours. Another member exerts pressure by draping themselves over the individual's back. Ask if the individual wants the weight of another person. Have them identify each new weight with a specific individual or life situation in which they are feeling restriction. Then process the experience.

If you want to do this on your own, use weights of two, five, and ten pounds. Place a number of weights in front of you. Identify each with a difficulty you are now having. Pick one and walk back and forth with it. Without letting go of the first weight, carry another one around, and then pick up the next, and so on. Pay close attention to how you feel as you add more weights. Can you arrange the weights to make them easier to carry? Is there anything you can let go of? Express feelings to the group or nonverbally by drawing a picture.

Life Cycles

Most people are aware of the rhythmic process of natural events such as the daily cycle of night and day, the moon's cycle from new to full and back again. But few are aware of how extensively cycles permeate our lives. Our bodies have a multitude of cycles— our red blood cells regenerate approximately every 128 days, the ovaries release every 28 days, the stomach contracts about three times a minute, the heart beats 76 times a minute, and the brain's various Alpha, Beta, Theta and Delta rhythms pulse near 10 cycles per second. These hidden cycles are the life forces of a human being. But we can also observe broader, longer rhythms in life.

Typically, we see our lives in phases, as a baby, a child, a teenager, a young adult, an adult, middle-aged, and elderly. Using these categories, go back in your life and look at each of these periods as a distinct unit of time. How was your babyhood? What key events can you remember that marked it? What words come to mind when assessing it? Do the same for each of the other periods. Compare them. Which phases were more difficult? Easier? More fulfilling? Examining our life in its cycles can bring us more conscious clarity.

Foundations

Either individually or as a group, draw a picture of your current foundation. Does it feel firm, strong? Is it weak in an area? Where? What does that weakness look like? What aspect of your life does it symbolize? Is this situation demanding major reconstruction? Do you have the means to "shore up" this weakness? Ask each person to do these exercises individually, then share what was discovered.

If your intention is for group members not only to clarify, but to work through a Saturn issue, ask them to identify what resources they possess that could possibly help them improve the limiting situation in their lives. Each participant should then draw up a strategic plan to execute in the coming months.

Clay

Playing with soft clay is a superb antidote for Saturn transits. Because we feel so stuck, so encased under difficult Saturn transits, feeling and working with soft clay unconsciously reminds us about flexibility and the fresh, pliable phase that follows the breaking up of old, dry forms. This is particularly effective with a Saturn return chart in which the clay becomes a symbol of the new foundation and structure you are starting to build.

History around Your Birth

We know that babies, like soft clay, are impressionable. We each absorb the psychic energy around us before and after our birth. What series of events were going on in the world for the nine-month period before your birth? At your birth? During your first year of life? What feelings did you unconsciously absorb? Can you relate any of these world events to the ways you feel about life?

Saturn Return

Because the Saturn return represents the culmination of a thirty-year cycle, it is obviously an important transit. Try this experience when Saturn returns to its natal position for you, a friend, or a client.

Many long-term transits can be more easily understood in metaphor. One of the better images I have found for the Saturn return is hiking down a railroad track tunneled into the mountains. The six to nine months preceding the exact Saturn return is symbolized by the conditions approaching the tunnel; the one-year period of the exact transit is symbolized by the journey through it, and the six to nine months immediately after the return is symbolized by the new vista and the conditions on the other side of the tunnel. Use this metaphor in guided imagery for your group. Modify the experience to focus on particular phases of the life cycle. Working with this metaphor over a period of time will help to crystalize your understanding of this transit.

To guide your client through this "tunnel," ask some of the following questions: Have you ever backpacked in the mountains? If not, imagine what this is like. Envision carrying all your gear—tent, poles, food, and pack. As you begin to approach the tunnel, create a picture that represents your life now. Identify each piece of gear you are carrying with specific situations in your life. Venture into the dark tunnel carrying all the gear. What are you getting tired of carrying? What feelings do you associate with the burden? What can you drop off? Let go of the items you don't need. What does it feel like to be free of the excess baggage? Look ahead of you. Can you see some light at the end of the tunnel? Walk through the tunnel until you are standing at the other end. What do you see? What new visions and unexplored vistas open up? Create a final picture of what you envision in this new phase of your life.

In my experience, this process helps people to vividly express their feelings about this often troublesome period, to restore clarity of purpose, to redirect their focus on the future, and to renew hope and anticipation.

Variation: Let the vista before the tunnel represent the thirty-year cycle. What do the first thirty years look like? What features, qualities and experiences mark the time period? Can you represent them symbolically in a drawing? What successes, disappointments, challenges, completions took place? What colors or tones dominate the different stages of the thirty years?

Or draw the vista after the tunnel to represent the next thirty-year cycle. What features, qualities and experiences are you hoping for?

Saturn Retrograde

Any time that Saturn is retrograde by transit and has eased off a difficult aspect to your natal chart is a "grace" period giving you a potentially valuable chance to assess your responses to the first transit of Saturn. Some of us waste this time, feeling so relieved the pressure is off that we slip back into our old ways or think we have solved our problem. Use this reprieve to look at your life. Have you approached a recent problem in a constructive way? What new methods can you continue to employ to meet the challenge that will likely resurface as Saturn goes direct and aspects your natal planet once again?

Asteroid Belt

Under difficult Saturn transits, this exercise is helpful to crystalize what is limiting in your life. Envision yourself traveling through the asteroid belt between the planets. Draw a picture of your surroundings; include big and little asteroids, and label each asteroid with a limitation you are currently feeling. Identify your biggest obstacle with the biggest asteroid. Giving a name to difficult Saturn influences can be therapeutic.

Which of these obstacles can you most easily get rid of? What is the biggest obstacle? What resources do you have to help you around this obstacle? Do you have any upcoming positive Saturn transits you can use? Initiate a strategy to implement when you have the help of a good transit.

Draw Your Current Problem

This exercise can be done alone, but is most effective when done in an ongoing therapeutic group. Ask each participant to draw a picture of their biggest current problem. Take turns showing the drawings. As a group, assess each picture for vividness of image. Note its strengths and weaknesses. How well are the components integrated? What is the degree of symbolism?

Discuss these questions—How well is the person coping with the problem? Is its seriousness being denied? Who's winning? Who or what does this person feel is responsible for the problem? For the healing? How indicative is the drawing of a good outcome? What resources, defenses and supports can help them solve the problem? Are there any supporting transits?

The Shadow

Recognizing our own darkness seems to be the prerequisite for self-knowledge. List the personality traits you have the most difficulty dealing with in others. Once this is done, you will have produced an accurate description of the repressed characteristics in your own unconscious! You have described your own shadow. Precisely what bothers us about others are the key unintegrated elements of our own psyche that we project out onto the world. This exercise may stir some uncomfortable feelings, but offers plenty of "food for thought."

Old Age

In a group, discuss the role of the elderly in our society. How are the elderly treated in other cultures by comparison? Because of the advancing age of the "baby boomers," within twenty years our culture will experience an enormous demographic change. There will be many more older people than we have now. What potential problems result from the growing numbers of elderly in our society? What creative solutions can the group devise?

An Old Person I Remember from My Childhood

Either alone or with a group member, lie down and get comfortable. Let your mind drift back into your past and recall an older person who was close to you when you were a child. Focus on visualizing that person. Describe them as fully as possible. What were they like? What kind of feelings did you have toward them? What gifts of wisdom did they give you?

The Old Wise One

In many cultures, elders are respected and revered. Saturn is time, and time teaches through experience. Many of us have known one or two elders who have taught us much.

A rewarding experience is to sit with an older person and ask them about their life; their memories, joys, pains, lessons, and accomplishments. Through them we see a glimpse of our own lives. Record the personal history of this elder. Include their significant moments: meeting their spouse, their first home, his leaving for the war, her taking a bus alone to the hospital to deliver her first child, etc. My husband's mother sent us an audiotape of just such information. We realized how important it is to have some record from our family elders, some memento of the history of our personal lineage. You might ask your parents to do this. Or perhaps interview them on video tape. Down the road, you may find it a treasured possession.

Strengthening Your Foundation

A harmonious Saturn transit is an auspicious time to strengthen your base. What aspect of your life could use more discipline? What part of your foundation needs reinforcement? Once you've identified that area, develop a strategy to strengthen it.

Corrections made now with diligence and hard work will solidify your base and advance your goal.

For example, there are several productive ways to make good use of a Saturn trine to your Sun. This is the time life runs more smoothly, when you can accomplish much, and make your position in the world strong. Spend a few minutes a day to consciously impact your psyche with positive Saturn energy. See your body and your life force getting stronger. If you have a weak part in your body, imagine that it is receiving vital, life-giving energy. Use the daily affirmation, "Every day, in every way, I am getting stronger. " Or decide now to begin some physical regimen—quit smoking, start daily exercise, etc. Speak this intention with conviction. By maintaining that conviction and self-discipline, you will see successful results. In a group, you can further empower your Saturn trine Sun transit by facing each person separately and speaking your intention *with resolve*.

Being positively recognized can strengthen your psyche. Let the group compliment you about your accomplishments and successes. Write them down to have to read when Saturn is squaring your Sun, or when you are having a difficult Saturn day.

Variation: Being acknowledged by others is important for each of us. Start a file of appreciative notes and letters you receive from clients or friends. This can be a useful psychological resource when dealing with the discouragement or lack of appreciation you might experience when Saturn squares or opposes your Sun.

Goals
Planning and developing concrete strategies can be most realistically assessed and effectively implemented under good Saturn transits. What goals have you set for this next year? Next five years? If you haven't got concrete future plans, take the time to do it now!

Role-Playing Difficult Saturn Transits
What if you have transiting Saturn opposite your Uranus, and you want to use an experiential method to bring it to conscious expression? Remember, the more you deny the existence of a problem or resist facing it, the more likely your problem will surface suddenly or explosively. This exercise can be done effectively with one other friend or

in a group. What specific problem is causing you a sense of uneasiness? Whose authority are you resisting? What do you want to break away from?

A metaphor for this transit is a wild stallion in a corral, restless and straining against the rope that is feeling restrictive. Breaking out may be your impulse, but you need to watch how you go about it. Uranian energy is so unpredictable that you might impulsively jump the fence and get snagged on the barbed wire, or escape the confines only to find you are unprepared to fend totally for yourself.

Role play with someone what it feels like to be in a tug-of-war between yourself and an authority figure or issue. You might literally get a rope and act out a tug-of-war. First, breathe deeply and get focused on your feelings. Now have someone representing the "other side" pull against you, testing you and challenging your validity or position. Keep your focus on your inner process. Keep breathing. Express these feelings aloud. Do you feel tension in your body? Specifically where? Act out this tension by kicking on a mattress or pounding on a pillow. The point of this exercise is to help you release and diffuse some of the unconscious tension and bring more awareness to a potentially explosive situation.

If after releasing some of the tension you still feel stirred up, you might evoke Jupiter within. Visualize a beam of healing light intervening, bringing you insight, understanding and a higher perspective about this situation. Who in your life can provide Jupiter support and perspective now?

Near-Death Experiences

Have you ever experienced a moment in your life when you thought you might die? Recall and reflect about that experience. In a group, share the experience. Did it change you? How? Do you feel differently about death now?

Death

Consider your feelings about death. Do you think about the possibility of your own death? Does it make you uncomfortable? Has anyone close to you died? In a group, divide into pairs and tell the story of the death of someone close. Let your partner be your Moon and quietly reflect your feelings. Although this exercise may restimulate sad or painful feelings, we can often find relief and healing just by "telling our story."

Study of Death

There are several excellent sources for those who want to study death. *Death and Dying in the Tibetan Tradition* (Glenn Mullin)[1] is a survey of nine Tibetan sources. It covers topics such as meditational techniques to prepare for death, inspiring accounts of the deaths of saints and sages, the experience of death and its secret and inner signs, and methods of consciousness transference.

Who Dies? (Stephen Levine)[2] is a sensitive and inspiring book to help you and loved ones face the process of death, and *Beyond Death* (Stanislav and Christina Grof)[3] draws illuminating parallels of concepts of the afterlife in different cultures, the accounts of those who survived a clinical death, the death and rebirth episodes by schizophrenic patients, and psychedelic states induced in experimental psychiatry.

MEDITATIONS AND VISUALIZATIONS

Saturn Walk

Saturn's gait is slow, heavy, laborious. Imagine that your feet weigh thirty pounds each. Better yet, attach wrap-around weights to your ankles, and move about.

Saturn Meditation

"I travel the roads of nature until the hour when I shall lie down and be at rest; yielding back my last breath into the air from which I have drawn it daily, and sinking down upon the earth from which by father derived the seed, my mother the blood, and my nurse the milk of my being" Emperor Marcus Aurelius, *Meditations*.[4]

SUGGESTED FILMS AND MUSIC

Saturn Films

Schindler's List; Breaking the Waves; Sophie's Choice; Death of a Salesman; Places in the Heart; They Shoot Horses, Don't They?; I Never Sang for My Father.

Suggested Music

"Fountain of Sorrow" (Jackson Browne), *Flesh and Bone* (Skeleton Woman), *Te Deum* (Arvo Part), *Ambient Music for Another Time* (Shadows and Light), *Working Men's*

Dead (Grateful Dead), *Symphony no. 3* (Gorecki), *Essential Blues Two* (The House of Blues), "Saturn" from *The Planets* (Holst), "Dance of Maya" (John McLaughlin), "I Want You (She's So Heavy)" *Abbey Road* (The Beatles), "Adagio for Strings" (Theme from *Platoon*—Samuel Barber), most Leonard Cohen songs: ("Dress Rehearsal Rag," "Nancy," "Desolation Row"), "Goin' Home" (Negro Spiritual), *Symphony no. 4* (Brahms), "Point Blank" *The River* (Bruce Springsteen).

URANUS AND AQUARIUS

The classical planets (those known since ancient times) from the Sun to Mars represent the sphere of personal ego. Jupiter and Saturn together represent the boundary or bridge between the personal ego and the collective unconscious. It is in this realm of the three outer planets—Uranus, Neptune, and Pluto—that we can reach an awareness of something more in life than what relates to our ego. A new dimension is added to the psyche, the awareness of energies that travel on the periphery of our everyday consciousness.

Uranus is the "primordial chaos" whose energy is erratic, unpredictable, and sudden. Like a lightning bolt, it shocks and disrupts, shaking up old foundations and patterns that have become too rigid. This can create liberating new forms which give the psyche breathing room and new possibilities for future development. If suppressed in the unconscious, this energy can explode, painfully demolishing and destroying hard-won structure. Uranus links to action that is original, creative, inventive, or even bizarre.

Individuals with strong Uranus/Aquarius energy can be highly independent. They experience change as life-restoring and they have an intuitive realization that there is more to the world than the realm of concrete thought bound by facts and the perception of the senses. If afflicted, one can exhibit categorial rejection of societal structures and explosive, unpredictable behavior. Those with little Uranus/Aquarius energy may express themselves more conservatively, fear change, or criticize those who "rock the boat."

Uranus—An "Electrifying" Experience

One of the more accessible places to experience Uranus if you're near a big city is on the trading floor of the commodities markets or stock exchanges. Visiting one can be

an exciting and unnerving experience. The intense, emotionally demanding, nerve-wracking scramble for a piece of the action where fortunes are made or lost in a matter of seconds, makes this one of the most unpredictable environments imaginable. From the early morning bell, the pits reverberate with frantic ear-crushing screams, chaos, high anxiety, pushing, pulling, and the extremes of human emotion—panic, elation, greed, insecurity, and joy. The highly unpredictable nature of the pits on a day-to-day basis, and the high risks and game playing attract those high rollers who love the freedom to be their own boss and who thrive in this environment.

Movement

Uranian movement is erratic, bizarre, and abruptly changeable. To give yourself a taste of it, turn on heavy metal rock music, and start shaking your hands vigorously. Now shake your arms, upper body, and whole body. Shake your head. Let yourself get disoriented. That's Uranus.

Unexpected Events

Expect the unexpected. One of the hardest transits to predict with accuracy is Uranus. Inevitably, you can imagine ten different possible ways to anticipate the effect of a particular Uranus transit and, true to its nature, Uranus will manifest in a way you never thought of. Try this as an experiment: Imagine ten possible manifestations of your next Uranus transit, keeping a record. Check later for any ways Uranus manifests that you hadn't considered.

Accidents

One of Uranus' favorite ways to manifest suppressed energy is through accidents. Have you had any accidents in recent years? This past year? Can you go back immediately *before* your accident and identify what was going on in your mind? Was there any anger, rebellion, or repression?

Creativity and Originality

Uranus encourages an appetite for experimentation, creativity, and the creation of new forms. Try these:

You have just inherited a suspender-making factory from your dear Auntie Nell. Because the fashion of suspenders has gone out of style, the factory has lost money.

What other uses can you think of for all those suspenders? Brainstorm as many possible alternatives as you can.

It is well-known that as human beings develop, we use less and less of our brain capacity. By the time we are grown, most of us use less than ten percent of our brain. You have been hired to come up with solutions to this problem. Brainstorm as many possibilities as you can.

Newspaper Tower

Using two sheets of newsprint and twenty-four inches of Scotch™ tape, construct the tallest tower that you can in thirty minutes. Cut, fold, or form these materials any way you like.

Space Fantasy

You are a crew member of the spaceship *Intrepid,* and you have just entered a previously unknown solar system. Your ship lands on a planet nearest its central star. Draw the environment you are now seeing for the first time.

Science Fiction

Try reading one of the plethora of science fiction books that are available. Books by Isaac Asimov, Robert Heinlein, and Clifford D. Simak are some of the best written. Stretch your own imagination to include these strange universes, worlds, and beings.

Bizarre Humor

Two cartoonists with Uranian humor, are Gary Larson (*The Far Side*) and Gahan Wilson (*Playboy* and other magazines). *The Far Side Gallery*[1] by Gary Larson is a collection of cartoons depicting his often odd humor—cigarette-smoking dinosaurs, grandmothers in bumper cars, an elephant on crutches in a phone booth. Very funny. Very strange.

Brainteasers

The last pages of the monthly magazine *Omni* is a good source of Uranian brainteasers and games of mental challenge. Or buy *Classic Puzzles*[2] by Gyles Brandreth, which includes three hundred classic puzzles involving numbers, words, shapes, and more.

Planetarium

Visit your local planetarium and see a sky show. Many sky shows create an experience of traveling outside the solar system and beyond by using sophisticated lasers, images, music, and sound effects. In Chicago, the sky show at the planetarium changes every two months, so there is always something new to see and learn about.

Uranian Art

The creative geniuses who have helped us perceive the world in new ways are examples of Uranian/Aquarian expression: the art of Pablo Picasso and Mark Chagall, or the architecture and vision of Paolo Soleri and Buckminster Fuller. If an art gallery is near, spend time experiencing their art or get books about them from your local library. Spend an evening being absorbed into their unique world of creative images and ideas.

Genius

Read biographies of the lives of individuals whose minds demonstrate creative Uranian thought processes, such as *Einstein: The Life and Times,*[3] by Ronald Clark; *The Unknown Leonardo,*[4] edited by Ladislao Reti; or *Prodigal Genius: The Life of Nikola Tesla,*[5] by J. O'Neil. Or treat yourself to the ideas in Thomas Kuhn's *The Structure of Scientific Revolution*[6] or James Gleick's *Chaos: Making a New Science.*[7]

Aliens

The phenomena of UFO's and alien abduction experiences are Uranian. Try reading books like *Communion,*[8] by Whitley Strieber, who recounts his abduction experiences, and *Intruders,*[9] by Budd Hopkins. Hopkins' book presents the results of his investigation of 135 subjects claiming abductions by aliens. These books stretch our credulity and our notions of reality.

Space Programs

What do you think is the future of our role in space? Should we plan trips to Mars or beyond? The fields of science and space have most successfully engaged the spirit of cooperation between nations. Should nations work together on joint projects in space? How do you envision this? This makes a good discussion for a group.

Electronics

Any computer or video games are Uranian. Spend the afternoon in a video arcade. Play an adventure game on your computer. If you have a modem, plug yourself into a computer conversation.

Uranian Weekend

Here is a helpful strategy for any time you are feeling bored and at the mercy of habit. Take one weekend to do as many things that vary from your normal routine as possible. Go to new places, do new things, eat foods you have never tried, wear your clothes in new combinations, hang out in Uranian environments, even brush your teeth with the other hand. It's a playful challenge to try to think of as much divergence as you can. My husband and I usually do this in February when winter sets in. We've had some great fun and pretty bizarre experiences being this spontaneous!

Future Transits

Speculate or predict what you think we'll see manifesting as Pluto continues to transit through Sagittarius? Neptune into Aquarius in 1998? Or Jupiter into Aries in 1999? How will these transits affect the field of astrology? In what new ways will astrology be a part of our culture? Can you envision astrology's potential with these particular transits? Get a group of your astrology friends together. As a group, what can you envision? Brainstorm. Let yourself imagine.

The Year 2050

What do you imagine the year 2050 will be like? What advances do you think we will have made as a species? Draw a series of sketches to depict what you guess your daily routine might be like?

MEDITATIONS AND VISUALIZATIONS

Uranus Walk

Walk quickly and erratically as if someone is zapping you with an electrical shock—spin, jump, do whatever comes into your mind. Don't censor, just do it!

Uranus Meditation

Take a trip in your imagination out of the solar system and galaxy, out of our local group of galaxies, past the galactic center to the furthest reaches of the universe. (There are some guided imagery tapes that do this.)

There is a fine film short entitled *Powers of Ten*[10] that dramatically illustrates relative distances that are so hard for us to visualize. It begins with a couple on a picnic blanket in Lincoln Park in Chicago and sequentially magnifies to images above the targeted area, past our solar system, past the galaxy, then rapidly returns through images to the couple on the picnic blanket. Although just a short ten-minute film, it puts space into perspective and gives us a direct experience of the enormity of the universe in which we live. There is also a book by the same title, describing the process of the filming, but by all means, if you get the opportunity, see the film.

SUGGESTED FILMS AND MUSIC

Uranus Films

All of the *Star Trek* films; *Alien (I, II, and III); Men in Black; Independence Day; Ed Wood; Mondo Cane; Clockwork Orange; Blade Runner; F/X; Mad Max: Beyond Thunderdome; The Man Who Fell to Earth; The Last Days of Man on Earth; Slaughterhouse Five; 2001: A Space Odyssey; The Star Wars Trilogy.*

Uranian Music

Techno music, *Dig Your Own Hole* (The Chemical Brothers), *Dead Cities* (The Future Sound of London), *Homework* (Daft Punk), *In Sides* (Orbital), the music of most electronic, heavy metal, or progressive Jazz artists. Much New Age music, especially Kitaro. "Hard Rock" (John Mclaughlin), "One Word"(John Mclaughlin), "Sheena is a Punk Rocker," "We're a Happy Family" and "I Don't Care" *Rocket to Russia* (The Ramones), "We Want the Airwaves" *Pleasant Dreams* (The Ramones), "Choke on This" and "Can't Change the World" *Choke on This* (Rhythm Pigs), "Rated X" from *Get Up with It* (Miles Davis), "Uranus, the Magician" *The Planets* (Holst).

19

NEPTUNE AND PISCES

Neptune is the most difficult planetary energy to understand because, by its nature, it symbolizes phenomena that are vague, subtle, illusory, and unclear. The urge of Saturn is to build a psychic foundation, an ego, from which to operate. Neptune is a contrary force in the psyche which is ego-denying and ego-dissolving; it grants us an awareness that the ego is not ultimately what one is.

Neptune is epitomized by the principle of entropy. A given amount of energy when released into the environment gradually becomes diluted or diffused until it appears to be dissolved into its surroundings. The amount of energy remains the same but is so diffuse that it can no longer be restored to its original form.

Neptune is a feminine force which allows us to sacrifice the goals of the ego and to immerse ourselves in the whole, into the void of the cosmic womb, returning with richer imagination, inspiration, greater sensitivity, receptivity, and human dedication. Neptune is linked to dreams, intuition, imagination, illumination, and true mysticism.

Individuals with strong Neptune/Pisces energy in their horoscope can be sensitive, idealistic, spiritual, romantic, and compassionate. If afflicted, Neptune can produce fears and phobias, cloudy misunderstanding, dependence, and escapism, especially through alcohol and drugs. Neptune is particularly difficult in a weak ego, for it can open the individual to these powerful unconscious energies with sometimes drastic consequences. Those with little Neptune/Pisces energy may not be aware of the subtle dimensions of spirit. They may be intolerant, rigid, and have little human compassion.

Neptune—An Experience

(This is best facilitated by a guide).

Imagine you are a one-celled organism living in a tiny puddle of water. This puddle is the totality of the world you know. Focus your attention on the one cell of your body. See it clearly. Now see the puddle you live in. It begins to rain again. Your puddle gets bigger. It merges with a smaller puddle on the ground next to you. Focus on your one-celled body. It continues raining. The many little puddles around you merge into a small rivulet. Now see the rivulet you live in.

You begin to float, flowing down, into more and more water. Focus on your one-celled body. The rivulet becomes a stream. See the stream you live in. You are moving with the flow of water, down into a creek. You are being propelled faster by the cumulative force of the water. Focus on your one-celled body. Now the creek joins a small river. See the river you now live in. The river gains more momentum, more volume. It winds its way into a bay and into the open ocean. Focus on your one-celled body. A wave carries you along, further and further from shore, moving you out into its great body, propelling you with its full force into its huge dimension. Feel yourself free floating moved by the rhythm of the waters.

(Guide brings you back into the bay, river, stream, rivulet and puddle, continuing to remind you to focus on the one cell of your body.)

Movement

Neptune's movement is best to visualize in water. Imagine you are a fish moving freely and fluidly. Your spine is supple, bendable, and you turn easily. You can ride the currents up and down like a roller coaster, or surface and be moved along by the wave.

Float Tank

If you live in a major metropolis, you might have access to a "samadhi tank," or float tank. Invented by dolphin researcher John Lilly, it is a large, enclosed "bathtub" which you enter by stepping through a door. After closing the door, you are in total warm darkness. The tub is filled with a saline solution so it is easy to lay down and float. The sensory deprivation and warm floating sensation feels like a return to the womb. At first, this may be scary for some. Others may adapt to it quickly and find it a nurturing, blissful experience of free-floating.

Blind Walk

Neptune deals with difficulty in seeing, the subsequent feelings of being out of control and the response of surrender. Here is an effective experience to get more deeply in touch with these feelings within ourselves. This is an ideal exercise for anyone with a strong Neptune, either natally or by transit. It can be done with one friend or in a group. (You'll need a large handkerchief or scarf for this.)

First, find a partner. One of you covers the other's eyes with the blindfold then leads the blindfolded partner preferably outside and around the block, or if time permits, to a grocery store or other public setting. Whether you are the guide or the blindfolded one, keep in touch with the different feelings you experience. Afterward, share your feelings. How does it feel to not be able to see or know where you are? How do you feel being dependent? Does this stir up feelings about current dependence or control issues? How did the guide feel? How did it feel to be depended upon?

Now switch roles and repeat the exercise. Examine your natal charts. Check for current transits. Does this reveal more to you about this experience?

Neptune/Saturn Variation: This is a good exercise for someone with a difficult Neptune/Saturn combination. It is better done indoors in a house. Ask the individual to take particular notice of the room she is in. How big is it? Where is the furniture? The doorways? The walls? Walk around with her into other rooms, helping her get familiar with the layout of the house and the relationship of the rooms to each other. Come back to the original room. Now have her cover her eyes with the blindfold. Once blindfolded, lead her into another room of the house. Give her six to eight books to carry, heavy enough to make it difficult. With you as a guide to keep them from falling into furniture, ask her to find her way back to her position in the original room. (As a guide you want to help her only when she might hurt herself, or if she appears at a high point of frustration.) This experience of feeling blind and burdened replicates what one feels like with this combination in a difficult natal or transiting aspect. Process these feelings.

Group Healing

Form a circle, sitting down. Get comfortable, loosen tight clothing, take off your shoes, and relax. Join hands and begin to breathe deeply. Become aware of a point of healing light between your eyebrows. Let it slowly grow and intensify. Let it fill your whole head. Now expand it to include your whole body. When you've done this, envision going around the circle to every person, bathing them with your healing light. Now take turns, one at a time, sitting in the center of the circle. With each new person, focus your full attention on them. Send them healing. Repeat their name silently, asking that your healing light be received. Those in the center should try to be as receptive as possible to the subtle spiritual energy being generated on their behalf.

Variation: Sit in a circle and begin to chant as a group. A most effective chant is the universal cosmic sound, "Aum " (pronounced "ah-omm. ") Repeat it at your own rhythm and soon there will be a beautiful vocal symphony all around you. Let it stop of its own accord.

Vocables

I am a part of a ritual group in Chicago that (among other things) chants vocables. We begin with the "Aum" chant. Then we each express ourselves, allowing whatever sound feels appropriate to move through us. It produces haunting group sounds which linger into the silence.

Subtle Healing Forms

Neptune is symbolized by holistic subtle healing forms such as the Bach flower remedies, healing with gems and crystals, and Reiki energy balancing. Learn more about them. Have healing work done on you. Do you feel its effects?

A Contemplative Retreat

From time to time we all seek solitude and withdrawal from the world. Take a week or weekend retreat at a Zen Buddhist monastery or participate in a weekend intensive at a spiritual community.

Drugs and Addictions

If you want to learn more about the subtle, sometimes insidious process of Neptune, attend an open meeting of Alcoholics Anonymous or Adult Children of Alcoholics. Get a copy of the Twelve Steps Toward Recovery. Listen to what the group members have to say about their lives.

Are you the child of an alcoholic? Or an alcoholic or drug abuser yourself? Many of us have addictions of a different sort—sugar, smoking, sex, relationships, work, or success. They are still addictions, none the less. Do the characteristics of one affected by alcohol fit you? Do you need help?

Does your chart show a tendency toward addiction? If so, be very attentive toward yourself under difficult Neptune transits.

Activities of Neptune

Go to Neptune's world by swimming at your local pool or scuba diving on your next vacation. How do you feel in water? In a swimming pool versus the ocean? Have your fears ever gotten the best of you? Or do you feel no fear at all? Is this reflective of your natal chart?

Photography

Neptune is associated with the realm of images. Gather a group of photographs. Include personal ones and those you find in magazines. Is your Neptune in Virgo? Examine these photos for detail. Analyze what you see. Is your Neptune in Libra? Look for the sense of balance in the photos. How is it composed? Is there a balance of contrast? Color? Is your Neptune in Scorpio? What sense of feeling is expressed in the photo? What was the mood of the photographer who took the picture?

Visionary Art

There are increasing numbers of visionary artists. A stunning series of paintings depicting the Sun, Moon, planets and stars is *Visions of the Universe*,[1] painted by Kazuaki Iwasaki. It is published by The Cosmos Store, a division of Carl Sagan Productions. Any astrologer working with experiential methods will appreciate the beautiful images in this book.

MEDITATIONS AND VISUALIZATIONS

Neptune Walk

Walk as you might the moment after you have just met your soulmate. Move in a dreamy, flowing, light-hearted manner feeling blissful and at peace.

Neptune Meditation

In Eastern tradition, the subtle energy field that surrounds all living things is known as the aura. The aura is a constantly shifting pattern, color, and intensity much like what happens in the phenomena of the Aurora Borealis. From time to time our auras will be more porous, sucking up psychic energy from anyone around us. Sometimes you will feel this by experiencing inexplicable moods, feelings of inner fuzziness or confusion, or a clingy, dependent feeling. To resolve these feelings, first cleanse your aura by physically exercising and/or taking a shower. Allow the water to run over you from your head to your toes. Imagine the disturbing vibrations washing right off you. Dry yourself off, get dressed, sit down, and immediately try this meditation. Its purpose is to create the inner strength to protect your aura.

Take a few deep breaths and quiet your mind. Focus your attention on the Ajna chakra, the point between your eyebrows. See a silver thread coming out of it, circling you, and creating a protective silver cocoon. Now see a golden thread coming out, circling you and creating a protective golden cocoon. Feel the safety of being encircled in this lunar/solar cocoon.

See yourself engulfed in this totally protective energy. Mentally say to yourself, "I will only take in energy of light." Do this as long as it takes to feel a return of balance.

If you believe you are absorbing negative energy from an individual and still have to be around them, reinforce this visualization for a few minutes before being in their company. You can strengthen your aura consciously this way.

SUGGESTED FILMS AND MUSIC

Neptune Films

Leaving Las Vegas; Toy Story; any animated film, especially the animated spoof of Disney's *Fantasia*, by Bruno Bozzetto; *Allegro Non Troppo; Lady Sings the Blues; Days of Wine and Roses; One Flew over the Cuckoo's Nest; The Heart Is a Lonely Hunter.*

Suggested Music

Canticles of Ecstasy, Vision (Hildegard von Bingen), *Soma,* (Steve Roach), *Music for Zen Meditation* (Tony Scott, Shinicki Yuize, and Hozan Yamamoto), *Cape Cod Ocean*

Surf (Moods Recordings), *Sailboat Voyage* (Mood Recordings), "Sanctuary" (John McLaughlin), *Discrete Music* (Brian Eno), *Tibetan Bells* (Henry Wolff/Nancy Hennings), *Ancient Echoes* (Steve Halpern and Georgia Kelly), *Music for Airports* (Brian Eno), "Lucy in the Sky with Diamonds" *Magical Mystery Tour* (The Beatles), "Lullaby"(Brahms), "Song of the Seashore"(James Galway), "Hosanna" (Berlioz), *Inside the Taj Mahal* (Paul Horn), "When You Wish Upon a Star," Gregorian Chants.

20

PLUTO AND SCORPIO

As the planet farthest out in the solar system, Pluto symbolizes the deepest, most profound level of change possible in the human psyche. It is the primordial feminine power that intrudes on consciousness and cannot be placated by will or reason. Pluto, mythologically, is the ancient Sumerian goddess of the Underworld, Ereshkigal, whose origins predate that of the Greek god Hades and the Roman god Pluto. She symbolizes the deep inward journey that each of us embarks upon after losing something precious. For most of us, this is not done consciously or willingly, but by inner forces that compel us to enter the purifying fire that separates one level of existence from another.

Pluto sounds like a grim unwelcome process. Yet when seen from the full light of the soul, it is a necessary process that returns balance to the deep psyche. In responding to this urge to penetrate our own depths and to know "the self" fully, we confront the "demons" of an unbalanced ego *(hubris),* desire, and power. By sustaining our courage and tenacity, we release our particular demons, integrate this raw power, and emerge with the gift of wholeness that contains within it a storehouse of psychic and spiritual riches.

Individuals with strong Pluto/Scorpio energy exhibit great intensity and forcefulness, sexual magnetism and charisma, and a capacity for relentless effort and in-depth healing. If afflicted, one may be power hungry, ego-centered, jealous, possessive, coercive or cruel. Those with little Pluto/Scorpio energy may fall victim to the onslaught of their own repressed energy by chronically ignoring what needs to be changed, or they may fall victim to someone else's abuse of power.

Because Pluto is likely to express itself through intensity and complexity, many Pluto experiences require competent guides. We need to be aware of the possibility that an individual will feel overwhelmed by the unconscious forces they have unleashed.

Dealing with Pluto energies effectively require two prerequisites—expertise in dealing with deep, sometimes scary realms, and adequate time to fully process the resulting stimulated unconscious material.

Shamanic Wounding

Shamanism is a phenomena that spans millennia and has been a part of almost every culture on the planet. A shaman is a priest or priestess who acts as mediator between the worlds of the conscious and the unconscious. They are healers of the psyche who use systems of coded symbols and images, providing a language for the unconscious and a means to express otherwise inexpressible psychic states.

In ancient days, the astrologers were the shaman-priests. Now, more astrologers are returning to the vital healing role of "midwife" to the psyche, creating the means and methods to help ourselves and others effectively deal with Pluto energy.

The concept of the wounded healer is significant for astrologers working in a healing capacity today. Carl Jung considered the true healer to be one who has been wounded, who has experienced both the wound and the healing process. As astrologers, we can only accompany others as far as we have gone ourselves. To lead another beyond the threshold of the unconscious, we must have traveled there ourselves.

Pluto transits often activate spiritual, physical or emotional trauma that catapults us into the inner workings of this wounding crisis. Once these experiences of suffering, dying, and rebirth are integrated, we can use the special knowledge of these powerful states for healing ourselves and others. By guiding those who are facing Plutonian forces, some for the first time, we can help to release and relieve the unconscious pressures within and assist our friend or client toward understanding, transforming, and integrating Pluto's energy.

There is an excellent experience of the wounding of Pluto devised by Jean Houston called the "Sacred Wound." It is a three-hour process done alone with a guide or with a group. You are asked a series of questions to stimulate a retelling of the story of your wound and then to repeat it in its mythic proportions. The exercise can be found in *Magical Blend* magazine (issue no. 17, p. 56) or in Jean's book, *The Search for the Beloved*, published by Jeremy P. Tarcher (Los Angeles).

Other good general sources for reading about the world of the shaman is the series of books by Carlos Castaneda, relating his experiences with the sorcerer Don Juan,[1] as

232

well as *Black Elk Speaks*[2] (John Neihardt), *Lame Deer: Seeker of Visions* (John Lame Deer and Richard Erdoes), or *Shamanic Voices*[3] (Joan Halifax).

Shamanic Journeying

Shamanic journeying is a system of psychological and physical techniques to alter states of consciousness without drugs and to enter the "non-ordinary" realm of the shaman. Journeys are deep, imaginal trips to the "Underworld" and the "Upper World." By utilizing trance, drumming, and guided imagery, one enters through a crack in consciousness into shamanic territory.

One of the best and most available resource for shamanic journeying is *The Way of the Shaman*[4] (Michael Harner). Harner offers a basic introduction of techniques gathered from his research as an anthropologist and from his experience with South and North American Shamans.

Powerline

This is an exercise to be used with a group that has interacted at least several times before. It will not work well with a new group.

First, ask the group to form a line. Designate what direction represents the "Front" and "Back" of the line. Pay particular attention to each individual's changing responses as the exercise proceeds. (Participants pay attention to your own responses.) As a group, arrange yourselves in order of the most powerful group member standing at the front of the line to the least powerful standing at the back. Do this silently. Any member can move any other to a position they feel is appropriate for that person. Let the line keep changing until there is a consensus. (This may not happen.) As a facilitator, watch the process carefully. Does anyone immediately go to the back? Front? Stay noncommittal between the two? Who moves people? Who waits for others to decide their position? This is remarkably revealing of how each person feels about their power among others, as well as how they may be held captive by certain feelings about power. After the exercise, allow the group plenty of time to express their feelings and to process what came up. Share your observations. Have each individual examine Pluto, both in their natal chart and by transit. Does this clarify their particular reactions?

Variation: Here is an exercise you can do on your own. Analyze a current situation in which you are involved with others. Determine and observe the lines of power. Who has the most power by title? Who actually has more power? Who aligns with who? Draw up a chart showing these lines of power. Where do you fit in? Are you one of the most powerful? Least? Are you satisfied with your position in the line of power?

Secrets

This is an interesting way to activate your feelings about secrets. In a group, pass out identical paper and pens. Each person writes down a secret they have never told anyone. Put the secrets in a hat or bowl placed in the center. Each person takes a turn drawing out a secret. Read this secret aloud to the group as if it were your own. If you draw your own, read it anyway. Elaborate about the secret. Fill in its details. Stay aware of your feelings during this process. How do you feel about others' secrets? Did any secrets shock you? In your opinion, are there some "worse" secrets than yours? Can you sympathize with the writer of each particular secret? How does it feel to reveal a private part of yourself?

Body Therapies

Body therapies such as Reichian release work, Bioenergetics, and Rolfing deal with releasing blocked energy within the body. From the premise that repressed, unintegrated emotional and traumatic experiences get locked in the body as a form of body armor, these techniques focus on energy and releasing these traumas through specific, sustained body positions or deep tissue massage. *Rediscovery of the Body* by Charles Garfield is a useful overview of the body therapies.

Parts of Myself I Do Not Like to See

Pluto will put us in touch with aspects of ourselves we don't want to acknowledge. It is this repressed, dissociated energy that presses up from the unconscious in order to be seen and integrated. What parts of your psyche have you seen glimpses of within you that you haven't really looked at or reflected upon? If these parts continue to be pushed aside, you could expect your next Pluto transit to stir them up. What can you do now to begin to come to terms with these repressed energies?

Resentments

Make a list of resentments. Do you resent anyone in your life now? Why? Have similar feelings of resentment been stimulated before? Can you recognize an unconscious repetitive pattern at work? If you are in a group, break into pairs. Talk about your resentful feelings.

Do you feel resentment toward a particular person? Symbolically, place that person in front of you in your mind's eye. As directly and unemotionally as possible, tell them why you feel resentment toward them. Be specific. Try to surround that person and yourself in a circle of love to dissipate the Mars/Pluto energy. Say "I forgive you. I forgive myself." Repeat this.

Variation: Pair up with a partner. One person chooses to be their own Pluto. The other becomes that person's Moon. The Moon's function is to silently sit, witness, and reflect the feelings shared by Pluto. Those playing their Pluto tell the Moon about their desires, resentments, hurts, ambitions, etc. When Pluto has exhausted her feelings about these areas, switch roles (Source: Jeff Jawer).

Ceremonial Ritual

Ceremonial ritual is done worldwide in all healthy cultures. These deeply symbolic, often annual rites, allow an individual and the community a pause from daily activities to reintegrate and commune with the primal, archetypal undercurrents of the psyche. The annual Summer Solstice Sundance of Native American and other ceremonial communities is an example. Typically, the Native American ritual is four days and four nights of continuous dancing, drumming, and praying. Some of these are open to the public and offer an opportunity to observe these special ceremonial rituals.

Living "On the Edge"

Take a trip into Pluto's realm on a challenging and demanding wilderness river rafting trip. There are a number of groups for men, women, or both that offer this type of river rafting or canoeing trip. A week trip on a fast river has all the characteristics of Pluto. It is totally absorbing, demanding, and filled with physical and emotional highs and lows. There are points of pure exhilaration when you successfully navigate a difficult rapid, or heart-stopping moments of fear as a boat flips and you see your friend tumbling, totally at the mercy of the turbulent water. Worse yet is the prospect that you yourself might be thrown from the boat, or your boat sucked into a hole. Anything is possible as you face life on a challenging stretch of river. Experiences like these can offer a wonderful feeling of satisfaction.

Sexuality

Mars and the more intense Pluto are both associated with our sexuality. Either alone or in a group, spend time recalling your most exciting sexual experience! (Obviously, this would not work well with a new group, or in a group where trust has not been established.) When was your last exciting sexual experience? Can you describe it to one individual or to the group?

Variations: What part of your body don't you like? When you go to bed with someone the first time, what part of your body are you embarrassed by? What turns you on sexually? What parts of your body are most erotic?

Tantra

The ancient yogic practice of Tantra is a Plutonian pathway to higher states of consciousness and control. By beginning with the most accessible energy, sexual attraction, a springboard is created to more subtle realms. The practice cultivates sexuality by integrating the subtle forces in the human body with the goal of achieving a dynamic balance between the dual and opposing energies called yin and yang. Here are some recommended books on Tantra: *Tantrism: Its Secret Principles and Practices* (Benjamin Walker), *Tantra in Tibet* (H. H. Dalai Lama, Tsong-ka-pa and Jeffrey Hopkins), *Tools for Tantra* (Harish Gohari), *Tantra for the West* (Marcus Allen) and *Sexual Secrets* (Nick Douglas and Penny Slinger).

Taboos

Taboos, whether personal or societal, are usually instituted on grounds of morality. What societal taboos can you think of? What are your personal taboos? Have you ever violated a societal taboo? A personal one? If you are addressing this in a group, can you tell the others about it?

Nuclear Annihilation

In a group, discuss what you think the odds are of a nuclear war in your lifetime? Spend time processing the feelings summoned up by this discussion.

AIDS

This complex issue is facing all of us. How do we deal with AIDS on an individual level? As a culture? As a world community? How do we protect the rights of those carrying the virus, and the rights of those that are not? How do we pay for the enormous medical expenses for such a large group? How do we deal with issues of testing, confidentiality, and prejudice? Do you know anyone who has AIDS? Do you know anyone who has died of AIDS?

Magic

Magic and magical operations fall under the category of Pluto. Many of us unconsciously work magic daily. On the simplest level, magic is the ability to influence the world by psychic means. It is the power to influence and ultimately control one's own space-time reality and eventually to control the space-time reality of others. An excellent source to learn more about magic is *Natural Magic: The Magical State of Being* [5] by Barry Saxe. It is particularly lucid, well-documented, and fascinating reading. A respected and well-known series of five books on magic, *The Magical Philosophy*, [6] was written by Melita Danning and Osborne Phillips. *The Practice of Magical Evocation* [7] by Franz Bardon and numerous books by occultist Dion Fortune [8] are among other resources for specific use and technique.

One Hour to Live

You have seen the future and now know you have but sixty minutes left of your life on earth. What would you need to say to those around you? Who do you have unfinished business with?

Scruples

The board game of Scruples couldn't be more Scorpion. It is a game of self-evaluation in which you knowingly make a decision to tell the truth or an untruth. This game puts you and your friends into a number of provocative ethical situations to which you must, after some soul-searching, respond. Would you pose nude for a national magazine for $10,000? You and a stranger hail a cab at the same time. As the cab pulls up, do you insist the cab is yours? You witness a car accident in which one party is clearly to blame. Do you come forward to testify? Sometimes you answer truthfully. Or anticipating how your friends think you'll respond, you give the opposite reply. Then you must convince the group of the sincerity of your reply. Very Scorpion and thought-provoking.

MEDITATIONS AND VISUALIZATIONS

Pluto Walk

Pluto's walk is intense and intimidating. Walk with power, strength, and passion. Pretend you are Hades coming out of the bowels of the earth to capture Persephone.

SUGGESTED FILMS AND MUSIC

Pluto Films

Mulholland Falls; Shawshank Redemption; Pretty Woman; Fatal Attraction; Basic Instinct; Testament; Bang the Drum Slowly; Deliverance; Shoah; My Fair Lady; The Godfather; The Lion in Winter; The Burning Bed.

Suggested Music

Hearing Solar Winds (The Harmonic Choir and David Hykes), *Tantric Songs* (Popul Vuh), *Totem* (Gabrielle Roth), *Chaotic Meditation* (Music of the Shree Rajneesh Ashram), *Dark Side of the Moon* (Pink Floyd), "I'm Not in Love" (10 cc), "Prelude to Lohengrin" (Wagner), and much of the work of Wagner, *Apocalypse Now* soundtrack, Te Deum (Berlioz), "Battle of the Huns" (Liszt), "Night on Bald Mountain" (Mussorgsky), Gloria (Vivaldi), Cho-ga: Tantric and Ritual Music of Tibet.

AFTERWORD: EXPERIENTIAL ASTROLOGY AROUND THE WORLD

The recent history of experiential astrology has been quite exciting, with a number of my colleagues hard at work on its development. Two particular examples come to mind: the "Roots Conferences" and the "Planet Camps." Kelley Hunter (of Vermont and the Virgin Islands) organized "Roots," a series of experiential conferences held for six consecutive summers (1988–1993). Always focusing on concurrent dynamic astrological transits, these events drew on the planetary energy of the moment and included four to five days of interactive and contemplative group and individual activities. The groups of 40 to 100 were facilitated by six experiential astrologers, who took turns leading an evolving psycho-spiritual process toward a celebratory finale, usually a three-hour (sometimes all night!) outdoor Full Moon Dance complete with professional conga drummers, costumes, a bonfire, a glorious night sky, and exuberant, heart-felt dancing. Definitely astrology *alive*. Somewhat similar, but with their own unique flavors, were the "Planet Camps," sponsored in 1991 and 1994 by the *Mountain Astrologer* magazine (and in 1995 by another group of hardy experientialists), and the 1996 "New Zealand Planet Camp," organized by Christine Broadbent.

Jeff Jawer, one of the founders of experiential astrology, has been involved with experiential methods since the mid-1970s. He has written many articles on experiential astrology and been one of its most dedicated advocates in the United States and Europe. Jeff and his French wife, Danick, who is an astrologer, singer, and musician, have conducted experiential workshops in Europe every summer since 1990. Their unique and popular workshops emphasize the use of astrodrama and music; they regularly present their work in France, Germany, Switzerland, and Holland.

They are now in San Diego, California, where they will also be offering lively experiential workshops.

Importantly, many of the major astrological conferences now have experiential tracks included in their programs. The United Astrology Congress has had such a track since its inception in 1986 (thanks in part to Marion March), as have the annual Astrological Association conference in England, The World Congress in Switzerland, and the conferences sponsored by the Chiron Center in Melbourne, Australia. In the United States, experiential workshops and tracks have been regularly included at the conferences of ISAR (International Society for Astrological Research) and the ARC (Aquarian Revelation Conference.) In addition, six astrological schools around the world now either sponsor experiential workshops (Astrodata in Zurich, the Chiron Centre in Melbourne, the Dublin Astrological Center in Dublin), or offer extensive experiential training programs (The Empress Center in London, Astrologskolen in Copenhagen, and Stichting Achernar, i.e. "School for Astrology," in Amsterdam).

All around the world, experiential astrology is *alive and well!*

Finally, let me offer a resource for keeping track of these exciting developments, *Astrology Alive: The Website,* at this Internet address:

<http://www.lightworks.com/Astrology/Alive/>.

NOTES AND REFERENCES

Introduction

1 Gregory Bateson and Mary Catherine Bateson, Angels Fear, New York: Macmillan, 1987, p.18.

2 Manilius, Astronomics, vol. 5, paraphrased in Franz Cumont, Astrology and Religion among the Greeks and Romans, New York: Dover, 1960, p. 79.

3 Ptolemy, Anthol. Palat., ix, 577, quoted in Franz Cumont, Astrology and Religion among the Greeks and Romans, New York: Dover, 1960, p. 81.

4 Sally P. Springer and George Deutsch. Left Brain, Right Brain, (Revised Edition), New York: Freeman, 1985.

5 Jean Houston, The Possible Human, Los Angeles: Jeremy Tarcher, 1982, p. 11.

6 Ibid., pp. 134–145.

7 For Erickson, see Jay Haley, Uncommon Therapy, New York: W. W. Norton, 1973. Milton Erickson and Earnest Rossi, Hypnotic Realities, New York: John Wiley and Sons, 1976.
For Neurolinguistic Programming, see Richard Bandler and John Grinder, Frogs into Princes, Moab, Utah: Real People Press, 1979.
Steve Lankton, Practical Magic, Cupertino, California: Meta Publications, 1980.

8 Stephen Arroyo, Astrology, Psychology and the Four Elements, Davis, California: CRCS Publications, 1975, p. xiii.

9 Harvey Cox, cited in Doris LaChapelle and Janet Bourque, Earth Festivals, Silverton, Colorado: Finn Hill Arts, 1976, p. 63.

Chapter 1 Introducing Experiential Astrology

1 Jeff Jawer, "Living the Drama of the Horoscope," Astrology Now, Vol. 22, 1979, pp. 12–15, 55–58.

2 Jamake Highwater cites the "95,140 combined body movements which have been laboriously calculated" for ancient Greek dance in his Dance: Rituals of Experience, Methuen, Toronto, 1985, p. 42.

3 Aristophanes, Frogs, vv. 340–350, tr. B. B. Rogers, cited in Mylonas, Eleusis and the Eleusinian Mysteries, Princeton University Press, Princeton NJ, 1961, pp. 254–255.

4 Lucian, on dancing, 15, cited in S. Angus, The Mystery Religions, p. 90.

5 Themistios, preserved in *Stobaios, IV*, p. 107, (Meineke), cited in Mylonas, *Eleusis and the Eleusinian Mysteries*, pp. 264–265.

6 Pindar. *Fragm*. 102 (Oxford) cited in Mylonas, *Eleusis and the Eleusinian Mysteries*, 1961, p. 285.

7 George E. Mylonas, *Eleusis and the Eleusinian Mysteries*, Princeton NJ: Princeton University Press, 1961, p. 284.

Chapter 2 Ancient Roots: Nothing New under the Sun

1 Eugenio Garin in Victor A. Velen and Elizabeth Velen (Trans.), *Portraits from the Quattrocentro*, New York, 1972, p. 156.

2 Charles Boer (Trans.), *Marsilio Ficino's Book of Life*, Dallas, TX, Spring Publications, 1980.

3 *Grolier Encyclopedia*, Grolier Electronic Publications, 1992.

4 Marsilio Ficino in Charles Boer (Trans.), *Marsilio Ficino's Book of Life*, Dallas, TX, Spring Publications, 1980, p. 87.

5 Noel Cobb, in his Foreword to Thomas Moore, *The Planets Within: The Astrological Psychology of Marsilio Ficino*, Lindisfarne Press, 1982, unpaginated.

6 Charles Boer (Trans.), *Marsilio Ficino's Book of Life*, Dallas, TX, Spring Publications, 1980, p. xiv.

7 *Ibid.*, p. xvi.

8 James Hillman, *Archetypal Psychology*, Dallas, TX, Spring Publications, 1983, p. 6.

9 *Ibid.*, p. 10.

10 James Hillman, "Plotino, Ficino, and Vico," *Loose Ends*, Dallas, TX, Spring Publications, 1975, p. 155.

11 James Hillman, "Preface: A Memoir from the Author." *Re-Visioning Psychology*. Harper Perenial Edition, 1992, p. xi.

12 James Hillman, *Archetypal Psychology*, Dallas, TX, Spring Publications, 1983

13 James Hillman, *The Soul's Code*, New York, London House, 1996.

14 Thomas Moore, *Care of the Soul*, New York, Harper Collins, 1992.

15 Thomas Moore, *The Planets Within: The Astrological Psychology of Marsilio Ficino*, Lindisfarne Press, 1982, p. 58.

16 Marsilio Ficino, in Charles Boer (Trans.), *Marsilio Ficino's Book of Life*, Dallas, TX, Spring Publications, 1980, p. 20.

17 Thomas Moore, *The Planets Within: The Astrological Psychology of Marsilio Ficino*, Lindisfarne Press, 1982, p. 65.

18 *Ibid.*, p. 66.

19 *Ibid.*, p. 70.

20 *Ibid.*, p. 125.

21 D. P. Walker, *Spiritual and Demonic Magic*, Notre Dame University of Notre Dame Press, 1975, p. 31.

22 Richard Tarnas, *Prometheus, the Awakener*, Oxford, Auriel Press, 1993, p. 8.

23 Paul Oskar Kristeller, *Eight Philosophers of the Italian Renaissance*, Stanford, CA, Stanford University Press, 1964.

24 Marsilio Ficino, in Paul Oskar Kristeller, *Eight Philosophers of the Italian Renaissance*, Stanford, CA, Stanford University Press, 1964, p. 49.

25 James Hillman, *Archetypal Psychology*, Dallas, TX, Spring Publications, 1983, p. 25.

26 Marsilio Ficino, *The Letters of Marsilio Ficino*, New York, Columbia University Press, 1985, Vol. 2, p. 33.

27 For the date, see Paul Oskar Kristeller. Preface to *The Letters of Marsilio Ficino*, New York, Columbia University Press, 1985. I concur with Ruth Clydesdale ("A Solar Talisman: Marsilio Ficino's Holistic Astrology," in *Mountain Astrologer*, August–September, 1996, p. 24, that the many references in Ficino's letters suggest the time of 12:40 GMT.

28 Ioan Couliano, *Eros and Magic in the Renaissance*, Chicago, University of Chicago Press, 1987, p. 46.

29 Paul Oskar Kristeller, Preface to *The Letters of Marsilio Ficino*, New York, Columbia University Press, 1985, Vol. 1, p. xxi.

30 Marsilio Ficino, *The Letters of Marsilio Ficino*, New York, Columbia University Press, 1985, Vol. 1–3.

31 Charles Boer (Trans.), *Marsilio Ficino's Book of Life*, Dallas, TX, Spring Publications, 1980, p. viii.

32 D. P. Walker, *Spiritual and Demonic Magic*, Notre Dame University of Notre Dame Press, 1975, p. 30.

33 Marsilio Ficino, *The Letters of Marsilio Ficino*, New York, Columbia University Press, 1985, p. 123.

34 E. H. Gombrich, *Gombrich on the Renaissance*, Vol. 2: Symbolic Images, London, Phaidon Press, 1972, p. 41.

35 *Ibid.*, 1972, p. 36.

36 *Ibid.*, p. 40.

37 Thomas Moore, *The Planets Within: The Astrological Psychology of Marsilio Ficino*, Lindesfarne Press, 1982, p. 138.

38 *Ibid.*, p. 137.

39 Erwin Panofsky, *Renaissance and Renascences in Western Art*, New York, Harper & Row, 1960.

40 See, for example, Edgar Wind, *Pagan Mysteries in the Renaissance*, New York, W.W. Dutton, 1968; Charles Dempsey, *The Portrayal of Love*, Princeton, NJ, Princeton University Press, 1992; Joanne Snow-Smith, *The Primavera of Sandro Botticelli*, New York, Peter Lang, 1993.

41 Craft, Bob "Psyche and Eros." Unpublished address. The Astrology World Congress, Lucerne, May, 1996.

42 E. H. Gombrich, *Gombrich on the Renaissance*, Vol. 2: Symbolic Images, London, Phaidon Press, 1972, p. 41.

43 *Ibid.*, p. 41–42.

44 Marsilio Ficino, Thomas Moore, *The Planets Within: The Astrological Psychology of Marsilio Ficino*, Lindesfarne Press, 1982, p. 139.

Chapter 3 Modern Roots of Experiential Astrology

1 Dane Rudhyar, *Astrology and the Modern Psyche*, Vancouver WA: CRCS Publications, 1976, pp. 2–34.
2 *Ibid.*, p. 5.
3 *Ibid.*, p. vii.
4 Carl Jung, cited in Dane Rudhyar, *Astrology and the Modern Psyche*, 1976, p. 24.
5 Carl Jung, *Memories, Dreams, Reflections*, New York: Vintage Books, 1965, p. 158.
6 Joseph Campbell, *The Portable Jung*, New York: Penguin Books, 1976, p. xxii.
7 Carl Jung, "Archetypes of the Collective Unconscious," in *The Archetypes and the Collective Unconscious*, Second Edition, Princeton NJ: Princeton University Press, 1968, pp. 3–4.
8 *Ibid.*, p. 5.
9 Carl Jung, "Psychological Aspects of the Mother Archetype," in *The Archetypes and the Collective Unconscious*, p. 79.
10 Joseph Moreno, *Psychodrama*, Vol. I, Beacon House, Beacon NY, 1946.
11 Rudhyar, *Astrology and the Modern Psyche*, p. 69.
12 Michael P. Nichols and Melvin Zax, *Catharsis in Psychotherapy*, New York: Gardner Press, 1977, p. 73.
13 M. H. Klein, P. L. Mathieu, E. T. Gendlin, and D. J. Kiesler, *The Experiencing Scale: A Research and Training Manual*, Bureau of Audio-Visual Instruction, University of Wisconsin Extension, 1970.
14 Claudio Naranjo, "I and Though, Here and Now: Contributions of Gestalt Therapy," Chapter III in F. Douglas Stephenson, ed., *Gestalt Therapy Primer*, New York: Jason Aronson, 1978, p. 38.
15 Wilhelm Reich, *The Function of the Orgasm*, New York: World Publishing, 1971.
See also:
   Alexander Lowen, *The Language of the Body*, New York: Collier Books, 1971.
   Stanley Keleman, *Your Body Speaks Its Mind*, New York: Simon & Schuster, 1981.
16 Paramahansa Yogananda, *Autobiography of a Yogi*, Los Angeles: Self-Realization Fellowship, 1974, p. 279.
17 Ken Wilbur, *Up From Eden*, Shambhala, Boulder, CO, 1983.
See also:
   Stanislav Grof, *Beyond the Brain*, Albany NY, State University of New York, 1985.
   Robert N. Walsh and Frances Vaughan, (Eds.), *Beyond Ego*, J. P. Tarcher, Los Angeles, 1980.
18 Stanislav Grof, *Beyond the Brain*, Albany NY, State University of New York, 1985, 393–394.

Chapter 4 Using Experiential Astrology

1 Carl Fitzpatrick. Personal Communication, 1986.

Chapter 5 Birthing Venus Within: A Plantary Example

1 Ron Tanner and Cynthia Connop, *Secrets of Sacred Sex,* Triple Image Film Productions. Available in the US at 1-800-2LIVING.

2 Joseph Kramer, *Fire on the Mountain: An Intimate Guide to Male Genital Massage,* EroSpirit Research, Inc. Available in the US from *Tantra Magazine Bazaar,* 1-800-341-8272.

3 Annie Sprinkle and Maria Beatty, *Sluts and Goddesses.* Available in the US from *Tantra Magazine Bazaar,* 1-800-341-8272.

4 Hesiod, *Theogony: The Poems of Hesiod,* Norman, OK, University of Oklahoma Press, 1983, p. 25.

5 Thomas Moore, *The Planets Within: The Astrological Psychology of Marsilio Ficino,* Lindesfarne Press, 1982.

6 Margo Woods, *Masturbation, Tantra and Self-Love,* San Diego, CA, Mho and Mho Works, 1981.

7 Georg Feuerstein, *Sacred Sexuality,* Los Angeles, CA, Jeremy Tarcher, 1992, p. 140.

8 David Frawley, *Tantric Yoga and the Wisdom Goddesses,* Salt Lake City, Utah, 1994, pp. 29–30.

9 Margo Woods, Margo Woods, *Masturbation, Tantra and Self-Love,* San Diego, CA, Mho and Mho Works, 1981, p. 21–22.

10 Barbara Schermer, "Psyche's Tasks: A Path of Initiation for Women," in Gloria Star (Ed.), *Astrology for Women,* St. Paul, MN: Llewellyn, 1997.

11 Simone de Beauvoir, *Letters to Sartre,* New York, Arcade, 1990.

12 Apuleius, (*Metamorphoses*) *The Golden Ass,* Bloomington, IN, Indiana University Press, 1960.

13 Barbara Schermer," Psyche's Tasks: A Path of Initiation for Women," in Gloria Star (Ed.), *Astrology for Women,* St. Paul, MN: Llewellyn, 1997.

14 Nor Hall, *The Moon and the Virgin: Reflections on the Archetypal Feminine,* New York: Harper & Row, 1980, p. 11.

15 James Hillman, *The Thought of the Heart and The Soul of the World,* Dallas, TX, Spring Publications, 1992, p. 47.

16 (Novalis). Cited in Chistopher Bamford, "The Magic of Romance: The Cultivation of Eros from Sappho to the Troubadours," *Alexandria,* Vol. 2, Grand Rapids, MI, Phanes Press, 1993, p. 290.

17 C. G. Jung, "Civilization in Transition," *Collected Works,* Volume 10, p. 90.

18 Helen Fisher, *Anatomy of Love,* New York, Fawcett Columbine, 1992, p. 52.

19 Astrology flourishes there, too. See, for example, my web site:
    <http://lightworks.com/Astrology/Alive/>.

20 Henry Corbin, "The Jasmine of the Fedeli D'Amore," *Sphinx* Vol. 3, London, The London Convivium for Archetypal Studies, 1990, p. 195.

21 Marsilio Ficino. In Thomas Moore (Ed.), *The Education of the Heart*, New York: HarperCollins, 1996, p. 172.

Chapter 6 Do It Yourself!
1 Jose and Miriam Arguelles, *Mandala,* Berkeley and London: Shambhala, 1972, p. 12.
2 This is a useful oversimplification of ideas found in Wilhelm Reich, *The Function of the Orgasm.*
3 Ida P. Rolf, *Rolfing*, New York: Harper & Row, 1977.
4 Barbara Brown, *New Mind, New Body*, New York: Harper & Row, 1975.
5 Lucerne Valley, CA: Geetam Rajneesh Sannyas Ashram, 1979.

Chapter 8 Healing with the Power of Images
1 Jean Achterberg, *Imagery in Healing*, p. 7.
2 G. Prince. "Putting the Other Half of the Brain to Work," *Training: The Magazine of Human Resources Development*, 15 (1978): 57–61, cited in Sally B. Springer and George Deutsch, *Left-Brain, Right Brain*, p. 247.
3 David Galin, cited in Sally B. Springer and George Deutsch, *Left Brain, Right Brain*, p. 261.

Chapter 9 Balancing Your Difficult Transits
1 Jung, *Memories, Dreams, Reflections*, p. 346.
2 *Ibid.,* p. 345.
3 Edward Rice, *Eastern Definitions*, Garden City, NY: Anchor Doubleday, 1980, p. 409.
4 *Ibid.,* p. 408.
5 Swami Satyeswarananda Giri, *Lahiri Mahasay*, Self-published, 1983, p. 92.
6 Paramahansa Yogananda, *Autobiography of a Yogi*, San Rafael, California: Self-Realization Fellowship, 1974, p. 275–276.
7 *Ibid.,* p. 278.
8 *Ibid.,* p. 278.
9 *Ibid.,* p. 275.
10 Mohandas K. Gandhi, cited in Robert T. Jones' background article included with the libretto for the Chicago Lyric Opera performance of Phillip Glass' "Satyagraha," New York: CBS Masterworks, 1987.
11 *Ibid.*
12 Lama Anagarika Govinda, *The Way of the White Clouds*, Boulder, Colorado: Shambhala, 1970.
13 Peter Matthiessen, *The Snow Leopard*, New York: Bantam Books, 1978.
14 John G. Neihardt, *Black Elk Speaks*, New York: Pocket Books, 1972.
15 Stanislav Grof, *The Adventure of Self-Discovery*, Albany, NY: State University of New York Press, 1988, p. 30.
16 A. A. Milne, *Winnie the Pooh*, New York: Dell Publishing Company, 1982.

Chapter 10 Facilitating Groups: Tips, Techniques, and Skill Building

1 G. I. Gurdjieff, as reported by P. D. Ouspensky, in *In Search of the Miraculous*, cited in "ARCS," *Parabola*, Vol. 3, August, 1981, p. 42.

2 Frederic S. Perls, "Gestalt Therapy and Human Potentials," Chapter V in Stephenson, *Gestalt Therapy Primer*, New York: Jason Aronson, 1975, p. 77.

Chapter 12 The Moon and Cancer

1 Edward C. Whitmont, *The Return of the Goddess*, Crossroad, NY: Garber Communcations, 1984.

2 Sylvia Brinton Perera, *Descent to the Goddess*, Toronto, CAN: Inner City Books, 1981.

3 Robert A. Johnson, *She*, New York: Harper & Row, 1976.

4 M. Ester Harding, *Woman's Mysteries*, New York: Harper & Row, 1971.

5 Shakti Gawain, *Creative Visualization*, New York: Bantam, 1982.

6 Jean Houston, *The Possible Human*, Los Angeles: J.P. Tarcher, 1982, p. 102–110.

7 *Ibid.*, p. 91–94.

8 Vicki Noble and Karen Vogel, *Motherpeace Tarot Deck*, New York: US Games Systems, Inc., 1981.

Chapter 13 Mercury, Gemini, and Virgo

1 Jean Houston, *The Possible Human*, Los Angeles: J. P. Tarcher, 1982, p. 177.

Chapter 14 Venus, Taurus, and Libra

1 George Downing, *The Massage Book*, New York: Random, 1972.

2 Anais Nin, *Little Birds*, New York: Bantam, 1980, and *Delta of Venus*, New York: Bantam, 1985.

3 Kensington Ladies Society, *Ladies Own Erotica*, Berkeley, CA: Ten Speed Press, 1984.

4 Lonnie Barbach, *Pleasures*, New York: Harper & Row, 1985, and *Erotic Interludes*, New York: Harper & Row, 1985.

5 Jeanne Rose, *Herbal Body Book*, New York: Perigee (Putnam), 1982.

Chapter 15 Mars and Aries

1 *NASA Adventure Game*, School of Public Administration #786, University of Southern California.

Chapter 17 Saturn and Capricorn

1 Glenn Mullin, *Death and Dying in the Tibetan Tradition*, London: Routledge & Kegan Paul, Inc., 1986.

2 Stephen Levine, *Who Dies?*, Garden City, NY: Anchor Books, 1982.

3 Stanislav Grof and Christina Grof, *Beyond Death*, London: Thames & Hudson, Ltd., 1980.

4 Emperor Marcus Aurelius, *"Meditations"*, cited in *Death and Dying in the Tibetan Tradition*, p. 192.

Chapter 18 Uranus and Aquarius

1 Gary Larsen, *The Far Side Gallery*, Kansas City: Andrews, McMeel and Parker, 1985.
2 Gyles Brendreth, *Classic Puzzles*, New York: Harper & Row, 1985.
3 Ronald Clark, *Einstein: The Life and Times*, New York: Avon Books, 1971.
4 Ladislao Reti, *The Unknown Leonardo,* New York: McGraw-Hill Books, 1974.
5 John O'Neil, *Prodigal Genius: The Life of Nikola Tesla*, New York: McKay (Tartan Books).
6 Thomas Kuhn, *The Structure of Scientific Revolutions*, Chicago: University of Chicago Press, 1970.
7 James Gleick, *Chaos: Making a New Science*, New York: Viking, 1988.
8 Whitley Strieber, *Communion: A True Story*, New York: Morrow, 1987.
9 Budd Hopkins, *Intruders: The Incredible Visitations at Copley Woods*, New York: Random, 1987.
10 Film short entitled "Powers of Ten," from Phillip Morrison's, *Powers of Ten, a Book of the Relative Size of Things in the Universe and the Effect of Adding Another Zero*, Redding, CN: Scientific American Library, 1982.

Chapter 19 Neptune and Pisces

1 Kazuaki Iwasaki and Isaac Asimov, *Visions of the Universe*, Montrose, CA: The Cosmos Store, 1981.

Chapter 20 Pluto and Scorpio

1 Carlos Castañeda, *The Teachings of Don Juan: A Yaqui Way of Knowledge*, New York, Simon & Schuster, 1968. See also:
Carlos Castañeda, *A Separate Reality*, New York: Simon & Schuster, 1971, and *Journey to Ixtlan*, New York: Simon & Schuster, 1974.
2 John Lame Deer and Richard Erdoes, *Lame Deer: Seeker of Visions*, New York: Simon & Schuster, 1976.
3 Joan Halifax, *Shamanic Voices*, New York: E. P. Dutton, 1979.
4 Michael Harner, *The Way of the Shaman*, San Francisco: Harper & Row, 1980.
5 Barry Saxe, *The Magical State of Being*, New York: Arbor House, 1977.
6 Melita Denning and Phillip Osborne, *The Llewellyn Inner Guide to Magickal States of Consciousness: Working the Path of the Tree of Life*, Minneapolis, MN: Llewellyn Publications, 1985 and *Mysteria Magica*, 2nd, revised and extended edition, Minneapolis, MN: Llewellyn Publications, 1986.
7 Franz Bardon, *The Practice of Magical Evocation*, Wuppertal, W. Germany: Dieter Ruggeberg, 1975.
8 For example: Dion Fortune, *Psychic Self-Defence*, Wellingborough, Northamptonshire, Aquarian Press, 1985, and *Sane Occultism*, Wellingborough, Northamptonshire, Aquarian Press, 1985.

BIBLIOGRAPHY

Achterberg, Jeanne. *Imagery in Healing*. Boston: Shambhala, New Science Library, 1985.

Angus, S. *The Mystery Religions*. New York: Dover, 1975.

Arguelles, Jose, and Miriam Arguelles. *Mandala*. Berkeley and London: Shambhala, 1972.

Arroyo, Stephen. *Astrology, Karma, and Transformation*. Davis, Calif.: CRCS Publications, 1978.

——. *Astrology, Psychology and the Four Elements*. Davis, Calif.: CRCS Publications, 1975.

Bandler , Richard, and John Grinder. *Frogs into Princes*. Moab, Utah: Real People Press, 1979.

Barbach, Lonnie. *Pleasures*. New York: Harper & Row, 1985.

——. *Erotic Interludes: Tales Told by Women*. New York: Harper & Row, 1985.

Bateson , Gregory, and Mary Catherine Bateson. *Angels Fear*. New York: Macmillan, 1987.

Bettelheim, Bruno. *The Uses of Enchantment*. New York: Arthur A. Knopf, 1977.

Bolen, Jean Shinoda. *Goddesses in Everywoman*. New York: Harper & Row, 1984.

Brendreth, Gyles. *Classic Puzzles*. New York: Harper & Row, 1985.

Brown, Barbara. *New Mind, New Body*. New York: Harper & Row, 1975.

Campbell, Joseph. *The Hero with a Thousand Faces*. Princeton: Princeton University Press, 1973.

——. *The Portable Jung*. New York: Penguin Books, 1976.

——. *The Mythic Image*. Princeton: Princeton University Press, 1981.

——. *Way of the Animal Powers*. San Francisco: Harper & Row, 1983.

Castañeda, Carlos. *The Teachings of Don Juan: A Yaqui Way of Knowledge*. New York: Simon & Schuster, 1968.

——. *A Separate Reality*. New York: Simon & Schuster, 1971.

——. *Journey to Ixtlan*. New York: Pocket Books, 1972.

Clark, Ronald. *Einstein: The Life and Times*. New York: Avon Books, 1971.

Clydesdale, Ruth. "A Solar Talisman: Marsilio Ficino's Holistic Astrology," in *Mountain Astrologer*, August–September 1996.

Collin, Rodney. *The Theory of Celestial Influence*. Boulder, Colo.: Shambhala Publications, 1984.

Corbin, Henry. "The Jasmine of the Fedeli D'Amore." In *Sphinx*. Vol. 3. London: The London Convivium for Archetypal Studies, 1990.

Couliano, Ioan. *Eros and Magic in the Renaissance*. Chicago: University of Chicago Press, 1987.

Coward, Harold. *Jung and Eastern Thought*. New York: State University of New York Press, 1985.

Craft, Bob. "Psyche and Eros." Unpublished address. Lucerne: The Astrology World Congress, May 1996.

Cumont, Franz. *Astrology and Religion Among the Greeks and Romans*. New York: Dover, 1960.

Cunningham, Donna. *Healing Pluto Problems*. York Beach, Maine: Samuel Weiser, Inc., 1986.

Dempsey, Charles. *The Portrayal of Love*. Princeton: Princeton University Press, 1992.

Downing, George. *The Massage Book*. New York: Random House, 1972.

Erickson , Milton, and Earnest Rossi. *Hypnotic Realities*. New York: John Wiley and Sons, 1976.

Feder, Elaine, and Bernard Feder. *The Expressive Arts Therapies*. Engelwood Cliffs, N.J.: Prentice-Hall, Inc., 1981.

Ficino, Marsilio. *Marsilio Ficino's Book of Life*. Translated by Charles Boer. Dallas, Tex.: Spring Publications, 1980.

——. *The Letters of Marsilio Ficino* (New York: Columbia University Press, 1985), 2:33.

Fisher, Helen. *Anatomy of Love* (New York: Fawcett Columbine, 1992), 52.

Fluegelman, Andrew. *The New Games Book*. New York: Doubleday, 1976.

Garin , Eugenio. *Portraits from the Quattrocentro*. Translated by Victor A. Velen and Elizabeth Velen. New York: 1972.

Gawain, Shakti. *Creative Visualization*. New York: Bantam, 1972.

Gleick, James. *Chaos*. New York: Viking Penguin Inc., 1988.

Gombrich, E. H. *Gombrich on the Renaissance*. Vol. 2 Symbolic Images, London: Phaidon Press, 1972.

Govinda, Lama Anagarika. *The Way of the White Clouds*. Boulder, Colo.: Shambhala, 1970.

Grof , Stanislav, and Christina Grof. *Beyond Death*. London: Thames & Hudson, Ltd., 1980.

Grof, Stanislav. *Beyond the Brain*. Albany, N.Y.: State University of New York, 1985.

——. *The Adventure of Self-Discovery.* Albany, N.Y.: State University of New York Press, 1988.

Grolier Encyclopedia. Grolier Electronic Publications, 1992.

Grossinger, Richard. *The Night Sky*. San Francisco: Sierra Club Books, 1981.

Growtowski, Jerzy. *Towards a Poor Theatre*. New York: Simon & Schuster, 1968.

Haley, Jay. *Uncommon Therapy.* New York: W. W. Norton, 1973.

Halifax, Joan. *Shamanic Voices.* New York: E. P. Dutton, 1979.

Hall, Nor. *The Moon and the Virgin: Reflections on the Archetypal Feminine.* New York: Harper & Row, 1980.

Hamaker-Zondag, Karen. *Astro-Psychology.* Wellingborough, Northampton: The Aquarian Press, 1980.

Harding, M. Esther. *Woman's Mysteries.* New York: Harper & Row, 1971.

Harner, Michael. *The Way of the Shaman.* San Francisco: Harper & Row, 1980.

Hesiod. *Theogony: The Poems of Hesiod.* Norman, Okla.: University of Oklahoma Press, 1983.

Highwater, Jamake. *Dance: Rituals of Experience.* Toronto: Methuen, 1985.

Hillman, James. *Re-Visioning Psychology.* New York: Harper & Row, 1975.

——. "Plotino, Ficino, and Vico." In *Loose Ends.* Dallas, Tex.: Spring Publications, 1975a.

——. *Archetypal Psychology.* Dallas, Tex.: Spring Publications, 1983.

——. *The Thought of the Heart and the Soul of the World.* Dallas, Tex.: Spring Publications, 1992.

——. *The Soul's Code.* New York: London House, 1996.

Holst, Imogen. *Holst.* London: Faber & Faber, Ltd., 1974.

Hopkins, Budd. *Intruders: The Incredible Visitations at Copley Woods.* New York: Random House, 1987.

Howell, Alice. *Jungian Symbolism in Astrology.* Wheaton, Ill.: The Theosophical Publishing House, 1987.

Houston, Jean. *The Possible Human.* Los Angeles: Jeremy Tarcher, 1982.

Jawer, Jeff. "Living the Drama of the Horoscope." *Astrology Now* 22 (1979): 12–15, 55–58.

Johnson, Robert A. *She.* New York: Harper & Row, 1976.

Jung, Carl. *Man and His Symbols.* New York: Doubleday, 1964.

——. *Memories, Dreams, Reflections.* New York: Vintage Books, 1965.

——. *The Archetypes and the Collective Unconscious.* Second edition. Princeton: Princeton University Press, 1968.

——. "Civilization in Transition." In *Collected Works.* The Bollingen Series Vol. 10. p. 90.

Iwasaki , Kazuaki, and Isaac Asimov. *Visions of the Universe.* Montrose, Calif.: The Cosmos Store, 1981.

Kensington Ladies Society. *Ladies Own Erotica.* Berkeley, Calif.: Ten Speed Press, 1984.

Klein, M. H.; P. L. Mathieu; E. T. Gendlin; and D. J. Kiesler. *The Experiencing Scale: A Research and Training Manual.* Bureau of Audio-Visual Instruction. Madison: University of Wisconsin Extension, 1970.

Keleman, Stanley. *Your Body Speaks Its Mind.* New York: Simon & Schuster, 1981.

Kramer, Joseph. *Fire on the Mountain: An Intimate Guide to Male Genital Massage.* EroSpirit Research, Inc. Available in the U.S. from *Tantra Magazine Bazaar,* 1-800-341-8272.

Kristeller, Paul Oskar. *Eight Philosophers of the Italian Renaissance.* Stanford, Calif.: Stanford University Press, 1964.

Kriyananda, Swami. *The Spiritual Science of Kriya Yoga.* Chicago: The Temple of Kriya Yoga Press, 1985.

Kuhn, Thomas. *The Structure of Scientific Revolutions.* Chicago: University of Chicago Press, 1970.

LaChapelle, Doris, and Janet Bourque. *Earth Festivals.* Silverton, Colo.: Finn Hill Arts, 1976.

Lame Deer, John, and Richard Erdoes. *Lame Deer: Seeker of Visions.* New York: Simon & Schuster, 1976.

Larsen, Gary. *The Far Side Gallery.* Kansas City: Andrews, McMeel and Parker, 1985.

Levine, Stephen. *Who Dies?* Garden City, N.Y.: Anchor Books, 1982.

Lewis, Howard R. *Growth Games.* New York: Bantam Books, 1972.

Lingerman, Hal A. *The Healing Energies of Music.* Wheaton, Ill.: The Theosophical Publishing House, 1983.

Lowen, Alexander. *The Language of the Body.* New York: Collier Books, 1971.

Marieschild, Diane. *Motherwit.* Trumansburg, N.Y.: The Crossing Press, 1981.

Matthiessen, Peter. *The Snow Leopard.* New York: Bantam Books, 1978.

McEvers, Joan. *Metaphysical, Spiritual and New Trends in Modern Astrology.* Minneapolis: Llewellyn Publications, 1988.

McKim, Robert H. *Experiences in Visual Thinking.* Boston: PWS Engineering, 1980.

Milne, A. A. *Winnie the Pooh.* New York: Dell Publishing Company, 1982.

Moore, Thomas. *The Planets Within: The Astrological Psychology of Marsilio Ficino.* Lindesfarne Press, 1982, p. 58.

——. *Care of the Soul.* New York: HarperCollins, 1992.

—— (Ed). *The Education of the Heart.* New York: HarperCollins, 1996.

Moreno, Joseph. *Psychodrama.* Vol. I. Beacon, N.Y.: Beacon House, 1946.

Morrison, Phillip. *Powers of Ten: A Book of the Relative Size of Things in the Universe and the Effect of Adding Another Zero.* Redding, Conn.: Scientific American Library, 1982.

"Motherpeace Tarot Deck." New York: U.S. Games Systems, Inc., 1981.

Mullin, Glenn. *Death and Dying in the Tibetan Tradition.* London: Routledge & Kegan Paul, 1986.

Mylonas, George E. *Eleusis and the Eleusinian Mysteries.* Princeton: Princeton University Press, 1961.

NASA Adventure Game. School of Public Administration #786. University of Southern California.

Neihardt, John G. *Black Elk Speaks*. New York: Pocket Books, 1972.

Nichols, Michael P., and Melvin Zax. *Catharsis in Psychotherapy*. New York: Gardner Press, 1977.

Nin, Anais. *Little Birds*. New York: Bantam, 1980.

——. *Delta of Venus*. New York: Bantam, 1985.

Novalis, in Christopher Bamford, "The Magic of Romance: The Cultivation of Eros from Sappho to the Troubadours," *Alexandria*, Vol. 2, Grand Rapids, Mich.: Phanes Press, 1993.

O'Neil, John. *Prodigal Genius: The Life of Nikola Tesla*. New York: McKay (Tartan Books).

Panofsky, Erwin. *Renaissance and Renascences in Western Art*. New York: Harper & Row, 1960.

Perera, Sylvia Brinton. *Descent to the Goddess*. Toronto: Inner City Books, 1981.

Reich, Wilhelm. *The Function of the Orgasm*. New York: World Publishing, 1971.

Reti, Ladislao. *The Unknown Leonardo*. New York: McGraw-Hill, 1974.

Rice, Edward. *Eastern Definitions*. Garden City, N.Y.: Anchor Doubleday, 1980.

Rolf, Ida P. *Rolfing*. New York: Harper & Row, 1977.

Rose, Jeanne. *Jeanne Rose's Herbal Body Book*. New York: Putnam Publishing Group, 1976.

Rudhyar, Dane. *Astrology and the Modern Psyche*. Vancouver, Wash.: CRCS Publications, 1976.

——. *Person Centered Astrology*. New York: Aurora Press, 1980.

Satyeswarananda, Swami Giri. *Lahiri Mahasay: The Father of Kriya Yoga*. Self-published, 1983.

Saxe, Barry. *The Magical State of Being*. New York: Arbor House, 1977.

Schermer, Barbara. "Psyche's Tasks: A Path of Initiation for Women." In *Astrology for Women*, edited by Gloria Star. St. Paul: Llewellyn, 1997.

Snow-Smith, Joanne. *The Primavera of Sandro Botticelli*. New York: Peter Lang, 1993.

Spolin, Viola. *Improvisation for the Theater*. Evanston, Ill.: Northwestern University Press, 1963.

Springer, Sally P., and George Deutsch. *Left Brain, Right Brain*. Revised edition. New York: Freeman, 1985.

Sprinkle, Annie, and Maria Beatty. *Sluts and Goddesses*. Available in the U.S. from *Tantra Magazine Bazaar*, 1-800-341-8272.

Starhawk. *The Spiral Dance*. New York: Harper & Row, 1979.

Stephenson, F. Douglas. *Gestalt Therapy Primer*. New York: Jason Aronson, 1975.

Strieber, Whitley. *Communion: A True Story*. New York: Morrow, 1987.

Tanner, Ron, and Cynthia Connop. *Secrets of Sacred Sex*. Triple Image Film Productions. Available in the U.S. at 1-800-2LIVING.

Tarnas, Richard. *Prometheus, the Awakener*. Oxford: Uriel Press, 1993.

Walker, D. P. *Spiritual and Demonic Magic*. Notre Dame: University of Notre Dame Press, 1975.

Walsh, Robert N., and Frances Vaughan, eds. *Beyond Ego*. Los Angeles: J. P. Tarcher, 1980.

Whitmont, Edward C. *The Return of the Goddess*. Blauvelt, N.Y.: Garber Communications, 1984.

Wilber, Ken. *Up from Eden*. Boulder, Colo.: Shambhala, 1983.

——. *A Sociable God*. New York: McGraw, 1982.

Williamson, Ray A. *Living the Sky*. Boston: Houghton Mifflin, 1984.

Wind, Edgar. *Pagan Mysteries in the Renaissance*. New York: W. W. Dutton, 1968.

Woods, Margo. *Masturbation, Tantra and Self-Love*. San Diego: Mho and Mho Works, 1981.

Yates, Frances. *The Art of Memory*. Chicago: University of Chicago Press, 1966.

Yogananda, Paramahansa. *Autobiography of a Yogi*. Los Angeles: Self-Realization Fellowship, 1974.

A

abundance, meditation for, 202
accidents, 174, 217
accommodation, in experiential astrology, 25
activities, for teaching astrology, 50
addictions
    and drugs, 226-227; foundations of, 24; Neptune affecting, 130; to food, 182; Venus affecting, 182
Adventure, 192-193, 235-236
affirmations. *see also* visualization
    for positive enhancement, 123, 152, 211, 228
aggression, Mars affecting, 189
AIDS, 237
Air
    affecting groups, 138; communion with, 10; teaching with, 50, 51
aistheses, 71
alchemy, processes of, 24-25
alcoholism. *see also* addictions
    Neptune affecting, 130, 226-227
De Amore (Ficino), 29
ancient mysteries, discussed, 14-18
anecdotes, 112-113
anger, 194
Animus-Anima, 36
Aquarius
    dance forms for, 88; Saturn in, 27-28; Venus in, 76-79
Aquarius/Uranus, astrodrama techniques, 215-221
archetypes
    astrological, 18-19, 41, 83; Gods as, 21; masculine and feminine, 64; mythological, 19, 36-38; of soul, 22; theory of, 35
Arguelles, Jose and Miriam, 83
Aries
    dance forms for, 88; Venus in, 60-62
Aries/Libra Pushing, 193-194
Aries/Mars, astrodrama techniques, 189-195
art. *see also* visual arts techniques
    devotion to, 29; exploring, 185; Uranian, 219; visionary, 227
art supplies, resources for, 81, 185
The Art of Sexual Ecstasy (Anand), 61
Asteroid Belt, 209
astrodrama. *see also* living horoscope
    art astrodrama, 105-106; breathing in, 105, 154; discussed, 95-107; how to do it, 96-98; and Jung's psyche model, 106-107; living horoscope, 98-104; meditative astrodrama, 105; "New Center of the Moon" conference, 12-14; nonverbal astrodrama, 106; Noyes

Cultural Arts Center performance, 42-50; origins for, 38-40; and psychotherapy, 53-55; Theater of Planetary Memory, 12-14
astrodrama techniques, 134-144
    discussed
        Jupiter/Sagittarius, 196-202; Mars/Aries, 189-195; Mercury/Gemini/Virgo, 166-176; Moon/Cancer, 156-165; Moon/Mercury, 88-90; Neptune/Pisces, 222-229; Pluto/Scorpio, 230-238; Saturn/Capricorn, 203-214; Sun/Leo, 147-151; Uranus/Aquarius, 215-221; Venus/Taurus/Libra, 177-188
experiential groups outline, 140-141
    closure, 142; introductions, 140-141; process, 141; warm-ups and ice-breaking, 141
group
    Affirmation, 152; AIDS, 237; Aries/Libra Pushing, 193-194; Boundaries, 204-206; Ceremonial Ritual, 235; Charades, 173; Childbirth, 161; Childhood Home, 160; Childhood Photo, 159; Childhood Toy, 160-161; Cocktail Party, 171; Contact, 180; Contact Games, 180; Contacting Others, 181; Dictionary Game, 173-174; Doubling, 142-144; Draw Your Current Problem, 209; Eating with Mindfulness, 182; Eating Out Together, 182; Exaggeration, 199; Feminine Issues, 161; Follow the Leader, 172; Foundations, 206-207; Freeze!, 142; Gibberish, 173; Giveaways, 200-201; Goddess Worship, 186; Group Healing, 225-226; Home, 160; Jupiter experiencing, 197; King or Queen, 153; Learning to Listen, 172; Massage Line, 180; Memorize a Poem, 151; Memory Games, 170; Miming, 172; Mirror Dancing, 164; My Ideal Trip, 173; My Most Attractive Features, 183; Name Chant, 151-152; NASA Adventure Game, 189-192; Nuclear Annihilation, 237; Old Age, 210; Oranges, 180; Pillows, 181; Powerline, 233-234; Primum non nocere, 139-140; Relaxation, 172; Resentments,

235; Rocking, 159-160; Sand Play, 163; Saturn Return, 207-208; Scruples, 237-238; Secrets, 234; Sheet Game, 181; Space Programs, 219; Spoon Touch, 180-181; Stand Up, 181; Surprise Trip!, 199; Taboos, 236; Telephone, 170-171; Tell About a Leo Experience, 152; Telling Stories, 152; Theme Party, 199; This is Your Life!, 161; Time Line Charts, 162; Trivial Pursuit, 174; Vocables Chants, 226; Warm Fuzzies, 152-153; What's Good About You?, 151; Where You Grew Up, 160; Women's Issues, 161-162
group dynamics, 137-140
    feedback, 139; feelings, 137-138; Primum non nocere, 139-140; structure and timing, 138
personal
    Abundance/Healing Meditation, 202; Accidents, 217; Adventure!, 192-193, 235-236; Affirmation, 123, 152, 211, 228; Aliens, 219; Amusement Parks, 193; An Old Person Remembered From Childhood, 210; Anger, 194; Art Exploration, 185; Art, Uranian, 219; Art, Visionary, 227; Asteroid Belt, 209; Athletics, 192; Autobiography, 162; "Ball of Light" Meditations, 154-155; Beliefs, 197; Birthday Ritual, 153-154; Bizarre Humor, 218; Blind Walk, 225; Body Therapies, 234; Brainteasers, 218; Cancerian Planet Walk, 163; Clay Play, 207; Clothing, 183, 186; Computer Games, 220; Conceptualize the Sky, 171; Contemplative Retreat, 226; Creativity and Originality, 217-218; Death, 212-213; Dialogue with a Planet, 169-170; Drugs and Addictions, 226-227; Emergencies, 193; Erotica, 184; Famous People, 199; Fingerpaint, 201; Float Tank, 223; Food and Eating, 182; Foreign Films, 200; Foreign Journeys, 200; Foundations, 206-207; Foundations Strengthening, 210-211; Friends, 199; Future Transits, 220; Genius, 219; Goals, 99-100, 129, 135-136,

RELATED BOOKS FROM THE CROSSING PRESS

Soul-Centered Astrology: A Key to Your Expanding Self
By Alan Oken

Complete with detailed astrological charts and diagrams, meditations, and visualizations, this is the definitive guide to enlightenment for professional and amateur astrologers alike.

$18.95 • Paper • 0-89594-811-7

Experiential Astrology: Symbolic Journeys Using Guided Imagery
By Babs Kirby

Explore astrology in a more personal way without an interpreter. Guided imagery is an innovative technique that will translate the astrological symbols into a more personal set of images, offering a better understanding of what these symbols actually mean to us.

$14.95 • Paper • 0-89594-798-6

Healing with Astrology
By Marcia Starck

Bring balance and energy to your life using the correspondences between your horoscope and a wide range of natural healing systems—vitamin therapy, herbs, music, color, crystals, gemstones, flower remedies, aromatherapy, and unification rituals

$14.95 • Paper • 0-89594-862-1

An Astrological Herbal for Women
By Elisabeth Brooke

An extensive guide to the use of herbs in healing the mind, body, and spirit, organized by planetary influence. Includes the astrological significance of 38 common herbs, as well as their physical, emotional, and ritual uses.

$12.95 • Paper • 0-89594-740-4

Pocket Guide To Astrology
By Alan Oken

Astrology serves as a way to explain events in life that otherwise appear inexplicable or arbitrary. This Pocket Guide covers the twelve signs of the zodiac and what they mean, the planets and how they affect your life, and the Houses and their role in your experience.

$6.95 • Paper • 0-89594-820-6

To receive a current catalog from The Crossing Press,
please call toll-free, 800-777-1048.
Visit our Website on the Internet at: www.crossingpress.com